Scandinavian Scotlan‹

The Proceedings of

held on 19 February 2007

Edited by

Alex Woolf

ST ANDREWS
St John's House Papers No 12

2009

Frontispiece: Map of North Sea and North Atlantic
Showing bishoprics in Norway and the 'Scattlands'.

LIST OF ILLUSTRATIONS ~~~~~~

Chapter 6

February 2007 saw the eighth St Andrews Dark Age Studies Day Conference, preceded as has become the tradition since 2005, by the Anderson Memorial Lecture. The theme chosen for the Conference 'Scandinavian Scotland: twenty years after' was the result of a number of coinciding strategies. The Dark Age Studies Committee has always tried to encompass as wide a range of subject areas relating to early Scotland and its neighbours as possible but it had been some time since any of our Conferences had focused on the Norse element. The fact that it was twenty years since Barbara Crawford's seminal work, and still essential reading on the topic, Scandinavian Scotland had appeared in print, encouraged us to take the opportunity to see how research in the field had moved on (or not) since its publication. This also allowed us to utilise the Conference as something of a smoke screen. The editors of Barbara's Festschrift, Beverley Ballin Smith, Simon Taylor and Gareth Williams, were in the final stages of putting together the impressive volume West over Sea: Studies in Sea-Borne Expansion and Settlement Before 1300 (Brill, 2007), and Simon Taylor, also a member of the Committee, suggested to me that having a Norse-themed conference which made explicit reference to Barbara's work, would be a way of gathering together an audience comprising many of the contributors of the Festschrift, and would provide a venue for presenting the finished product to Barbara. Simon and I also considered that if Barbara got wind that some sort of Festschrift was in the air, she might well imagine the proceedings of the Conference (the book you are reading now) to be it, and thus, by sleight of hand, be distracted from any evidence regarding the production of West over Sea. This feint seems to have worked and Barbara claims, to this day, to have suspected nothing.

Of course the Conference was not simply a scam designed to delude a senior colleague. The papers presented were themselves of a high standard and reflected ongoing research in different aspects of Viking Age and Late Norse history and archaeology. The week-end events commenced with Professor Steinar Imsen of University of Trondheim giving the 3rd Anderson Memorial Lecture (in honour of A.O., and Marjorie Anderson) on the Friday night. He spoke on the topic of developing relations between the Scottish and Norwegian crowns in the Late Norse period. On the Saturday we heard papers on Scandinavian toponymy in Caithness and the West Coast, from Doreen Waugh and Andrew Jennings respectively, and on the archaeology of Norse settlement in the Western and Northern Isles, from Niall Sharples and David Griffiths. David felt that his contribution was not appropriate for the published proceedings since his field project was in a far earlier and less conclusive stage than Niall's and it is our regret that this area, so close to Barbara's own heart, has not been adequately represented in the volume. Orkney, however, did figure largely in the final session of the day when Ian Beuerman and Judith Jesch produced very substantial papers based largely upon saga material; Ian constructing a political biography of Sveinn Ásleifarson and Judith investigating the reflections of Norse myth in medieval Orkney.

Production of the final volume has taken somewhat longer than one might have hoped. Some contributors were able to present us with full texts fairly promptly but others, doubtless operating under the exigencies of the notorious Research Assessment Exercise, were forced to prioritise other projects. The final papers arrived at a time when my own university obligations were pressing particularly heavily and Barbara valiantly took over the crucial final stages of the editing process, for which I am very grateful. [1] Twenty years after (and more) she still remains a dominant force in the study of Scandinavian Scotland!

Alex Woolf
January 2009

---

[1] The editors would like to express their appreciation of the speed and efficiency with which Margaret Smith, Reprographics Unit, enabled this volume to be prepared in time for the Ninth Dark Age Conference.

Third Anderson Memorial Lecture
The Scottish-Norwegian Border in the Middle Ages
Steinar Imsen

Up to the latter half of the 15th century the kingdoms of Norway and Scotland were close neighbours, and had been so for a couple of centuries. Here I will discuss two questions, first: how is the border between Scotland and Norway in the Middle Ages to be understood, and second: what kind of border country regime did Norway develop in the 13th century as contact between the two kingdoms grew closer?

The Border

Perth, the definition of sovereignty and the new state-border

On 2nd July 1266 Magnus IV Håkonsson of Norway and Alexander III of Scotland concluded a treaty of lasting peace, which involved the drawing up of a permanent state border between the two monarchies that ran through the Pentland Firth. The Treaty of Perth was later renewed in Inverness in 1312 and in Bergen in 1426.[1]

When I venture the claim that a permanent state border between Norway and Scotland was defined in 1266, I base this on how the peace treaty defined the territorial dominion of the kings: there it states that they and their descendants shall "[...] *hold, own and possess (the Hebrides [Sudreys]-Man, and Orkney-Shetland respectively) with crown lands, rights over men, income, services and all other rights connected to the mentioned islands, without curtailment* [...]". What we are dealing with, then, is not indirect rule or overlordship of the type which characterises the relationship between the suzerain and his vassal; but undivided and direct territorial rule defined according to legal principles. Others who might have had an historical basis for laying claim to lordship over the islands, such as the kings of Man and the Isles, or the Earl of Orkney, are not mentioned in the treaty. Further on in the document Orkney is described as "the territory of the King of Norway". What is being expressed, in other words, is the sovereignty of the Kingdoms of Scotland and Norway over the islands to the west and north of Scotland respectively.[2] This is how the nascent European states understood territorial dominion at the end of the 13th century, which in principle excluded overlapping lordships and unclear boundaries.[3]

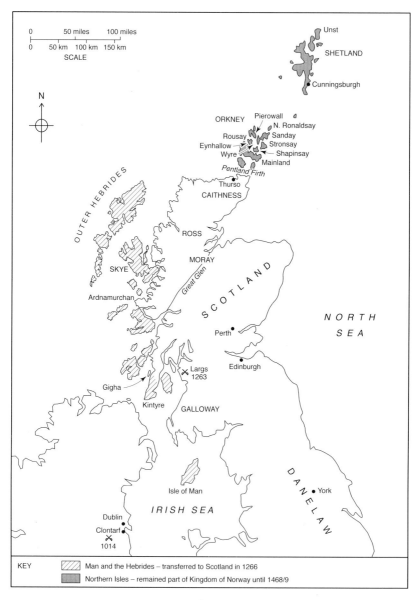

Figure : 1.1 Map of Scandinavian Scotland showing places
mentioned in Chapters 1 and 3.

Even though the Pentland Firth can be characterised as *a front-line area* in the early 1260s with a Scottish army in Caithness, and Orkney under Norwegian military rule, the new state border should be open for social and cultural exchange in the centuries to come.[4] However from then on people on each side of the Pentland Firth were defined as subjects of the King of Scots and the King of Norway. For the Orcadians the Caithnessians were now turned into Scots and foreigners, even though the Orcadians themselves were of mixed Scottish-Norse breed, and the other side of the Firth became foreign territory. All this can be read from late medieval documents.[5] The events in the early 1260s and the treaty of 1266 brought two kingdoms with ambitions of ruling their territories directly in close contact with each other.

Our first question then is: how can we characterise neighbourhood-relations between the Kingdoms of Norway and Scotland up to the turning point in the 1260s?

From March to Border

In his *Gesta Hammaborgensis* from about 1070 Adam of Bremen describes Norway and the land of the Norwegians as an almost boundless territory, ending somewhere up in the Arctic mist or the boundless Western sea.[6] Adam avoids referring to Norway as a Realm or Kingdom, or to any kind of political arrangements in the Norse territories overseas; his reference in this context is purely ethno-geographic, not political. Nor does he say anything about Scotland or neighbourhood-relations in the Western sea. Then only some twenty years later, in 1098, King Magnus III Olavsson of Norway and King Edgar of Scotland reached an agreement about the extent of their respective dominions in the western seaboard of northern Britain.[7] And about the same time the Norwegian kings also accepted that the Norse earls of Orkney kept Caithness, the mainland part of their earldom, as a fief from the Scottish crown. So, from the end of the 11th century the Pentland Firth was some kind of boundary, though not a state border. An equivalent understanding of territorial lordship was reached between King Magnus and the Swedish king Inge Stenkilsson in 1101, defining the upper western part of the Göta-river region as Norwegian territory. Thus the reign of Magnus III Olavsson marks the point of departure for a process of territorial consolidation that ended up with fixed state-borders in the latter half of the 13th century, in northern Britain as well as in Scandinavia.

However the 1098 agreement was not about borders in a strict sense; it should rather be understood as a mutual understanding of territorial pretensions in the western seaboard of northern Britain between two expanding kingdoms. There was nothing like a Norwegian — or a Scottish — state in 1100; the kingdoms were in fact patchworks of principalities and lordships and borders were correspondingly flexible. Moreover joint kingship was customary in Norway until the 13th century, and the king's power was dependant on his ability to mobilise men and money, on loyalty from local princes and lords, and on royal presence and unpredictability.[8] Besides, Norwegian kings hardly visited Norse Britain between 1103, when King Magnus died after having forced his overlordship upon the king of Man and the Isles, and 1263, when King Håkon IV's military campaign to defend Norse territory in the Western sea failed.

Nevertheless, the mutual understanding of territorial overlordship made the kings of Norway and Scotland neighbours, though not yet close neighbours. Until 1266 there was an area off the British Isles of more or less autonomous Norse and Norse-Gaelic principalities under some sort of Norwegian overlordship, which served as a buffer between Norway and Scotland. The process of territorial consolidation and state formation that ended up in Perth in 1266 had however, begun.

Even though Caithness came in principle under the Scottish Crown in the late 11th century, the united Earldom of Orkney-Caithness seems to have retained its Norse character throughout the 1200s in terms of language and culture as well as social organisation. Barbara Crawford writes that in terms of both geography and communication Caithness had closer ties to the islands in the north than to the rest of Scotland, and that up to 1266 Caithness "[…] *was linked emotionally and economically with the Norwegian earldom*". Furthermore, she writes that "[…] *the overlord of Norway was far more at home in the waterways and harbours of Caithness than the king of Scotland could ever dream of being.*" During his campaign in 1263 the Norwegian King Håkon IV Håkonsson controlled Caithness. When he addressed a letter to its inhabitants, it was probably written in Norwegian which, according to Crawford, was still the common language among the Caithnessians. Moreover, she adds that as late as 1231 the Caithness community was entirely Norwegian, both in social and structural terms.[9] The Scots element in Caithness was not represented by the monarchy, but above all by the church; and contrary to the bishop's wishes, the Earls largely held on to Norse traditions, even after the

Earldom of Orkney-Caithness had come into the possession of Earls of Scots descent.[10]

Up to 1266 then the Norwegian, or Norse, parts of Northern Britain should be regarded as a political, social and cultural continuum extending from the islands in the north and down the Western Seaboard of Scotland to the Irish Sea. In this sense, Orkney-Caithness and Man and the Isles can be regarded as a Norse or Norse-Gaelic frontier or march.[11] Even after the joint Earldom of Orkney-Caithness under Earl Harold Maddason had been brought under stricter royal control at the close of the 1100s by both the Scottish and Norwegian Crowns (particularly by the latter), the northern part of Scotland remained as a kind of Norse-British frontier. This was to change after 1230, and the war in 1263 inserted a wedge through the joint Earldom of Orkney-Caithness, which was confirmed in principle in the 1266 treaty.

The Norwegian concept of "skattland", and their relations to the Norwegian king until the 1260s

In the anonymous *Historia Norwegie*, probably from the 1160s, the Faeroes, Orkney, Shetland, the Hebrides and Man are characterised as tributary islands under the Norwegian crown, and the political category "skattlandene" i.e. the tributary countries, becomes common during the 13th century.[12] At the end of the century Norwegian kings style themselves as kings of Norway and the tributary countries.

The Norse principalities in the Irish Sea as well as the North Sea were the original "skattlands", which meant that the kings of Man and the Isles and the earls of Orkney-Shetland paid tribute to the Norwegian king as recognition of his overlordship. We do not know for certain when they acquired this status. Even though medieval historians like Snorre Sturlason and the author of the Orkney saga maintain that the "skattland" story reaches back into the time of Harald Finehair in the 9th century, it is probably not older then the late 11th century. The earls of Orkney and the kings of Man up to the 1060s and 90s can be regarded as more or less independent princes like their Norse colleagues in Dublin, who never accepted Norwegian overlordship. From the 1260s Iceland and Greenland too accepted the King of Norway as their lawful lord and acquired the status of "skattlands". The tributary countries were thus regarded as royal dominions beyond the borders of Norway proper. Consequently, the population of these areas is not described as Northmen, which was the common term applied to people in Norway in the Middle Ages, as it still is. They were "orknøyinger" (Orcadians), "islendinger" (Icelanders), "hjaltlendinger" (Shetlanders), "grønnlendere" (Greenlanders) and so on, though from the 1260s subjects of the Norwegian king as well.

When it comes to the Hebrideans ("Sudrøyingene") and the Manx, I doubt if they were ever considered subjects of the king of Norway. The Norwegian kings related first and foremost to the Norse-Gaelic kings of Man and the Isles, who in turn paid them tribute in acknowledgment of their overlordship. There are no traces of any Norwegian rule in the area, no Norwegian laws were introduced — as far as I know — and no institutions established to take care of the political interests of the Norwegian king. I doubt that a few military campaigns and short term occupations, and an outspoken will to assert royal overlordship and royal hegemony in the area during the reigns of Magnus Olavsson and Håkon IV Håkonsson deserve to be called "Norwegian rule". But a common language, allied with a concept of some sort of historical and cultural community, linked people in the Norse world together. It is interesting to notice that throughout the Middle Ages the Norse communities in the west are described by the inhabitants of mainland Scotland (and Ireland) as the 'islands of the foreigners' ("Innse Gall"). This continued despite the expansion of the Gaelic language into the area during the Middle Ages.

Through their sagas and annals, the Icelanders have contributed considerably towards the conception of a Norse community in the Irish and Norwegian Seas, with the Norwegian monarchy as a common point of political and historical reference. This is what Norwegian historians since the 19th century like to call "Norgesveldet", which can be translated as the "Empire of Norway". However in contemporary usage "Norgesveldet" refers to the King's right to rule his realm, above all Norway proper.[13] There is nothing imperialistic about the concept, at least not in a broader territorial sense, i.e. as a political superstructure over the Norse territories. Until c 1200 there was no Norwegian rule at all in the Norse colonies overseas. However from the end of the 12th century a process starts to incorporate the Faeroes, Orkney and Shetland in the Norwegian monarchy. A rudimentary royal administration was established together with a system of native royal liegemen.

So, gradually, the parts of Norse Britain least affected by Gaelic language and culture were going to have stronger ties to Norway during the 13th century together with the new tributary lands in the North Atlantic. However, there is not the least suggestion of a Norwegian political nation emerging in Norse

Britain or the Norwegian Sea during the Middle Ages – in contrast to the situation in continental Norway. The Norwegian realm was, and remained, a conglomerate of peoples and communities – although the population was probably more homogenous than in the Scottish realm after 1266.

The Treaty of Perth once more, historiography and outcome

The Treaty of Perth was a consequence of Håkon IV's failed 1263 campaign in the Hebrides. In a sense, Håkon's campaign constitutes a Norwegian-Scottish parallel to Harold Hardrada's invasion of England in 1066. Both operations failed, and both bring to a kind of close – at least for historians – Norwegian and Scandinavian history in England and Scotland, respectively. Many Norwegian historians have seen the Treaty of Perth as an omen of the national disaster that was to hit the country in the 1300s, with the Black Death and Nordic unions resulting eventually in annexation by the Danish monarchy in 1537. Norway as it is defined by Norwegian historians following the dissolution of the union with Denmark after the Napoleonic Wars corresponds to the territory that remained after land had been ceded to Scotland in the 1460s, to Sweden in 1645, and to Denmark by the Treaty of Kiel in January 1814. Consequently, there has been no place in our national historiography for the provinces in the west, or for the old landscapes on the Swedish border.

Although historians seem to consider 1266 the terminal point of Norse history in Scotland, the fact is that it was from this point onwards that the Norwegian authorities established themselves fully in Orkney and Shetland. We will now look closer at Orkney as a border country in the Norwegian kingdom, in other words the political situation in the islands during the last two centuries of Norwegian rule, and we will concentrate on the three main components of the Norwegian regime on the islands: the king, the earl, and the country – which in contemporary documents is described as "Communitas Orchadensis".

The Border Country regime

The King

Unlike his father Håkon IV Håkonsson, Magnus IV Håkonsson (1263-80) was a peace-loving monarch. He built the land by law, thus gaining the nickname 'Lawmender' – and he sought territorial consolidation rather than territorial expansion by reaching an understanding with his neighbours. The peace negotiations with Alexander III and the drawing of a border with Scotland were not unique examples of Magnus' peace work: during his reign, negotiations were also initiated with the neighbours in the east, the Swedes, and a permanent border was then drawn up between the two countries, stretching from Jemtland in the north to the Göta river in the south. As a result of this extension, negotiations were also begun with the Russians, resulting in the first border treaty between Norway and Novgorod in 1326.[14]

As we have seen, dominion according to the Treaty of Perth was primarily a matter of access to material resources and the right to reign over people. The purpose of the political design of the tributary countries from about 1280 was generally to secure these interests for the Norwegian crown in its most distant territories, and we should add that the new system of province-communal rule was based on predictability (rule by law), participation by the community (consensus), and royal representation. The king himself never visited any of his tributary provinces after 1266. In the case of the border country of Orkney the introduction of the Norwegian law-code and the establishment of a provincial commune also aimed at reducing the position of the earl and strengthening the ties between king and country. Moreover the new border country regime should be viewed in relation to the Scottish king, who was a potential threat to Norwegian dominion over the islands. Communications must have been an enormous challenge to Norwegian authorities.

We do not know much about how royal rule functioned in Orkney prior to 1267. Therefore I will not enter into a discussion of whether the system of royal management through royal officers, called *sysselmen*, was to become a permanent feature in Orkney before 1300. However after 1267 at the latest the earls lost all trace of being princes, a process that had started in 1195. Instead they should be looked upon as some sort of royal governors. Moreover for most of the 134-year period from Magnus V's appointment as earl in 1300 to William Sinclair's installation in 1434 there was, according to W. P. Thomson, no *sui juris* earl on the islands, which meant that the country had to be ruled by royal officers and ombudsmen, many of them of local or Scots descent.[15] The last in a string of *sysselmen* was to be Alexander le Ard, one of the pretenders to the title of earl after Earl Malise of Strathearn who died in the 1350s. Alexander was installed "for a trial period" in 1375, but another of Malise's descendants was appointed earl of Orkney four years later in 1379, namely Henry Sinclair. At that point, the position had been vacant for close on thirty years. The last person we know of with an equivalent authority over the islands was the Scotsman David Menzies. He was appointed royal governor in 1423, but in all likelihood, he never actually took up the position. Before him, Bishop Thomas Tulloch was governor, and he probably took part in the running of the islands on behalf of both the king and the earl right up to his retirement in 1461.[16] In Norway it had become commonplace by then to furnish bishops with royal offices and to involve them in the council of the realm.

In their turn, these royal officers surrounded themselves with an entourage of subordinate servants or bailiffs. Moreover, from the beginning of the 13th century, the kings had already started to build up a network of clients, the so-called hirdmen (royal liegemen), from among the leading men in Orkney. We encounter them already in the early 1220s, and the system was further amended during the reign of King Magnus IV. Royal liegemen were still found in the islands during the reign of King Eric the Pomeranian in the first half of the 15th century – and as late as the close of the 1500s, the winter session of the Lawthing in Kirkwall is described as a gathering of royal liegemen.[17]

The Earl

The Norwegian king, then, had indisputable and undivided secular dominion over the Orkneys; he was the one and only lord of the country. We may say that the king's previous supremacy or indirect control was replaced by direct royal dominion because of the settlement between Earl Harold and King Sverre in 1195.[18] This control was further strengthened by the agreement with Scotland in 1266, and was confirmed during the 1267 talks between Earl Magnus Gilbertsson and King Magnus Håkonsson which took place in Bergen.[19] After 1195 the relationship with the earls was to be considered an internal matter between the king and his liegemen – and it was at a Norwegian gathering of royal liegemen in Bergen that unqualified submission to the king was forced upon Harold Maddadson.

Despite the curtailment of the earl's authority embedded in the agreement from 1195, the earldom must nonetheless have been perceived as an anomaly in the state that was being created by the kings during the late 1200s. It is symptomatic that the *Hirdskrá* from the 1270s draws up very strict parameters for the powers invested in the earl's office; at the same time as it is stated elsewhere that entertaining earls is something to be avoided.[20] As already mentioned from the 1270s the earl was little more than a royal deputy or officer. All authority was delegated to him by the king, and in principle his duty was to manage the country on behalf of the sovereign, which he probably did using local ombudsmen when in charge of the earldom. In all practical matters there was no difference between the office of the earl and that of the other royal governors, be they sysselmen or the late medieval lensmen, though the military obligations of the earls may have been more extensive. It is not stretching things by any means to interpret the sources between 1267 and 1434 as expressions of a conscious royal policy aimed at keeping the earls of Orkney within the constitutional parameters defined by the Norwegian law.

However, when Håkon V Magnusson in 1308 abolished the title of earl in Norway an exception was made for the earls of Orkney[21], who had a sort of hereditary right to the dignity of the title; though this right was not automatically implemented, and the hereditary claim was not unconditional, as we see from disputes about the succession in the 1350s, the 1370s and the 1430s. And the prime interest of the claimants was not the office of earl as such, but the earl's benefice since royal appointment gave them usufruct to the earldom revenues, i.e. rent from earldom land, fines, and probably part of the taxes as well.

Originally, this hereditary right seems to have been understood as applying undisputedly to only the dynasty of the earls. Hence, several earls could be in office at the same time. This was analogous to the Norwegian system of joint kingship, which was abolished after 1163. Ascension to joint earlship required acceptance from one of the other earls – unless the pretender had the support of the king, or the power to do whatever he liked. After the rule of the joint earls Pål and Jon (1232), individual succession was introduced in the Orkney earldom – a change that was probably connected to the fact that the earl was now regarded as a royal Norwegian governor and officer. We do not know of any regulations with regards to the practical implementation of the hereditary right. The king thus seems to have had free rein in such matters, as in 1379 for example, when Håkon VI appointed Earl Malise's grandchild Henry Sinclair earl of Orkney at the expense of his older cousin Alexander le Ard.

From the 1230s, the earls were all of Scottish descent, though this had probably no impact on the alleged Scotification of Orcadian culture and community, which does not become noticeable until the latter half of the 14th century or even later. Barbara Crawford is almost certainly correct in saying that the church was the main source of Scottish influence in the islands during this period. In this sense, the 1379 appointment of Henry Sinclair heralded a change. The active participation of the Sinclairs in Scottish politics also meant that Orkney was pulled closer to Edinburgh. As Barbara Crawford has pointed out, there is a direct line from Earl William's involvement in Scots national politics to the mortgaging of Orkney in 1468 and the subsequent property exchange between King James and Earl William in 1470.[22] Furthermore, the Sinclairs were earls for no less than three generations beginning in 1379, their tenure interrupted only by a period of vacancy from ca. 1420 to 1434 following the death of Earl Henry II. This gave a degree of stability to the institution and functioning of the earldom that was unmatched in the entire period from 1266, even though the earls may hardly have set foot on the islands after 1400.

The Country

After 1266 Orkney, called "Landet" (the country), and the Orcadians were regarded as a commune incorporated in the kingdom and directly subordinated to the king. Late medieval sources therefore take care to distinguish between *the country*, on the one hand, and *the earldom in the same locality* on the other. We don't know for certain when the old principality was turned into a commune, but we can be sure that it started with the introduction of the Norwegian Landlaw, which should contribute towards securing a Norse social organisation in the Orkney Islands long after they had become *de facto* Scottish.

The provincial commune, in other words, was part of the new state system that took its definitive form under Håkon V Magnusson (1299—1319), and as such an instrument of royal rule.[23] At the same time, however, the Lawthing also represented the Orcadians, the Shetlanders, the Icelanders etc. vis à vis both the monarchy and the outside world, as can be evidenced on several occasions during the 1300s. Hence, it was this "Communitas Orchadensis" which the prominent Scotsman Duncan Anderson addressed in 1357 on behalf of one of Earl Malise's heirs. Duncan was claiming that, after Malise's death in 1350, the Norwegian king should have suspended the earldom's income. Moreover, he asked the Orcadians not to let funds be taken out of the country before the heir had been given an opportunity to make an appearance before them. Any failure to comply with his directive would be regarded as inheritance fraud, and he threatened financial sanctions in reprisal. We know that this claim had no warrant in contemporary legislation, and that it must be understood as a pretension rather than a right. The Orkney community passed the request on to the king, and matters cooled down.[24]

Then in 1369, when an open conflict erupted between the bishop on the islands and King Håkon's *sysselman* and close relative, Håkon Jonsson, the country's most prominent men were drawn into the conflict. The settlement states that henceforth, the bishop and the best men in Orkney and Shetland would rank first and foremost in all councils relating to the king, the church, and the people, in accordance with the country's laws and customs. Furthermore, the settlement states that like other bishops in the kingdom of Norway, the bishop would have good native men from Orkney and Shetland in his service.[25] We see that these "best men of the country" have both Norwegian and Scottish names, suggesting that the new state border was no obstacle to immigration from the Scottish mainland: we see too that some of the Scotsmen even gained entry into the Orcadian elite.

There is no evidence of any Norwegian fear that the islands would become "Scottified", and it is unlikely that people thought along the lines of national boundaries at the time. On the other hand we can observe that in the 15th century this mixed Norse-Scottish elite look upon themselves as true natives fighting to protect the system of provincial self rule and their own political privileges against foreigners, i.e. Scots intruders. They even refer to 'wild Scots', as in the substantial Letter of Complaints presented by the Orcadians to the state leadership in Copenhagen in 1425. The main grievance was that David Menzies, Henry Sinclair II's brother-in-law and ombudsman in Orkney had appropriated both the country seal and the lawbook and violated the political privileges of the native 'good men'.[26]

Orkney in the 15th century, Norse community and Scandinavian-British frontier

After 1379 connections between the Western provinces and the Norwegian monarchy loosened. This applied to Iceland and the Faroes as well as to Shetland and Orkney. In part, this development was probably due to the fact that during the reign of Håkon VI Magnusson and his queen Margrete, the Norwegian state leaders became more and more involved in Nordic politics, and the Nordic question came to dominate Norwegian and Norwegian-Danish politics as the 1380s progressed. Moreover, the western parts of the realm were probably regarded as unproblematic. After all, Scotland did not constitute a threat, and no-one was challenging the authority of the monarch on the islands. Furthermore, after Norway, Denmark, and Sweden formed the Nordic union in 1397, leadership of the state was transferred to Denmark.

The new union monarchy was primarily oriented towards the Baltic. In relation to the rest of Scandinavia, Norway's old Atlantic dominions thus ended up in a geopolitical backwater. After 1400, traditional Norwegian national interests had to give way to the Baltic-German policies of the Nordic union.[27] Up to 1460 the attention of the union's kings was completely absorbed by the province on its southern border – that is to say, the dukedom of Slesvig. Nonetheless, the 1426 negotiations in Bergen about renewing the Treaty of Perth suggest that there was a certain understanding that the Northern (our Western) Isles and the relationship to Scotland were primarily a Norwegian concern.

The tributary countries were managing well on their own. The provincial communities functioned even without the presence of royal bailiffs and envoys, in Orkney as well as in Iceland. Letters from Orkney in both the 14th and the 15th centuries bear witness to a strong sense of regional identity. As we have seen a clear distinction is made between the country's native men and foreigners, and a primary concern was to secure the land for the country's own men. Having the support of a sovereign in this struggle was a clear advantage. At the same time, the Orcadians also developed reasonably good relations with the new dynasty of earls, as indicated by their support for William Sinclair's candidature for the earlship in the 1420s. Moreover, it does not seem that the transferral to Scotland had any undue influence on conditions in the provincial communes for the first couple of generations after 1468. It was only as a consequence of the transition to Scottish sheriff rule from 1540 onwards, and the new large-scale immigration of Scots threatening the positions of the native farmers, that the Norwegian traditions started to fall apart. Nevertheless, it was going to take another couple of generations before local public life had adopted a predominantly Scottish flavour, and even after 1611 remnants of the Norse community traditions continued to exist.[28]

The 15th century thus turns out to be a golden age for Orkney (and Shetland). Extensive self rule and only modest involvement from outside authorities, Norwegian or Scottish, also meant that the Northern Isles for a short while returned to their former position as a Norse-British frontier.

Conclusion

Not only did the Treaty of Perth bring together two states with a new common border at the northern tip of Scotland – the two states divided by the Pentland Firth also represented different systems of government. North of the Firth there was a (geographically speaking) very extensive, sea-based realm with a shared language, a shared code of law, and uniform bodies of government. The Norwegian realm extended from Greenland in the west to the present-day Gothenburg in the south-east and to the Kola Peninsula in the north-east. The ceding of the semi-Celtic areas in the west strengthened its homogenous Norse character. The relative homogeneity – ethnically, socially and politically speaking – does not, however, mean that the Norwegian realm was a national state in the modern sense: in comparison with today's Norway, the Norwegian realm of medieval times must be considered a political and cultural conglomerate; but it was a conglomerate in which there existed some important common denominators. Some like to talk about a Norwegian Atlantic empire in the Central Middle Ages, I would prefer to call it a Norse Commonwealth.

The new state border also cut deeply into the old earldom of Orkney. Where the border between Norway and Scotland had earlier been more of a continuum, both in political and ethnic terms, it was now a line on the map. The active state building on both sides of the Pentland Firth also had the consequence of severing the political bond between the two parts of the old Norse earldom. The joint earldom ceased to exist in 1375. And while the Orcadians strengthened their regional Orcadian identity, the Caithnessians became Scots and foreigners. We must assume that Orcadians of Scottish descent also mastered the local language, and they may have provided a link to the English-speaking part of Scotland. There is reason to believe that the Orcadians, like the Shetlanders, remained bilingual for centuries to come.[29]

South of the Pentland Firth lay Scotland with a population of approximately the same size as Norway's, but occupying a considerably smaller area of space, and with substantial ethnic and linguistic diversity.[30] None of the Scottish historians I have consulted seems to consider that a Scottish nation developed in the Middle Ages, although many tend to talk of a national monarchy. This common monarchy is thus seen as an umbrella covering a number of peoples, where the Norse element seems to have had no place up to the mid 1500s, although Scandinavian Scotland continued to exist not only after 1098, but also after 1266 – and for that matter, even after 1468. In Scots historiography, the national question is primarily concerned with the relationship to England.[31] However, even if the Scottish realm qualifies even less than the Norwegian one for the term nation in the Middle Ages, the most important difference between the two realms was political: whereas the Norwegian medieval state was to a large extent built on a communal and federal principle, the Scottish realm was founded on feudal institutions and traditions, with lords, earls, and clan chieftains as the country's real masters. This is a paradox, since it must be admitted that the Norwegian realm's enormous geographical extent and scattered population were considerable obstacles to central political government and the execution of power. The secret must lie in the shared law, as well as in the development of systems of provincial self-government within the parameters of the realm, in principle under the auspices of the monarchy.

It is difficult to ascertain how far these two cultures – Scottish and Norse – had a mutual influence on each other: but it is a fact beyond dispute that the Norse culture in the Northern Isles was flavoured by Scottish influence. As far as I am concerned, we may well talk of Scotification, but we should guard against believing that what we are witnessing here is a cultural and social amalgamation which was virtually fore-ordained to lead to the ceding of Orkney to Scotland, and with it the annexation into something that with time starts to look like a Scots nation. The mortgaging of the islands and acquisition of the earldom title in 1468-70 was purely a matter of politics, engineered by King James III in Edinburgh. And, even though he was eager to secure Orkney and Shetland for the Scottish Crown, he did not think in terms of any form of national integration of Orcadians and Shetlanders into Scotland. However it certainly signified that more than four centuries of long and mostly peaceful neighbourhood had come to an end.

Notes

[1] *Norske Middelalderdokumenter* (NMD), Sverre Bagge et al. (eds.) no. 25, cf. *Diplomatarium Norvegicum* (DN) VIII no. 9, *Regesta Norvegica* (RN) III no. 788, cf. no. 787, DN VIII no. 276.

[2] Moreover, the renewal in 1426 is described as a "Composicio inter regem Noruegie et Skocie [...]"; in other words as a treaty between the Kingdoms of Norway and Scotland (DN VIII p. 310).

[3] M. J. Wilks: *The Problem of Sovereignty in the later Middle Ages*, Cambridge 1963 pp. 525; Matthew Strickland: "In Coronam Regiam Commisereunt Iniuriam: The Barons' War and the Legal Status of Rebellion, 1264-66", in *Law and Power in the Middle Ages. Proceedings of the Fourth Carlsberg Academy Conference on Medieval Legal History 2007*, edd. Per Andersen et al., Copenhagen 2008, pp. 172.

[4] Barbara E. Crawford: "The Earldom of Caithness and the Kingdom of Scotland 1150—1266", in *Essays on the Nobility of Medieval Scotland*, ed. K.J. Stringer, Edinburgh 1985, p. 38, cf. the fragment of King Magnus the Lawmender's saga in *Norges kongesagaer*, vol 4 ed. Finn Hødnebø and Hallvard Magerøy, Oslo 1979 p. 351-55.

[5] F. ex. DN II no. 691.

[6] *Adam av Bremen. Beretningen om Hamburg stift, erkebiskopenes bedrifter og øyrikene i Norden*, edd. Bjørg Tosterud Danielsen et al., Oslo 1993, p. 210f and 214f. Adam of Bremen, *The Archbishops of Hamburg-Bremen* trans. F.T. Tschan, 1959, New York, pp. Cf. Tore Nyberg: "Adam av Bremens syn på Norden", in *Dokumentation av medeltidssymposiet i Lidköping 21-22 april 1990 i anledning av Götiske Förbundets 175-årsjubileum*, Lidköping 1990; Laurtitz Weibull: "Geo-etnografiska innskott och tankelinjer hos Adam av bremen", in *Scandia. Tidskrift för historisk forskning*, vol. Iv, Lund 1931.

[7] The agreement is referred to in Snorre Sturlasson's *Magnus Berrføtts saga* (written c. 1230, *Norges Kongesagaer,* vol. 2, eds. Finn Hødnebø et al., Oslo 1979 p. 232, cf. *Heimskringla* III, *Íslenzk fornrit* XXVIII, Reykjavík 2002, p. 224) and in *Håkon Håkonssons saga* (written 1264-65, *Norges Kongesagaer* vol. 4, Oslo 1979, p. 241). We should notice that Magnus' saga is rather vague with regard to the geographical extent of the agreement. According to Snorre (over)lordship over the islands west of Scotland, the so-called Suðreyar (the Hebrides), was the prime concern of King Magnus. The saga-text does not explicitly include Man in the agreement, which came about after the Norwegian king had ended his military campaign in the Irish Sea and conquered Man, Anglesey and one third of Bretland (Wales). Then he conquered the Hebrides from King Gudrød, and finally, after having attacked Scotland, Magnus reached an agreement with the King of Scots who accepted Norwegian dominion over the Western Isles and part of the western seaboard of Scotland. King Håkon's saga confirms that King Melcolm (Edgar) in 1098 accepted formally King Magnus' territorial claims on the western seaboard of Scotland. Man is not mentioned in this connection, only the Hebrides. This corresponds to the contemporary *Chronicle of the Kings of Man and the Isles* (ed. George Broderick, Manx National Heritage 2004, p.f.34r.-f.35r), which does not mention the Scots-Norwegian agreement at all, neither any Norwegian overlordship over the kingdom. Instead the Manx Chronicle tells us a story about King Magnus who chose to leave Norway after having violated St Olav's tomb, and who took over Man almost peacefully after some kind of civil war between the Manxmen in 1098. And from there he ruled his newly conquered territories in the Irish Sea and the western seaboard until he

died (in 1103), which is not true since King Magnus at the turn of the century was busy in Scandinavian politics. Nevertheless, the 1098 agreement should make a basis for Norway's claim of supremacy over the Kingdom of Man and the Isles later in the medieval period, and both in principle and de lege the 1098 agreement lasted until 1266.

[8] Hans Jacob Orning: *Unpredictability and Presence. Norwegian Kingship in the High Middle Ages*, Leiden-Boston 2008.

[9] Crawford op. cit. 1985 p. 25ff.

[10] Barbara E. Crawford: "Norse Earls and Scottish Bishops in Caithness", in *The Viking Age in Caithness, Orkney and the North Atlantic*, ed. Colleen E. Batey et al., Edinburgh 1993.

[11] In his doctoral thesis, *Masters of the Narrow Sea. Forgotten Challenges to Norwegian Rule in Man & the Isles 1079—1266* (Oslo 2007, p. 111 and p. 156, cf. pp. 213-20), Ian Beuerman claims that the Irish Sea, which admittedly constituted one geopolitical area until well into the thirteenth century, stopped being a frontier from 1171 with Henry II's move to Ireland. According to Beuerman the Irish Sea from the later twelfth century was inland water within the Angevin sphere of interest, and the southern part of the Kingdom of Man and the Isles, the political centre of Man itself, lay in its centre. And he concludes that "The area outwith the 'English Empire' had shrunk to northwestern Ireland and the Scottish Western Seaboard." Beuerman is certainly right in stressing the new political situation in the Irish Sea brought about by the English expansion in the area. Nevertheless Norwegian claim of overlordship over Man was in principle not questioned either by English or Scottish authorities prior to 1266. According to Norwegian sources from the 13th century, the only threat to Norwegian overlordship over Man and the Isles came from Scotland under Alexander II and III. Besides, as far as I can see the English expansion in the Irish Sea did not affect the nature of the political march-character of the Norse principalities in the region prior to 1266.

[12] Inger Ekrem and Lars Boje Mortensen: *Historia Norwegie*, Oslo 2003 p.55-75, cf. Randi Bjørshoel Wærdahl: *Norges konges rike og hans skattland. Kongemakt og statsutvikling i den norrøne verden i middelalderen*, Trondheim 2006.

[13] See Ebbe Hertzberg's combined index and glossary of *Norges gamle Love* (NgL) vol. V, Christiania 1895, under "veldi", p. 701.

[14] Steinar Imsen: *Grenser og grannelag i Nordens historie*, Oslo 2005, pp. 147ff. See also Carsten Pape, "Rethinking the Medieval Russian-Norwegian Border", in *Jahrbücher für Geschichte Osteuropas*, vol. 52, 2004.

[15] *The New History of Orkney*, Edinburgh 2001, p. 181.
[16] Barbara E. Crawford: "The Bishopric of Orkney", in S. Imsen (ed.): *Ecclesia Nidrosiensis*, Trondheim 2003 pp. 151ff.
[17] J. Storer Clouston: "The 'goodmen' and 'hirdmen' of Orkney", in *Proceedings of the Orkney Antiquarian Society*, iii, 1924-25.
[18] Steinar Imsen: "Earldom and Kingdom. Orkney in the Realm of Norway 1195—1379", in *The Faces of Orkney. Stones, Skalds and Saints*, ed. Doreen J. Waugh, Scottish Society for Northern Studies 2003 pp. 66-73..
[19] Steinar Imsen: *Hirdloven til Norges konge og hans håndgangne menn*, Oslo 2000 p.80f..
[20] Ibid. pp. 82ff.
[21] NMD p. 248.
[22] Barbara E. Crawford: "The Earldom of Orkney and Lordship of Shetland. A Reinterpretation of their Pledging to Scotland 1468—70", in *Saga-Book*, xvii, parts 2-3, London 1967-8.
[23] Steinar Imsen: "Det norske grenselandskapet Jemtland", in Harald Gustafsson and Hanne Sanders (eds.): *Vid gränsen. Integration och identiteter i det förnationalle Norden*, Stockholm and Gothenburg 2006, pp.63-74.
[24] DN II no. 337, cf. RN VI nos. 458, 459.
[25] DN I no. 404.
[26] DN II no. 691.
[27] Steinar Imsen: "The Union of Calmar — Nordic Great Power or Northern German Outpost?", in *Politics and Reformations: Communities, Polities, Nations and Empires*, edd. Christopher Ocker et al., Leiden-Boston 2007.
[28] Steinar Imsen: "Public Life in Shetland and Orkney c. 1300—1550", in *New Orkney Antiquarian Journal*, vol. 1, Kirkwall 1999.
[29] Berit Sandnes: "Fra norn til skotsk. Det Norrøne språkets skjebne på Versterhavsøyene ca.1300-1750" in S.Imsen 2005, pp.164ff.
[30] Matthew H. Hammond: "Ethnicity and the writing of Medieval Scottish History", *The Scottish Historical Review*, vol. lxxxv, 1: no. 219, April 2006.
[31] A.A.M. Duncan: *Scotland. The Making of the Kingdom*, Edinburgh 1975, p. 111, cf. ibid. pp. 101ff: Ranald Nicholson: *Scotland. The Later Middle Ages*, Edinburgh 1978, p. 24f.; *Historical Atlas of Britain*, ed Malcolm Falcus and John Gillingham, 1981, p. 90f.; Bruce Webster: *Scotland from the eleventh century to 1603*, 1975, p. 12; T.C. Smout: *A History of the Scottish People 1560—1830*, London 1969, p. 18f.

Bibliography

Printed Sources

Adam av Bremen. Beretningen om Hamburg stift, erkebiskopenes bedrifter og øyrikene i Norden, edd. Bjørg Tosterud Danielsen & Anne Kari Frihagen, Oslo 1993

Chronicles of the Kings of Man and the Isles, ed. Georg Broderick, Manx National Heritage 2004

Diplomatarium Norvegicum (DN), vol. 8, edd. C. R. Unger & H. J. Huitfeldt, Christiania 1871

Heimskringla III, Íslenzk fornrit vol. XXVIII, ed. Bjarni Aðalbjarnason, Reykjavík 2002.

Hirdloven til Norges konge og hans håndgangne menn, ed. Steinar Imsen, Oslo 2000

Historia Norwegie, edd. Inger Ekrem & Lars Boje Mortensen, Oslo 2003

Norges gamle Love (NgL) vol. 5, ed. Ebbe Hertzberg, Christiania 1895

Norges Kongesagaer, vol. 1-4, edd. Finn Hødnebø et al., Oslo 1979

Norske Middelalderdokumenter (NMD), edd. Sverre Bagge, Synnøve Holstad Smedsdal & Knut Helle, Bergen, Oslo, Tromsø 1973

Regesta Norvegica (RN) vol. III, edd. Sverre Bagge & Arnved Nedkvitne, Oslo 1983, vol. VI, ed. Halvor Kjellberg, Oslo 1993

Literature

Beuerman, Ian, 2007, *Masters of the Narrow Sea. Forgotten Challenges to Norwegian Rule in Man and the Isles*. Doctoral dissertation, Faculty of Humanities, University of Oslo

Clouston, J. Storer, 1924-25, "The 'goodmen' and 'hirdmen' of Orkney", in *Proceedings of the Orkney Antiquarian Society*, iii, pp.9-20

Crawford, Barbara E., 1967-8, "The Earldom of Orkney and Lordship of Shetland. A Reinterpretation of their Pledging to Scotland 1468-70", in *Saga-Book*, xvii, parts 2-3,pp.156-76

Crawford, Barbara E., 1985, "The Earldom of Caithness and the Kingdom of Scotland 1150-1266", in *Essays on the Nobility of Medieval Scotland*, ed. K. J. Stringer, pp.25-43

Crawford, Barbara E., 1993, "Norse Earls and Scottish Bishops in Caithness", in *The Viking Age in Caithness, Orkney and the North Atlantic*, ed. Colleen E. Batey et al., pp.129-47

Crawford, Barbara E., 2003, "The Bishopric of Orkney", in *Ecclesia Nidrosiensis*, ed. S. Imsen, Trondheim, pp.143-58

Duncan, A. A. M., 1975, *Scotland. The Making of the Kingdom*, Edinburgh
Historical Atlas of Britain, edd. Malcolm Falcus et al., London 1981
Hammond, Matthew H., 2006, "Ethnicity and the writing of medieval Scottish History", in *The Scottish Historical Review*, vol. LXXXV, 1: no. 219,
Imsen, Steinar, 1999, "Public Life in Shetland and Orkney c. 1300-1550", in *New Orkney Antiquarian Journal*, vol. 1, pp.53-65
Imsen, Steinar, 2003, "Earldom and Kingdom. Orkney in the Realm of Norway 1195-1397", in *The Faces of Orkney. Stones, Skalds & Saints*, ed. Doreen J. Waugh, Scottish Society for Northern Studies, pp.65-80
Imsen, Steinar (ed.), *Grenser og grannelag i Nordens historie*, Oslo 2005
Imsen, Steinar, 2006, "Det norske grenselandskapet Jemtland", in *Vid gränsen. Integration och identiteter i det förnationella Norden*, edd. Harald Gustafsson & Hanne Sanders, Stockholm & Göteborg, pp. 61-85
Imsen, Steinar, 2007, "The Union of Calmar – Nordic Great Power or Northern German Outpost?", in *Politics and Reformations: Communities, Polities, Nations, and Empires*, edd. Christopher Ocker et al., Leiden & Boston, pp. 471-90
Nicholson, Ranald, 1978, *Scotland. The Later Middle Ages*, Edinburgh
Nyberg, Tore, 1990, "Adam av Bremens syn på Norden", in *Dokumentation av medeltidssymposiet i Lidköping 21-22 april 1990 i anledning av Götiska Förbundets 175-årsjubileum*, Lidköping pp.13-21
Orning, Hans Jacob, 2008, *Unpredictability and Presence. Norwegian Kingship in the High Middle Ages*, Leiden & Boston
Pape, Carsten, 2004, "Rethinking the Medieval Russian-Norwegian Border", in *Jahrbücher für Geschichte Osteuropas*, vol. 52, pp.161-87
Sandnes, Berit, 2005, "Fra norn til skotsk. Det norrøne språkets skjebne på Vesterhavsøyene ca. 1300-1750", in S. Imsen ed. *Grenser og grannelag i Nordens historie*, pp. 163-75
Smout, T. C., 1969, *A History of the Scottish People 1560-1830*, London
Strickland, Matthew, 2008, "In Coronam Regiam Commiserunt Iniuriam: The Barons' War and the Legal Status of Rebellion, 1264-1266", in *Law and Power in the Middle Ages. Proceedings of the Fourth Carlsberg Academy Conference on Medieval Legal History 2007*, edd. Per Andersen et al., Copenhagen.
Thomson, William P. L., 2001, *The New History of Orkney*, Edinburgh
Webster, Bruce, 1975, *Scotland from the eleventh century to 1603*, Cambridge
Weibull, Lauritz, 1931, "Geo-etnografiska innskott och tankelinjer hos Adam av Bremen", in *Scandia. Tidskrift för historisk forskning*, vol. IV, Lund, pp. 210-23

Wilks, M. J., 1963, *The Problem of Sovereignty in the Later Middle Ages*, Cambridge

Wærdahl, Randi Bjørshoel, 2006, *Norges konges rike og hans skattland. Kongemakt og statsutvikling i den norrøne verden i middelalderen.* Doktoravhandlinger ved NTNU, 107, Trondheim

CHAPTER 2

Caithness: Another Dip in the Sweerag Well

Doreen Waugh

Introduction

In 1989, I wrote a chapter on Caithness place-names (see Bibliography), and drew towards a conclusion with the following words:

'An obscure Scots place name in Dunnet Parish could be used as a metaphor for place-name studies as a whole. The name is *Sweerag Well* (*ND261744) and the derivation is from Scots *sweerie-well* 'a spring which flows plentifully for a while after rain, but cannot be depended on for a constant stream'. I take these words out of context but the metaphor proved unintentionally prophetic. My PhD thesis, completed in 1985, covered only six coastal parishes of Caithness – Reay, Thurso, Olrig, Dunnet, Canisbay and Wick – and I did not have the opportunity to complete the remaining four parishes at that time (Fig. 2.1). I have now returned to the county of Caithness with the aim of revitalising the wellspring of my personal place-name studies with ideas which have been revised, or are in the process of revision, in the light of intervening toponymic research.

To an extent I regret having focused solely on the north-east coast of Caithness in my original work but I was privileged to have such excellent local informants in these parishes that I would have missed out on a great deal of valuable information had I opted to do otherwise. I should say that I am sure I could have found equally good local informants in the areas which I did not cover (i.e. Halkirk, Bower, Watten and Latheron) but time was against me and them in the mid-1980s. Sadly, two of my original informants, Mr James Gunn of Reay and Mrs Margaret Gunn of Canisbay, have died in the intervening years and I would like to pay tribute to them here. As far as I am aware, although they had the same common Caithness surname, Gunn, they were unrelated but they shared a love of Caithness and its cultural history, and both had a most impressive depth of knowledge of the areas in which they lived. The local informant is essential to place-name research, particularly in the north of Scotland where documentary sources are sparse.

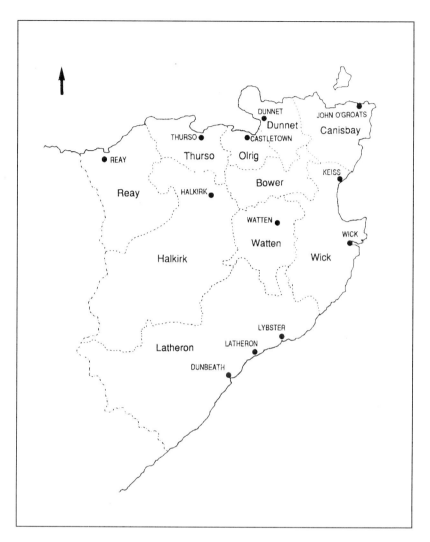

Figure : 2.1 Map of Caithness parishes

A proposed dictionary of Caithness place-Names

My current project is the production of a dictionary of Caithness place-names, which, with her permission, is modelled on Diana Whaley's recently published volume entitled *A Dictionary of Lake District Place-Names*. I shall also frequently turn to Simon Taylor's impressively detailed volumes of *The Place-Names of Fife* (see Bibliography).

The index of my thesis has approximately 1500 entries but there will not be 2,500 entries in the dictionary, as a mathematical calculation might lead you to expect, because the place-names will be organised differently in the dictionary. There is much revision to be done but some draft sample entries are included here to give the reader a foretaste:

A Dictionary of Caithness Place-Names

Draft Sample Entries

ACHUNABUST NC995645 (hab.), A~ BRIDGE NC988648 (Reay par.).
Achunabust 1876 (*6" OS*). [ax"Vn@bist]

▶ The generic in Achunabust is Gaelic *achadh* m. a field, farm. Lack of early written references makes it difficult to propose a convincing interpretation for the second part of the name, although the stress placed on the second syllable of the name in pronunciation supports the suggestion that *Unabust was once a place-name in its own right, most probably Nordic rather than Celtic. The most probable source of the generic within this putative lost name is ON *bólstaðr* m. a homestead, which often takes the form *–bust* or *–bost* in Gaelic-speaking parts of Scotland. The specific could be the Old Norse personal name *Uni*, gen. *Una* m. (*Lind 1931, 804*) which is thought to occur in place-names in Orkney and Shetland, but the documentation for this Caithness name is much too scanty to be confident of its origin.

BIELD, THE ND008642 (Reay par.).
The Bield 1876 (*6" OS*). [D@ "bild]

▶ Scots ***bield*** a shelter for animals, usually cattle. This name, however, applies to a freestone quarry on Isauld Hill and it could be referring metaphorically to the hollowed-out shape of the quarry or, literally, to its use by sheep who find it offers gratuitous shelter.

CANISBAY, EAST ND344725, CANISBAY, WEST ND338724 (hab. & par.). ["kan@sbi]
Canenisbi 1222 x 45 (*CSR*), prebenda de *Cranesby* 1275-78 (*Bagimond's Roll*), *Canysby* 1437 (*CSR*), *Canesbi* 1445 (*CSR*), *Cannasby* 1480-81 (*REO*), *Kannesbie* 1508 (Mey), *Kanesby* 1539 (*RMS*), *Cannesbie* 1542-43 (*RMS*), *Cannisbe* 1554 (Mey), *Canespie* 1582 (Mey), *Canesbey* 1631 (Mey), *Canesbay* 1640 (Mey), *Conansbay* 1654 (*Blaeu*).

▶ Assigned as a prebend of Dornoch cathedral by Bishop Gilbert in his constitution of 1224 x 45 (Cowan 1967, 26). There are numerous early forms of this name but the examples listed above give a clear impression of the variant spellings which occur. Derivation is problematic. The generic most probably derives from Old Norse *bœr* m. a farm, the vowel in which is weakened to [i] in unstressed position (Waugh 2006, 298). The problem is that it is unusual to find personal names combined with *bœr* in the north of Scotland but both Canisbay (probably) and neighbouring Duncansby (certainly) have personal-name specifics. Canisbay Church was dedicated to the Celtic Saint *Drostán* whose name is associated with the founding of the monastery at Deer in Aberdeenshire and in the Gaelic notes in *The Book of Deer* mention is made of a Clann Chanann who held lands locally. The actual reference is to the 'taesec Clande Canan' or 'chief of the *Clann Chanann*', in which Chanann is the genitive form of the name *Cano*, a rare name probably of Pictish origin (Jackson 1972, 32). It would have to be supposed that the Norse knew the occupant of the farm by name and added an ON genitive singular masculine inflexional ending *–s* to *Cano*, or that they might have known him as a member of the *Clann Chanann* and added a further ON genitive singular masculine ending to the genitive form of the name *Cano,* in which case his own name could have been something quite different.

DOUNREAY NC982669 (hab.), D‑‑ BURN NC990645, D‑‑ QUARRY NC997668, LOWER D~ NC986669, UPPER D~ NC998661 (Reay par.). [dun"re ; dun"ra]
Dunray 1369 (*REO*), *Dunra* 1542-43 (*RMS*), *Downra* 1562 (Mey), *Donraa* 1577 (Mey), *Dounra* 1610 (*RMS*), *Dunra* 1654 (Reay), *Dounrae* 1654 (*Blaeu*), *Downreay* 1753 (Forse), *Downreay* 1770 (Freswick).

▶ The first element is Gaelic *dùn* m. a fortified house or hill; a fortress. For a detailed discussion of the second element see REAY.

DUNCANSBY ND385727 (hab.), D~ HEAD ND406732, BIEL OF D~ ND388708, BOARS OF D~ ND388743, BURN OF D~ ND391710, HA' OF D~ ND376732, NESS OF D~ ND390738, STACKS OF D~ ND400719 (Canisbay par.). ["dVNk@nsbi]
Dungalsbær 12th cent. (*OSaga*), *Duncasbe* 1552 (*RMS*), *Duncasbie, Dunkasbie* 1592 (*RMS*), *Dungasbe* 1573 (Mey), *Dungysbÿ* 1573 (*Ortelius*), *Dungusbe* 1574 (Mey), *Duncans Bay* 1654 (*Blaeu*), *Boers of Dungysby* 1654 (*Blaeu*), *Dungysby* or *Duncans Bay Head* 1654 (*Blaeu*), *Dungsbay Head* 1755 (*Roy*).

▶ The generic most probably derives from Old Norse *bær* m. a farm (cf. CANISBAY). The *Orkneyinga saga* form strongly suggests that the specific is the Celtic personal name *Dungal*. *Duncan* first appears as a clear alternative to *Dungal* on Blaeu's map although, arguably, it was already present in forms such as *Duncasbe* 1552. The present-day local pronunciation used by older people is ambivalent but tends towards *Dungal* [>>dauN'nsbi]. Younger locals give [>>dVNK'nsbi], citing the modern map form as the source of their pronunciation.

bore, boar (Sc.) a big wave breaking on the beach amid smaller ones; also used as a place-name for a bad roost (tidal race), as in the *Bore of Papay* (ORK 1929 Marwick) and the *Boars of Duncansby* ND388743. ["bo@r]

PAPEL ND342731 (Canisbay par.).
Papel 1876 (*6" OS*) ["pap@l]
▶ This name refers to a small rock, covered at high tide, lying off-shore from the Kirk of Canisbay. The present church is listed as probably dating from the fifteenth century (*Inventory of Monuments* 1911, 7), but it probably built on a much older religious site. The specific derives from *Papar* which was the Norse name for the early Irish anchorites or priests whose presence can be traced in place-names throughout the area which came subsequently under Norse control (see Crawford (ed.) 2002; and the *papar* website www.paparproject.org.uk under Caithness). There are at least two possibilities for the generic in this name. The name *Papil* is recorded by Jakob Jakobsen in three places in Shetland (North Yell, Haroldswick and Burra Isle) and he suggests that it corresponds to ON *Papýli*, from **Papabýli* (*býli* = *bæli* from **ból*), the residence of the priest (Jakobsen 1993 reprint, 172). An alternative possibility is that the Caithness name derives from *Papahólmi* (*hólmi* being a weak form of ON *hólmr* m. an island), although *hólmr* is not normally used of islands which are submerged at high tide.

REAY NC967647 (hab. & par.), R~ BURN NC969632, DOUNR~ NC982669, NEW R~ NC960645. ["re]

Ecclesie de Ra 1222 x 1245 (*Caithness and Sutherland Records*), *landis of Ra* 1439 (*CSR*), *Raa* 1507 (*RSS*), *Ray* 1554 (Mey), *Raa* 1557 (Mey), *parochia de Rei* 1616 (*RMS*), *Rae* 1619 (*RMS*), *Rhae* 1640 (*Retours*), *Rae* 1635 (Reay), *Rea, Rheay* 1649 (Reay), *Reay* 1755 (*Roy*), Reay 1876 (*6" OS*).

▶ Almost certainly one of the six churches of the diocese reserved to the bishop's mensa in the constitution of Gilbert, bishop of Caithness (1224 x 45) (Cowan 1967, 169). There are at least two possibilities for the etymology of this name. Both Watson (1926, 117-118) and MacBain (1922, 11) suggest Gaelic *ràth* m. fortress, artificial mound, but none of the earliest written forms contains any hint of final *-th* in the orthography, which might be expected even though already silent in speech (see MacDonald 1981-82, 32-56) and it is worth asking why the apparently pleonastic *Dounreay* (Watson suggests *dùn* m. fortress, plus *ràth* m.) should have been coined, because there is no positive evidence for the existence of two neighbouring forts. This etymology is, nevertheless, worthy of serious consideration in a possible chronological sequence. Another possibility is Old Norse *rá* f. 1) a corner, nook; 2) a pole (used metaphorically of 'a long, stretched-out elevation). The farm-name *Re* which occurs at least five times in Norway is an interesting and very relevant parallel (*Norske Gaardnavne* v.10, 140; v.12, 478-9; v.14, 155; v.15, 34 and v.15, 92). Gaelic speakers in Caithness often borrowed earlier Norse place-names as part of their own later toponymic constructions.

The ordering of names in the main body of the dictionary will be alphabetical, as in this excerpt, but the names discussed hereafter are not in alphabetical order, starting with Reay and Dounreay to illustrate some points about layout. Note that the root names (i.e. the first name in the capitalised lists of names) are taken from the 1st edition of the 6" Ordnance Survey maps of Caithness, dating from the mid-1870s. After each root name there is a six-figure grid reference, followed by a bracketed indication of the status of the place. In the case of Reay, it is both village and parish name, so hab. for 'habitative' and par. for 'parish'. Secondary names are then listed in the order you see here: names with Reay as first element are followed by those with Reay as second element, in alphabetical order where there is more than one name in each of these categories. A simple phonetic transcription of the root name has been added, (thanks to a useful suggestion made by Simon Taylor at the Day Conference). Dounreay is included in the list because it plays a significant part in the discussion of the name Reay, but Dounreay also has a dictionary entry in its own right as a recognisably distinct location which people might wish to check. Onomastic jargon will be kept to a minimum, but a few expressions such as compound, simplex, specific, generic and so on will be used and will be defined at the start of the dictionary. Where there is some uncertainty about the elements in a name, the neutral descriptions 'first element' and 'second element' will be used.

Following the root and secondary names, an italicised selection of early forms are listed when sources are available. More often than not, the list of early forms is very small indeed and all can be included. Written and published map sources are italicised and local estate papers – many now housed in the National Archives of Scotland – are in ordinary script. Sources such as *Caithness and Sutherland Records* are written out in full here but there will, of course, be a list of bibliographic and other abbreviations in the dictionary, as in '*landis of Ra* 1439 (*CSR*)'. The bibliographic details of sources are only included here when reference is made to them in the course of discussion. In other words, some references are included in the excerpt the details of which will appear in the dictionary but not in this brief article.

After the list of early forms, there is a comment on the root name, indicated by a triangular pointer. For the most part, the elements which occur in secondary names will be dealt with separately through inclusion in an alphabetical list of elements used in Caithness place-names. This should avoid too much repetition of explanation. Occasionally, a focused comment on an individual secondary name will be included in the text following the root name, such as the comments on Dounreay which are included under Reay. If the root name is a medieval parish the comments will begin with a reference to Cowan's *The Parishes of Medieval Scotland* (1967)), as in the cases of Reay and Canisbay. On occasion, reference will be made to *Origines Parochiales Scotiae* (1855). Thereafter an etymology (or more than one) will be proposed. For Reay there are at least two etymological possibilities. One is Watson's and MacBain's suggestion of a Gaelic etymology for the name (Watson,1926), 117-8; (MacBain, 1922), 11, and the other is my suggestion of an Old Norse origin.

It seems probable that both Old Norse and Gaelic have their chronological place in the toponymic history of the name and this entry may be further revised to reflect that belief more fully, with the additional suggestion that a "Celtic" name may well have preceded the later Norse re-interpretation of it. The question here really is whether the Gaelic-speaking people mentioned at the end of the current entry for Reay were post-Norse and were reinterpreting a Norse name which was itself a reinterpretation of an earlier "Celtic" name. It is not a question that can be easily answered.

Dounreay will, of course, appear at an earlier point in the dictionary than Reay but the reader is referred back to the discussion of its generic under the root name Reay, because Dounreay is essentially a secondary name, although now a place of some significance or even notoriety in Caithness and beyond. Where a place is not a parish name, its status will be listed after the root name, if habitative, and the parish name will appear in brackets after all secondary or non-habitative place-names, as it does for Dounreay. It is difficult to think of a single term which can describe all non-habitative place-names because they are not necessarily all topographical. In fact, the comment can generally be left to explain the nature of the individual name.

Before moving on to Canisbay Parish in the east, there are two further place-names in Reay Parish which illustrate commonly encountered problems or perhaps just 'matters for consideration' rather than 'problems'. Both of these place-names, regrettably, come into the category of names for which I have, as yet, found no forms earlier than the 1876 6" OS map reference, which is surprising for a habitative name like Achunabust. Part of the problem lies in not really knowing what to look for. It is frustrating, but Achunabust is a very small settlement and it may well be that it does not appear in the written record before the 19th century, although it may have come into existence long before that time. Names which have *achadh* as their generic tend to be elusive in written record in the north, even when they almost certainly incorporate earlier Norse place-names, such as the name *Unabust. Modern pronunciation can still be very helpful in unravelling the various linguistic layers of a place-name.

On a point of detail, the expression *Old Norse* will be reserved for the written language, as in the text below Achunabust where there is reference to the Old Norse personal name *Uni*. Old Norse or ON is also used for what the written form can reasonably be supposed to have been and, in that case, it will be introduced by an asterisk, eg. *Unabust. *Nordic* will be used as a general term for Scandinavian when in opposition to *Celtic*, and *Norse* for the actual people who settled in the north of Scotland.

The final example from Reay Parish is The Bield. All names of this common type (i.e. definite article + Scots or English word) are listed alphabetically in the dictionary under the first letter of the root name and the proposed generic element will be highlighted to show that it also appears in the separate list of elements. A longer explanation will be given in the text only where there is specific reason to comment on the location or other circumstances of an individual name. This Reay example of **bield** needs an explanatory comment because it refers to a freestone quarry rather than an actual purpose-built shelter for animals.

Let us now turn to Canisbay, which appears on the map as Canisbay East and Canisbay West, both of which, in a sense are secondary but are listed as root names. It is a very complicated and puzzling place-name, as the detailed comment on the name indicates, and the possible connection with the monastery at Deer in Aberdeenshire is particularly interesting and worth duplicating here:

> Canisbay Church was dedicated to the Celtic Saint *Drostán* whose name is associated with the founding of the monastery at Deer in Aberdeenshire and in the Gaelic notes in *The Book of Deer* mention is made of a Clann Chanann who held lands locally. The actual reference is to the 'taesec Clande Canan' or 'chief of the *Clann Chanann*', in which Chanann is the genitive form of the name *Cano*, a rare name probably of Pictish origin (Jackson 1972, 32). It would have to be supposed that the Norse knew the occupant of the farm by name and added an ON genitive singular masculine inflexional ending *–s* to *Cano*, or that they might have known him as a member of the *Clann Chanann* and added a further ON genitive singular masculine ending to the genitive form of the name *Cano*, in which case his own name could have been something quite different.

Moving on to Duncansby, you will see that the specific in Duncansby was certainly recorded as a personal name in *Orkneyinga saga*, 20, 45, 56, 66, 78, 82, 83, and I am really using that certainty to underpin my discussion of the specific in Canisbay when I suggest a personal name. Following the Duncansby entry there is an example of what might appear in the separate elements' section to which the reader would turn for an explanation of an element such as BOARS~. The importance of the local informant is again highlighted in the Duncansby entry.

These two *–by* names, with their Celtic personal-name specifics, one of which at least is certain, are misfits in a northern context. In fact, even in the

Danelaw, where personal-name specifics do occur with *bý* the vast majority of them are Scandinavian names, **not** indigenous personal names, which makes these two place-names even more difficult to explain; more unique one might also say. In her 1972 study of Scandinavian settlement in Yorkshire, Gillian Fellows-Jensen (G. Fellows-Jensen, *Scandinavian Settlement Names in Yorkshire* (Copenhagen, 1972)) identified 210 *býs* of which approximately 57% had either certainly or most probably a personal-name specific. Of these personal names, 'approximately 90% are Scandinavian, 7 English, 3 Irish, and one probably Continental Germanic' (Fellows-Jensen, *Yorkshire*, 9).

Caithness in the North Atlantic

This apparent divergence of Canisbay and Duncansby from the norm that one might expect in an integral part of the Orkney earldom leads me on to the second section of this paper. Some important work has been done in the years which have passed since the mid-1980s and it has informed my thinking on Caithness. In a nutshell, it has been beneficial to see Caithness in the wider northern Scottish and North Atlantic context which has been the focus of my own recent work and I have certainly also gained understanding from work done by other researchers in the neighbourhood of Caithness and further afield (P. Gammeltoft, C. Hough and D. Waugh (eds.), 2006).

You will note that Barbara Crawford's *Scandinavian Scotland* was published in 1987 two years after I had completed my thesis. Barbara's scholarly work has influenced me in all sorts of ways and I should like to thank her for all she has done to put Scandinavian Scotland, as she describes it, firmly on the map. There is also the important work done by Barbara Crawford and Simon Taylor to the south of Caithness in Easter Ross (B. E. Crawford and S. Taylor, 2003, 1-76). This, along with a paper read at a conference in Strathnaver in 1992 and published some years later (D. Waugh, 2000, 13-23), has helped me to see Caithness in its northern mainland context, which is just as important as seeing it in the northward-looking context of Orkney and, geographically more distant, Shetland. At the 1992 conference, I said:

'It is my opinion ... that we should give more weight than we do to topographical naming as evidence of Norse presence in a settled capacity in north and north-west Scotland. I find it difficult to accept that, on the one hand we argue that topographical names are often the oldest names in a region of Norse settlement ... and yet, on the other hand we tend not to cite these as sound evidence of any form of permanent settlement if *bólstaðr, setr, sætr* and other primary elements indicative of habitation and farming are not to be found in place-names in the vicinity. It is difficult to believe that Norse terms could attach themselves with such tenacity to topographical features if the Scandinavians were not present, on the land, in numbers large enough and permanent enough to perpetuate the names surrounding their dwellings' (Waugh, 2000, 15).

Since first writing these words in 1992, I have examined a number of Norse topographical generics in detail:

Coastal names:
D. Waugh, 'Toponymie et vocabulaire maritimes des îles Shetland', in Elisabeth Ridel (ed), *L'Héritage maritime des Vikings en Europe de l'Ouest.* (Caen, France, 2002), 377-399.
Nes-names:
D. Waugh, 'From Hermaness to Dunrossness: some Shetland ness-names', in A. Mortensen and S. Arge (eds), *Viking and Norse in the North Atlantic* (The Faroese Academy of Sciences, Faroe Islands, 2005), 250-256.
Eið-names:
D. Waugh, 'Place-Name Evidence for Portages in Orkney and Shetland', in C. Westerdahl (ed), *The Significance of Portages* (BAR International Series 1499, 2006), 239-250.

Topographical names deserve very serious attention from toponymists because they are often, in the case of names containing the elements *nes* and *dalr* for example, the stuff of which Norse livelihoods were made, indicating resources which were crucial to the Norse economy (e.g. places where fish could be caught at the coast, grazing and penning for animals and peat for fuel on the headlands, wood for various purposes in the valleys such Eskadale, in the Beauly/Strathglass area (Crawford & Taylor, 2003, 27) and, perhaps most important of all, routeways – whether river valley or island isthmus (Old Norse *eið*) (Waugh, BAR 1499, 239-250) – which offered opportunities for interaction of various kinds as people moved up and down rivers on the mainland or crossed over narrow necks of land while moving around their new island and mainland territories. However, I do also still believe that 'place-name generics which describe farms or other types of human habitation … are the most reliable indicators of extensive and prolonged Norse presence' (Waugh, 2000, 15) and we certainly find these in Caithness and, to a lesser extent, in Strathnaver. They are the building blocks of macrotoponymy but, viewing things from a local perspective, microtoponymy can often be more telling, if we know how to read it, and certainly more meaningful to the locals who use the names.

In her historical introduction to 'The Southern Frontier of Norse Settlement' Barbara Crawford first notes that the River Oykel was considered to be the southernmost limit of the territory which the earls held as the earldom of Caithness (Crawford & Taylor, 2003, 7). She then goes on to make a very important contribution to our understanding of the significance of the place-name Dingwall (= 'the field of the public assembly') as an indicator that the settlers in this area 'may have been allowed a degree of freedom from earldom control very different from Orkney or Caithness' (*ibid.*, 9) in that they had their own meeting place to regulate their own affairs. There is no certain example of Tingwall in Caithness to suggest any degree of independence from Orkney but, as has already been said with regard to Canisbay and Duncansby, there are a few indicators in the place-names of Caithness to suggest that there were interesting differences in this northern mainland part of the Orkney earldom which might suggest a degree of independence. There is a *Thing's Va Broch* in Reay Parish but I can find no references to *Thing's Va* which are earlier than the 19th century and I am consequently cautious about its possible interpretation as an ON *þing*-name. It is most likely to be a toponymic relict of Victorian antiquarian enthusiasm in the area.

Note that Caithness itself is a *nes*-name and, just as Canisbay and Duncansby do not quite fit the pattern of –*by*/-*bie* names in either Orkney or Shetland (Waugh, 2006, 298-321), so Caithness does not quite fit the usual pattern of *nes*-names. Nesses come in various shapes and sizes and it would be quite inaccurate to say that they are generally long and thin, but they do perceptibly jut out from the surrounding land and the whole landmass of Caithness, arguably, may fit that requirement. A study of other *nes*-names, however, reveals that personal-name specifics are very rare indeed with *nes* and although the specific in Caithness is a tribal name, as W J Watson has explained (Watson, *CPNS*, 30) rather than a personal name, it is still out of the usual run of specifics combined with *nes*, which describe some aspect of location, land use, orientation and appearance. Note that *nes*-names in the Northern Isles often become medieval parish, or multiple-parish, names, so *nes* is an element which can be used as a descriptor of a unit which had some kind of administrative cohesion, and that may be a more likely explanation of why we have a *nes* in Caithness, even though the specific does not quite fit the norm. A parallel could be drawn with Dunrossness, Shetland, in this respect.

Dunrossness is a name which would appear to have applied to the whole of the south end of Shetland for several centuries at least and, in my opinion, most probably from the time of its original coinage by the first Norse settlers. There is certainly no evidence to suggest otherwise.

By comparison with the present-day Northern Isles the element *nes* is not common in Caithness place-names in general, which is not altogether surprising given the landlocked nature of the county, but it makes it even more interesting that it should be chosen for the area as a whole. Using the Pathfinder map as a source there are 380 *ness*-names in Shetland, 252 in Orkney and only 11 in Caithness, five of which are of the post-Norse '*Ness* of X' type.

So, were the eponymous *Cats* still there when the Norse arrived? What language did they speak? The possibility of a pre-Norse "Celtic" language has already been mentioned in the discussion of the name Reay, and Dunnet, Mey and Latheron could have been added as other early Celtic possibilities, along with one or two other obscure names such as Olrig. W J Watson suggests with reference to Sutherland that the tribe of *Cats* 'apparently entered from Caithness, and occupied the eastern and south-eastern part of the modern county, – Sutherland proper, as opposed to Strathnaver and Assynt, and proposes that the tribe were in Caithness 'at some point antecedent to the Norse invasion' (Watson, *CPNS*, 30). Is it possible that the eponymous *Cats* could have survived to co-exist, however briefly, with the Norse in Caithness? Was there an early Celtic ecclesiastical elite powerful enough to survive and have places like Duncansby and Canisbay named after them by the Norse? Did the name *Papel* originally refer to an important ecclesiastical establishment of some kind at Canisbay, which was there in the centuries before the arrival of the Norse, as suggested in the duplicated text below, and was it displaced by the name *Canisbay* because of the importance of a particular cleric and/or the Norse perception that the farming activities surrounding the *býli* or church at Canisbay were centrally important?

PAPEL ND342731 (Canisbay par.).
Papel 1876 (*6" OS*) ["pap@l]
▶ This name refers to a small rock, covered at high tide, lying off-shore from the Kirk of Canisbay. The present church is listed as probably dating from the fifteenth century (*Inventory of Monuments* 1911, 7), but it was probably built on a much older religious site. *Papar* was the Norse name for the early Irish anchorites or priests whose presence can be traced in

place-names throughout the area which came subsequently under Norse control (see Crawford (ed.) 2002). There are at least two possibilities for the generic in this name. The name *Papil* is recorded by Jakob Jakobsen in three places in Shetland (North Yell, Haroldswick and Burra Isle) and he suggests that it corresponds to ON *Papýli*, from **Papabýli* (*býli = bœli* from **ból*), the residence of the priest (Jakobsen 1993 reprint, 172). An alternative possibility is that the Caithness name derives from *Papahólmi* (*hólmi* being a weak form of ON *hólmr* m. an island), although *hólmr* is not normally used of islands which are submerged at high tide.

The questions could be never-ending and there are very few conclusive answers.

Negative evidence also gives pause for thought. In fact, if we had a foolproof way of reading the absence of place-name evidence, our judgements about the past would be much more sound. Why, for instance, if we do have two *–by* names in Caithness is no trace of the *huseby* system to be found, when there are *huseby* names throughout Orkney, which Barbara Crawford has discussed in an important recent article (2006, 21-44). Perhaps it isn't quite so strange that there are no *husebys* in Caithness because there is no trace of the *huseby* system in Shetland either, but Caithness is a great deal closer to Orkney than Shetland is, and it is surprising that there is no evidence that the *huseby* system crossed the Pentland Firth. I understand that a Husbay has recently 'turned up' in South Ronaldsay so perhaps one will 'turn up' in Caithness as well. I have this information from W. Thomson who said in a personal comment that 'Husbay, South Ronaldsay, is associated with a big abandoned farm known as Mucklehouse under which is the Rood Chapel, rumoured to be the parish church of a lost mid-parish'. Canisbay would have been ideal *huseby* material but it was given a different specific. Why? Perhaps the dating of the *husebys* in Orkney is critical here and comment from historians would be welcome.

Place-name elements to ponder

I should like to conclude with a very brief and still embryonic consideration of the use, in Sutherland and elsewhere in the North Atlantic, of the Old Norse generic *land* n. This generic, of course, has an English equivalent which makes it readily understandable, or so we are inclined to think, carrying with us, as we do, our own cultural and linguistic preconceptions, but do we really understand its precise application in an early Norse context? Inge Særheim recently wrote an interesting paper about the use of this generic as a habitative name in Orkney and Shetland (I. Særheim, 'Norse Settlement Names in – *land* in Shetland and Orkney', in Gammeltoft, Hough & Waugh, 2006, 216-229). *Land* as an area or district name, occurs in Shetland, Sutherland (ON *suðrland*), Iceland and Greenland. Orkney and Faroe, on the other hand, have ON *ey, øy* f. 'an island' as the generic. Both *land* and *ey, øy* were available to the Vikings as generics to apply to the territories which they were colonising in the North Atlantic, so why choose one rather than the other?

Ancient district names in Norway, Sweden and Denmark could be called *land* (e.g. Hordaland and Rogaland in Norway), as could islands such as Gotland and Åland, so there is nothing inherently surprising about the use of the generic in Sutherland and Shetland, but what, if anything, may it have to tell us about the nature of the Norse movement into these areas? Orkney and Caithness both seem to have pre-Norse tribal names as specifics, compounded with Old Norse topographical generics which were commonly used of areas under Norse administration. These topographical generics – *ey* and *nes* – carry no implication of *landnám* or land-taking, so were the Norse able to move into these areas without too much opposition or do the generics simply signify that these were among the earliest places occupied, perhaps even in a fairly haphazard fashion at the start, in the period of Viking colonisation? It has been argued that topographical names are often the oldest names in a region of Norse settlement, although it is usually pointed out at the same time that they are notoriously difficult to date (e.g. G. Fellows-Jensen, 1984), 154-155), and that could be seen to apply to the district or area names for Orkney and Caithness. The land in both places – using the word in its literal, Modern English sense – is flat and easy to cultivate and might well have been very tempting to the earliest settlers.

Having established themselves in such desirable territory, did the Norse then plan to consolidate their holdings and decide to extend their territorial influence/domination to Sutherland in the south – the southern part of their province of Caithness, lying to the south of the Ord of Caithness – and perhaps even to Shetland in the north? Many would respond to this question by saying that it is wrong to think of a chronological sequence in this way and perhaps we should forget, for the moment, about issues of chronology and just consider whether the implication of choosing the place-name element *land* is that the settlement of Shetland, Iceland and Greenland were all *landnám* events indicating a major, planned influx of Norse settlers, although we only have the documentary evidence, in *Landnámabók*, to support such planned land-taking in Iceland? Faroe is akin to Orkney in that its generic carries no implication of planned land-taking.

Place-names are seldom as neatly systematic as we would wish them to be, however, and there are many toponymic conundrums to exercise the mind endlessly. I have touched on one or two here and left many questions unanswered for the moment. I hope to have the opportunity to revisit these conundrums many times and with many readers as I work towards completion of a dictionary of Caithness place-names.

Abbreviations

Blaeu= J.Blaeu, 'Theatrum orbis Terrarum, sive Atlas Novus' in D.G.Moir (ed.)*The Early Maps of Scotland* (Edinburgh, 1973)

CPNS, see Watson,W.J.

CSR =A. W. and A. Johnston (eds.), *Caithness and Sutherland Records*, Vol. 1 (London, 1909)

Forse=Sutherland (Forse), unpublished estate papers, in Scottish Record Office (NAS), cat. no.GD139

Freswick=Sinclair (Freswick), unpublished estate papers, in Scottish Record Office (NAS),cat.no.GD136

Inventory of Monuments 1911= *Third Report and Inventory of Monuments and Constructions in the County of Caithness,* RCAHMS, (Edinburgh)

Mey= Sinclair (Mey), unpublished estate papers, in Scottish Record Office (NAS), cat.no.GD96

Norske Gaardnavne, Rygh, O., 18 volumes 1897-1936 (Kristiania)

Origines Parochiales Scotiae, Vol. II, Part 2, Bannatyne Club (Edinburgh, 1855)

Orkneyinga saga (H. Pálsson and P. Edwards, Orkneyinga Saga (London, 1978))

Ortelius=Ortelius, Abraham. 'Scotiae Tabula 1573' in Moir. p.164

REO =*Records of the Earldom of Orkney1299-1614* ed. J.Storer Clouston (Scottish History Society, 1914)

Reay=Reay Estate papers, unpublished, in Scottish Record Office (NAS) cat.no.GD84

Retours = *Retours:Inquisitionum ad Capellam Domini Regis Retornatarum, quae in Publicis Archivis Scotiae adhuc Servantur, Abbreviatio,* edited T.Thomson (1811-1816)

*RMS=Registrum Magni Sigilli Regum Scotorum,*ed. J. M. Thomson and others (Edinburgh, 1908-)

Roy = Roy, William, 'The Military Survey of Scotland 1747-55' in Moir, 1973, p. 189.

RSS=Registrum Secreti Sigilli Regum Scotorum, ed. M. Livingstone and others (Edinburgh, 1908-)

Bibliography

Cowan, I., 1967, *The Parishes of Medieval Scotland,* Scottish Record Society, Vol. 93

Crawford, B.E., 1987, *Scandinavian Scotland* , Leicester

Crawford, B.E., (ed.) 2002, *The Papar in the North Atlantic. Environment and History*, St.John's House Papers no.10, (St.Andrews)

Crawford, B. E., and Taylor, S., 2003,'The southern frontier of Norse settlement in northern Scotland: place-names and history', *Northern Scotland*, vol. 23, pp.1-76

Crawford, B. E., 2006, 'Houseby, Harray and Knarston in the West Mainland of Orkney. Toponymic indicators of administrative authority?', in P. Gammeltoft & B. Jørgensen (eds), *Names through the Looking-Glass* Copenhagen, pp.21-44

Fellows-Jensen, G., 1984, 'Viking Settlement in the Northern and Western Isles – the Place-Name Evidence as seen from Denmark and the Danelaw', in A. Fenton & H. Pálsson (eds.), *The Northern and Western Isles in the Viking World*, Edinburgh, pp.148-68

Gammeltoft, P., Hough C., and Waugh, D.,(eds.), 2006, *Cultural Contacts in the North Atlantic: The Evidence of Names* Lerwick

Gammeltoft P., and Jørgensen, B.,(eds), 2006, *Names Through the Looking-Glass*,Copenhagen

Jackson, K., 1972, *The Gaelic Notes in the 'Book of Deer'*, Cambridge

Jakobsen J., 1993 reprint, *The Place-Names of Shetland*, Lerwick

Lind, E.H., 1931, *Norsk-Isländska Dopnamn ock Fingerade namn Från Medeltiden* (Uppsala, 1905-15, supplement Oslo, 1931)

MacBain, A., 1922, *Place-Names of the Highlands and Islands of Scotland,* Stirling

MacDonald, A., 1981-82, 'Caiseal, Cathair, Dùn, Lios and Ràth in Scotland, II' *Bulletin of the Ulster Place-Name Society,* Series 2, vol.4, pp.32-56

Marwick, H., 1929, *The Orkney Norn,* Oxford

Moir, D.G., 1973, *The Early Maps of Scotland*, 3rd ed., Edinburgh

Taylor S., with Markus G., 2006, *The Place-Names of Fife*, vol. I, Donington

Taylor, S., with Markus, G., 2008, *The Place-Names of Fife*, vol.2, Donington

Watson, W. J., 1926, *The History of the Celtic Place-Names of Scotland*, Edinburgh

Waugh, D.,1989, 'Place-names', in Donald Omand (ed.), *The New Caithness Book*, Wick, pp.141-155

Waugh, D., 2000, 'A scatter of Norse names in Strathnaver', in J. R. Baldwin (ed.) *The Province of Strathnaver* (Scottish Society for Northern Studies), Edinburgh,13-23

Waugh, D., 2002, 'Toponymie et vocabulaire maritimes des îles Shetland', in E. Ridel (ed), *L'Héritage maritime des Vikings en Europe de l'Ouest*, Caen, pp.377-399.

Waugh, D., 2005, 'From Hermaness to Dunrossness: some Shetland ness-names', in A. Mortensen and S. Arge (eds), *Viking and Norse in the North Atlantic* (The Faroese Academy of Sciences), Faroe Islands, pp.250-256

Waugh, D., 2006, 'Place-Name Evidence for Portages in Orkney and Shetland', in C. Westerdahl (ed), *The Significance of Portages* (BAR International Series 1499), pp.239-250

Waugh, D., 2006 'The --by/-bie names of Shetland', in Gammeltoft P., and Jørgensen, B.,(eds), 2006, *Names Through the Looking-Glass*,Copenhagen, pp.298-321

Whaley, D., 2006, *A Dictionary of Lake District Place-Names*, Nottingham

The Norse gods in Scotland

Judith Jesch

In 1987, Barbara Crawford presented what was then, and to some extent continues to be, the accepted view of the conversion of the Scandinavian settlers of Scotland to Christianity, which involved a gradual progress 'From pagan gods to Christ'.[1] Her discussion of the 'pagan gods' was divided between two chapters, on 'archaeological evidence' and on 'literary evidence'. The discussion of pagan beliefs and practices was focused mostly on burials,[2] while a subsequent section promisingly entitled 'Pagan and Christian sculpture',[3] conceded that 'The Scottish examples [of hogbacks] ... give no evidence of pagan associations'[4] and it is only in the Isle of Man, and possibly on one slab from Iona, that traditional, and possibly pagan, Norse motifs are found.[5] In a short section on 'Pagan beliefs and the cult of Odin' in a later chapter on 'literary evidence',[6] Crawford noted that 'The pagan element of early Norse society does not emerge strongly in the written sources'.[7] Nevertheless, she drew a brief sketch of a heroic warrior society using a variety of written sources (not all of them relating to Scotland) and largely focused on Odin. This section closed with brief comments on place-names and other landscape features and lore which have been associated with Odin or some of the other Norse gods.

In a recent book, Alex Woolf found little evidence for an Odinic warrior society in Viking Age Scotland, instead he conjured up a strong contrast between the 'intricate relationship between kingship and pagan ritual' of 'ancient Scandinavia' and the Scottish islands where 'pagan ritual may have been largely domestic and not dissimilar from ... folkloric practices'.[8] Part of the difference lies in the varying approaches and intentions of the two books – Crawford's pioneering work on Scandinavian Scotland used a broad sweep of evidence to reconstruct the impact of the Vikings in North Britain, while Woolf's book avowedly set out to complicate the narrative(s) of Scotland's past, emphasising the fragmentary and contradictory nature of the sources. Both scholars were critical of the sagas, but Crawford did use them, whereas Woolf eschewed them.

Also representative of this current trend to emphasise the difficulties of the evidence rather than to construct a narrative from any available source material, is Lesley Abrams's paper (in honour of Barbara Crawford) on the conversion of Scandinavians in the Hebrides.[9] She emphasised the difficulty of knowing anything at all about how this process happened, but usefully worked through a number of possible models and considered what evidence, if any, there was for them. Abrams did not go as far as Woolf, who claimed that 'Scandinavian Scotland slipped, without drama, into Christendom',[10] instead she assumed that some fairly positive act of conversion was needed in what she considered to have been a clearly pagan population. But her focus was on conversion and the Church, so she had little to say about what went before. Like Crawford, Abrams's main evidence for 'paganism' came in the form of a burial, the female grave from Barra, but she admitted that using changes in burial practice to measure religious conversion is 'doubtless too simplistic'.[11]

Inspired by all three of these works, the present paper attempts to clear some ground for the study of Scandinavian paganism in Scotland, by returning to first principles and attempting simply to assemble and assess whatever evidence there might be for the worship of the Scandinavian gods or the practice of the Scandinavian religion within the territory of present-day Scotland, with as close a focus on source-criticism as possible.[12]

The context for this attempt is the recognition of the diasporic character of the Norse migrations westwards.[13] Any migration causes dislocations which may particularly affect language, religion, and identities—migrant communities do not and cannot simply replicate the homeland. Scandinavian settlers in Scotland may have come from different parts of Norway (or indeed Scandinavia) which, with its great extent and diversity of geography, has always had a variety of language and culture. Moreover, the westward migrations of this period did not end in the British Isles, but continued to Iceland, Greenland, and even North America. The result of these migrations, originating principally though not exclusively in Norway, was what might be called a Viking diaspora, at least if we accept current definitions of

>...*migration* as physical movement, resettlement and re-establishment of key social institutions; *diaspora* as the consciousness of being connected to the people and traditions of a homeland and to migrants of the same origin in their countries; and *transnationalism* as the practices of exchange of resources, including people, across the borders of nation states.[14]

While this definition is primarily aimed at contemporary conditions, it has much that is relevant to the Viking Age expansion across the North Atlantic. From Shetland to Greenland, we can see evidence of migrations that resulted in diaspora and an early form of transnationalism. Thus, the physical movement of peoples (the 'migration') westward across this region led to the re-establishment in new communities of key social institutions such as the extended farming household, with its dependents and slaves, and the political and legal arrangements attached to the local or regional *þing*. The continuing contact between the colonies and with Norway encouraged a consciousness of connectedness, based on language, and cultural and historical traditions, fulfilling the requirements of a 'diaspora'. Recent definitions of 'diaspora' have tended to emphasise '[d]ecentered, lateral connections [which] may be as important as those formed around a teleology of origin/return'[15] and this connectedness was by no means unidirectional. Thus the colonies exchanged resources with each other and with the homelands, in the form of trade, and they exchanged people in social, religious and cultural networks that may be described as embryonically 'transnational'.

Since the full conversion to christianity of Scandinavians in the homelands postdated the westward migrations, an interesting question is that of the status of Norse mythology and the Norse gods in this diasporic culture. Our knowledge of this mythology comes largely from the evidence of texts written in medieval (and christian) Iceland. But if Iceland was part of a larger diaspora, and if Chesnutt is right that its subsequent isolation encouraged its preservation of cultural traditions,[16] then it is of some interest to ask whether other colonies in the diaspora once shared these traditions, derived from the homelands. If we see Iceland as preserving, in its literary art, a mythology originally exported there with the migration from the Norwegian homeland, then we would have to assume that such traditions were also exported to the other colonies of the diaspora and we can legitimately question what happened to them there.

It will not be possible in this short paper to come to any conclusions about the wider nature of Scandinavian paganism in North Britain, but a survey of the evidence (or lack of it) is a necessary first step in the process. In the discussion below I will consider a range of evidence that has previously been linked to individual Norse gods and some mythological figures. This evidence comes mainly from archaeology, place-names, and poetry, with occasional glances in the direction of folklore and personal names. All of this evidence is problematic in some way, yet none of it can be entirely dismissed, if only because much of it lives on in popular, and even some scholarly, accounts. The problems are surveyed first, then the evidence presented as it relates to particular gods or mythological figures or concepts.

What is usually considered the most obvious evidence for Scandinavian paganism in Scotland is the relatively large number of burials identified as pagan because of the presence of grave-goods and other features which distinguish them from contemporary christian graves.[17] Nevertheless, despite pagan features such as a Thor's hammer discussed below, or the burial of the dead with horses and boats, these burials 'may leave us uncertain with regard to pagan Norse views of the after-life, but instead ... provide glimpses of life in Scandinavian Scotland'.[18] Olwyn Owen has recently emphasised the difficulties of distinguishing between 'pagan' and 'christian', or 'Viking' and 'Pictish', graves in some Orkney cemeteries, and suggests that the situation in the tenth century was particularly fluid.[19] There may have been substantial chronological overlap between christian Pictish and pagan Viking burial practices, indeed there may even have been 'later waves of Viking settlers, born and bred in Norway, ... arriving as pagans in the Northern Isles in the tenth century, at a time when people of Scandinavian origin in the islands had already begun to adopt Christian burial practices'.[20] Other archaeologists stress 'the gradual adoption during the "pagan" Viking Age of Christianity at the local private landowner level reflected in small chapels at a date significantly earlier than that indicated by the written sources for the adoption of Christianity at the higher political level'.[21] The dividing line between paganism and christianity thus appears increasingly more difficult to define. And, while the archaeological finds do provide evidence of different burial rites practised by the Norse settlers, which might well be pagan, they have little or nothing that can serve as evidence for the cult of the Norse gods.

Place-names are even less fruitful. There is little evidence for theophoric or any sort of pagan names in Scotland. Most name-elements signify natural or topographical features, buildings, or ownership (in that they contain personal names). Such names as have religious reference in Scandinavian Scotland are more often than not christian. In the Northern and Western Isles, for instance, there are several *Papeyjar* and related names (the focus of a research project led by Barbara Crawford) and a substantial number of names in *kirkja*- 'church'. In Orkney, Eynhallow, or *Eyin helga* 'the holy island', is

presumably a christian name because it is a medieval monastic site.[22] Hugh
Marwick identified a number of place-names in Orkney that he thought might
refer to pagan gods or sites,[23] but his suggestions were without exception
cautious and few have been convinced by them.[24] In general, the place-names
are recorded very late, and many of Marwick's admittedly tentative 'pagan'
etymologies have alternative, and generally better, explanations.

Paradoxically, the most copious evidence for Norse myth is in the poetry
produced in, or associated with, twelfth- and thirteenth-century Orkney.
However, this emanates from a rather different cultural and a ligious milieu,
well after the conversion to christianity, and has no direct relevance to the
cults of the Norse gods in pre-christian times, so it will not be discussed in
this paper.[25] I also avoid considering literary versions of Norse myths, about
the gods or other supernatural or legendary figures, unless there is fairly
good reason to associate them with Scotland at a time when such myths may
still have had some religious resonance.[26] Such a source might be Arnorr
jarlaskáld's poetry from the eleventh century, at least that which he produced
for the Earls of Orkney. But in general his poetry contains few allusions to
mythological narratives. Like all poets, he does make use of mythological
names (though quite sparingly) but as these do not refer to specific myths they
are not necessarily evidence for mythological knowledge.[27] This general lack
of interest in Norse myth is to be expected in the eleventh century, when there
is a sharp drop in the use of mythological kennings in court poetry.[28] Some
stanzas ostensibly composed in Orkney before the year 1000 and preserved
in *Orkneyinga saga* are few in number and pose many problems.[29] While it
might be possible to construct an argument that these are genuine oral poetry
from early medieval Orkney, such an argument would be complicated and
problematic, not least because of the great time gap between their supposed
date of composition and their earliest manuscript records.

Folklore from more recent times has traditionally been regarded as a fertile
source for ancient beliefs, yet there is precious little that can convincingly be
linked to the Norse gods. Most of the popular tales of the Northern Isles
are in the common currency of pan-Scandinavian tales and beliefs, with
their 'trows' and other mythical creatures.[30] Moreover, the folklore evidence
derives from 'a set of older discourses constructed around the notion of
folklore as survivals from an earlier stage of culture'.[31] Such an approach is
viewed as problematic by folklorists, especially for verbal lore, though more
stable meanings may be found in the more enduring evidence of landscape
and place-names.[32]

Odin, norns and valkyries

Evidence for the worship of Odin is notoriously sparse, even in the Scandinavian material, although there the god can at least be traced in place-names,[33] and is widely represented in Old Icelandic poetry and prose. There is little or no reliable evidence for the cult of Odin in the pagan period in Scotland, as much of what has previously been associated with the god can be explained in other ways and all the evidence is of uncertain date.

As already noted, Hugh Marwick's few 'pagan' etymologies for Orcadian place-names have alternative, and generally better, explanations.[34] Thus, Odness (a pointed headland) in Orkney is more likely to be from ON *oddr* 'point' than from Odin, the god, despite recent assertions to the contrary.[35] Ernest Marwick's enthusiasm for seeing 'Odin in a place-name'[36] is also unwarranted, for Orkney is 'very largely devoid of theophoric place-names',[37] as indeed is most of Scandinavian Scotland. Even names which may allude obliquely to the god are problematic. Thus, place-names containing the element *hrafn* 'raven' could refer to a person of this name or just to the bird, without any Odinic associations.[38]

The so-called 'Odin Stone' on Mainland in Orkney, long thought to be a relic of Odinic beliefs, has recently been reinterpreted as an 'oathing stone'.[39] Although Ernest Marwick gives a tantalising reference to apparently unpublished 'old myths relating to Odin' recorded in Sandwick in the nineteenth century, his editor acknowledges that the particular informant's 'folklore is now regarded as suspect'.[40] References to 'Odin' in Marwick's 'retelling' of the story of 'Assipattle and the muckle mester Stoor Worm' do not seem particularly well-motivated in the story and their antiquity is questionable.[41] The retelling is derived from Dennison's version collected on Sanday in the mid-nineteenth century, which mentions 'the great Oddic', whose identity with Odin is entirely conjectural.[42]

Odin is however mentioned in the poetry of Arnórr jarlaskáld. The introductory stanza of *Þorfinnsdrápa*, his poem in praise of Earl Thorfinn of Orkney, uses an Odinic kenning for 'poetry': *hrosta brim Alfǫður* 'mash-surf (ale) of the All-Father', referring to the poem itself.[43] Such a reference would demand of Arnórr's Orcadian audience that they knew who the All-Father was, that they would recognise that the 'surf of mash' was ale, and that they knew that the ale of Odin was poetry, as outlined in a number of myths recorded mainly in *Snorra Edda* (which is also where this stanza is preserved). But anyone who could understand Arnórr's poem at all would have been familiar with this convention and anyone who could not would be lost in any case. This relatively rare mythological reference in Arnórr's poetry (another is discussed below) does not reveal much about knowledge of or interest in Odin at a more general level in Orkney.

It has been suggested that a stanza attributed to the otherwise obscure Ormr barreyjarskáld, apparently a poet from Barra, shows Odin welcoming him into Valhalla:[44]

Hvégi er, Draupnis drógar
dís, ramman spyr ek vísa,
sá ræðr—valdr—fyrir veldi—
vagnbrautar mér fagnar.

There are many uncertainties in this interpretation, not least whether the poet's nickname actually refers to Barra in the Hebrides rather than somewhere else, when Ormr lived, or even whether the stanza is pagan or christian. In contrast to Faulkes's 'pagan' interpretation, Hermann Pálsson and Paul Bibire preferred to see the stanza as an example of christian Hebridean poetry, referring to God:[45]

...In what way, goddess of Draupnir's cord,
—I hear the lord to be mighty;
that ruler governs the realm
of the cart-way—he will welcome me.

The choice of pagan or christian interpretation may well depend on the date one chooses for the poem and other interpretations are possible, for instance that the stanza draws both a parallel and a contrast between a secular lord and a pagan or the christian God. Unfortunately, the poetry is too fragmentary, and not sufficiently contextualised, to reveal much.

A more convincing poetic reference to Odin comes in a stanza whose connection with Scotland is however more difficult to establish. *Heimskringla* cites two stanzas by Glúmr Geirason, ostensibly about the raiding activities of the sons of Erik Bloodaxe.[46] One of these stanzas praises a warrior for having 'sent' a 'sword-beaten' army to Odin (who is referred to by his alias Gautr) in Scotland. But this is hardly evidence for the cult of Odin in Scotland, only among some of its conquerors at the moment of conquest. The Odinic imagery continues in the next stanza cited (which also uses the god-name Frey of the warrior being praised), but here the geographical context is Ireland.

If Odin himself is hard to identify in Scandinavian Scotland, might we see echoes of his cult in other references to his domains of war and fate? In one of Torf-Einarr's stanzas, he claims that the Norns arranged the death of Halfdan in revenge for that of Rǫgnvaldr of Møre.[47] This is the only mythological reference in these stanzas. The participants in this episode were all born in Norway, and the anecdote (which also includes a reference to Odin in the prose) may well represent the beliefs of the first generation of Orcadians. However, much work still needs to be done to establish a context of composition for Torf-Einarr's verses. Previous scholars have concentrated on literary interpretations that do not question the attribution, and even Russell Poole, who has argued that they represent 'an early poem (or perhaps a cycle of poems) about Torf-Einarr', was not able to be very specific about their date or place of composition.[48]

The most notable apparent survival of a mythological tale is Sir Walter Scott's well-known account of the inhabitants of North Ronaldsay in the late eighteenth or early nineteenth century. When their minister read Thomas Gray's ode 'The Fatal Sisters' to them, which was of course based on *Darraðarljóð*, they claimed to know the song well 'in the Norse language'.[49] *Darraðarljóð*, though preserved only in *Njáls saga* and therefore suspect as an ancient poem, is localised there to Caithness and Poole is inclined to date it to the tenth century.[50] While admitting that 'this proposition cannot be proved', Poole takes the Scott anecdote to demonstrate that this poem had 'the most lasting life of all in oral tradition'.[51] But even if this is true, the poem's evidence for mythological knowledge in northern Scotland is relatively meagre. Its mythological references focus on valkyries, six of whom are named, and their role in choosing the slain in battle, conceived as a macabre act of weaving a *vefr verþjóðar* 'woven fabric of warriors'.[52] There is certainly a thematic link here with the reference to Norns in Torf-Einarr's stanza (noted above), which might suggest that the Odinic mythology of war and fate was known in tenth-century Scotland, but this hangs on the uncertain dating of both poems.

The 'Unst Lay', a poetic fragment recorded on Shetland's northernmost island in 1865, appears to be 'a Christianised version of the Rune Rime of Odin from the *Háva-mál*', in which a 'he' who is most likely Christ is said to have hung 'nine days' and 'nine lang nichts' on a tree.[53] The poetic fragment was heard from an old woman of Unst by a 'Mr. George Sinclair, a young, well-read working-man, a native of Shetland' who regretted 'very much I did not make some attempt, however runic, to take notes'.[54] Although Sinclair had read Mallet's *Northern Antiquities*, the latter does not actually cite the relevant verse of *Hávamál* or indeed mention the hanging of Odin. Nevertheless, the value of this evidence for ancient Odinic beliefs is slight.

However, too much attention to source-criticism may obscure significant patterns in the overall material, particularly when different forms of evidence are brought together. For Iceland, Guðrún Nordal has argued that Turville-Petre was too reductive in claiming that Odin was never worshipped there.[55] She argued that an attention to place- and personal names and archaeology can reveal patterns which are then supported by the more problematic literary sources. A similar approach to Scotland suggests that there may, after all, be some evidence for an Odinic warrior cult there. In this approach, no one piece of evidence is conclusive, but the overall patterns in the conjunction of different kinds of evidence may be.

Nordal draws attention to both personal and place-names in Iceland with possible reference to Odin.[56] It is an onomastic axiom that people are not named after gods, at least in pagan Scandinavia. Though this axiom can be and has been challenged,[57] it still by and large holds true, for the exceptions seem, paradoxically, to come from christian contexts. However, Odin had many names and some of these are used in personal nomenclature, most notably Grímr. The name may be recorded on a fragment of a runic memorial stone from Cunningsburgh, Shetland.[58] One of the Icelandic settlers said in *Landnámabók* to have come via Scotland is a Grímr who spent time in the Hebrides.[59] In *Orkneyinga saga* we find one person called Grímr and one called Gauti (another of Odin's names was Gautr),[60] but it must be remembered that the saga reflects mainly the nomenclature of the eleventh and twelfth centuries and much less the earlier period. For this we may need to turn to place-names. The name Grímr is commonly found in place-names in both the Northern and the Western Isles.[61] Personal names deriving from Odin's favourite animals, the raven, the wolf and the eagle, are not found in *Orkneyinga saga* at all, despite their popularity throughout the Scandinavian world. However, place-names containing the element *hrafn* are found in both the Northern and the Western Isles, as already discussed, while *ulfr* occurs in Shetland and the Hebrides, and *ǫrn* 'eagle' in the Hebrides.[62]

Nordal also draws attention to Icelandic burials containing both a horse and a spear.[63] Both of these are common grave-goods in pagan burials, so neither is significant on its own, but she argues that they may represent Odinic beliefs when found together. As in Iceland, there are burials in Scotland that contain both, notably Kiloran Bay on Colonsay, but also Grave 8 at Pierowall on Westray.[64]

Is there a similar pattern behind some of the names on the Orcadian island of Wyre? The name comes from ON *vigr* 'spear' and is clearly derived from the spearhead shape of the island, visible from any nearby eminence.[65] This small island contains one farm Rusness 'headland of the horses' and another Helyie, containing some form of the ON word *heilagr* 'holy'.[66] None of this is significant on its own, for example a 'ness of horses' is most likely simply to be a place where such animals were habitually penned.[67] It is hardly even significant all together, yet it may be suggestive if it fits into a larger pattern. Further work on place- and personal names, and on the burials of Scotland, may indicate whether this emerging pattern is strong enough to bolster an argument that Scandinavia's Odinic warrior cult was exported to Scotland as well as Iceland.

Thor, giants and dwarves

The most popular of the Norse gods appears to be more reliably attested in Scandinavian Scotland than his father, though still not extensively so.

A Thor's hammer amulet, 'unique … in Scotland' was found in the female Viking grave at the Broch of Gurness.[68] While Thor's hammers are turning up regularly in England, particularly East Anglia, as a result of twenty-first century metal-detecting activities, this is not (yet?) the case in Scotland. A putative Thor's hammer mould that Barbara Crawford drew attention to is still awaiting confirmation but seems unlikely as it is from a Roman site.[69]

It has been argued that the Caithness place-name Thurso indicates a cult of Thor, as Thorson has argued it was originally *Þórshaugr*.[70] This evidence is very uncertain as the name is notoriously difficult to interpret.[71] In his book on Norn, Michael Barnes appears to suggest that 'several Orkney place-names' contain the god-name Thor.[72] The evidence does not however stand up to scrutiny. Even Hugh Marwick prefers to derive Hourston on Mainland (the oldest form, from 1492, is *Thurstath*) from 'a personal name, but exactly which is doubtful'.[73] Similarly, Thurvo on Walls (first recorded in 1492 as *Thurwaw*) most likely contains a personal name rather than the god's name.[74] Even the otherwise uncritical Frans-Arne Stylegar admits that Tor Ness on Stronsay is of uncertain origin.[75] The same name occurs on Mainland and there, as Berit Sandnes points out, the lack of a genitive and the late date of its earliest recording (1882) makes it unlikely that it includes the name of the Norse god rather than a form of the word *torf* 'peat'.[76] Elsewhere in Scotland, some place-names which appear to contain the name Thor in fact have a medial vowel which suggests that they actually contain the common personal name *Þórir*, also used in place-names in England.[77]

Thor does appear as a personal name in the south-east of Scotland in the early twelfth century.[78] This is however hardly evidence for veneration of the god, only for the curious emergence of Thor as a fashionable name in christian Anglo-Scandinavian England and its spread thence to Scotland. The appearance of the simplex Thor as a personal name in England is usually explained by its development as a short form of the many common compound names in Thor-.[79] Though Per Stille has argued for its occurrence in two late Viking Age runic inscriptions from Sweden,[80] one of these is in fact a christian grave-slab rather than a standing rune stone, demonstrating that this appears to be an onomastic development of christian times.

While veneration of Thor is difficult to demonstrate, there is some evidence for a more broadly-based telling of stories about him. Paul Bibire has argued that an anecdote told about Earl Rǫgnvaldr, and associated with *Orkneyinga saga*, is based on the myth of Thor fishing for the world serpent (though composed with a view to christian exegesis).[81] This is not in itself implausible, as the sources for this myth are widely scattered in space and time throughout the Scandinavian world. Sculpture indicates that this myth was known elsewhere in the British Isles at an earlier date and it is perfectly possible that the myth was known in Orkney before it was put to christian use. The Orcadian folktale 'Assipattle and the muckle mester Stoor Worm',[82] already discussed, is a conglomeration of folktale motifs, for instance the hero is an 'ash-lad', the Scandinavian male Cinderella figure, who marries a princess. But the story may also owe something to the story of Thor fishing for the world serpent. Thus, the 'Stoor Worm' that Assipattle kills is a large serpent whose body is 'coiled … around the earth' and he goes out in a small boat to engage with it. His successful killing of the monster is accompanied by apocalyptic imagery as people thought it 'the end of the world'.

Some Orcadian evidence seems to reflect Old Norse myths about Thor's enemies, the giants. Yetnasteen in Rousay, the name of 'a large standing stone', is derived by Hugh Marwick from Old Norse *jötna-steinn*, referring to Norse mythology in which 'giants are represented as residing in rocks and hills'.[83] This conceit is indeed familiar and is clearly summarised in Old Icelandic poetological texts such as that known as *Litla Skálda*: ...*er rétt at ... kenna dverga til steina eða urða, en jǫtna til fjalla eða bjarga*.[84] A better example is the Dwarfie Stane on Hoy, a large rock-cut tomb. Of interest here is not only the name of the rock, but a story recorded in the sixteenth century which makes it clear that it was imagined as the residence of giants.[85] This source, written in Latin in 1529, uses the word *gigans*, the opposite of what we today would imagine as a 'dwarf'.[86] However, there is no evidence that the defining feature of dwarves and giants in Norse mythology was their size; more important is the fact just outlined that they both inhabited rocky places. Size is not a factor in the descriptions of giants in Eddic poetry; even in the *fornaldarsögur*, giants may be large but are not necessarily so.[87] There is also a close connection in both types of text between giants and dwarves and, in the *fornaldarsögur*, dwarves can take over some of the functions of giants.[88] The Dwarfie Stane demonstrates this close connection between the two and may also reflect the transition from giant to dwarf that can be traced in the Icelandic *fornaldarsögur*.

The dwarf Austri, one of the four imagined in Norse mythology as holding up the disc of the earth, is referred to in Arnórr's *Þorfinnsdrápa*, in which the sky is called 'Austri's toil'.[89] But as this reference is embedded in the well-known apocalyptic imagery of this stanza, it probably owes as much to christian traditions of the conversion period as to established Norse paganism.

Frey and Freya

Ole Crumlin-Pedersen's suggestion that boat burials provide an indication of the cults of Frey and/or Freya can be difficult to substantiate in the absence of other evidence and may in any case be difficult to extend to all burials of this type.[90] Graham-Campbell and Batey prefer to see the boat graves of Scotland (of which there are at least thirteen currently known) as marking their occupants 'as being of some social standing' rather than as having 'particular priestly status'.[91] One of the most spectacular of these graves is that at Scar, on Sanday in Orkney, a boat burial containing three individuals (an elderly woman, an adult male and a child) with rich grave goods. The excavators tentatively interpreted the grave goods as suggesting that the woman buried there was a devotee, possibly even a priestess, of Freya. This interpretation combines Crumlin-Pedersen's general suggestion about boat-burials with an interpretation of the whalebone plaque found among the woman's equipment as associating her with the goddess because of its possible use in the preparation of linen.[92] Olwyn Owen has recently concluded that the whole burial may represent 'a self-conscious flourishing of pagan belief and ritual in the face of encroaching acceptance of Christianity in the tenth century',[93] but it has to be said that the religious symbolism in the grave, if that is what it is, is not as clear as the excavators imagined.

There is no evidence of either Frey or Freya in place-names: Per Thorson rejects this etymology for Freswick in Caithness and Frans-Arne's Stylegar's suggestion of such an etymology for the Point of Freyageo on Stronsay is particularly ludicrous.[94]

Other

The question of the buildings or other locations in which the Norse gods were venerated is a vexed one on which much scholarly ink has been spilt, even in Scandinavia. Evidence for 'temples' in Scandinavian Scotland tends to melt away under scrutiny. A name which might appear to indicate a pagan cult site and is recorded as early as in *Orkneyinga saga* (ch. 92) is *Hofsnes* on Stronsay.[95] Hugh Marwick identifies this place with Huip (< ON *hóp* 'small, tidal bay') and describes the saga form as a 'mistake for … *Hópsnes*', and he must be right.[96] Stronsay is a small island, and its northern headland with its tidal inlet is such a distinctive feature that it would be perverse to argue that this name is evidence for a 'temple ness' as Frans-Arne Stylegar has done recently.[97] Jakob Jakobsen lists one compound and two simplex names in *Hof-* in Shetland.[98] He interprets the latter as 'a fenced-in place, a farm', but *Hovland* in Fetlar 'is possibly rather to be accepted in sense of: land, belonging to a (heathen) temple', parallel to the rather frequent examples of this name in Norway. One of the buildings at Jarlshof was interpreted by its excavator as either a temple or a bath-house, though the former seems highly uncertain.[99]

Another word which may refer to a heathen cult site is ON *hǫrgr*. It is indeed recorded in place-names both in Orkney and Caithness.[100] However the complication is that it can also mean 'heap of stones' and this meaning is just as likely as, if not more likely than, 'heathen cult site' in these instances.

Similarly, the element *haugr* may refer to any mound rather than a burial mound. In Orkney, where there were, and still are, many mounds covering the ruins of pre-Viking monuments, names with this element cannot be particularly significant of paganism. However, in a few cases where the element is compounded with a personal name in the genitive it could be argued that the name indicates a pagan burial mound rightly or wrongly attributed to its original inhabitant.[101]

Finally, it is worth drawing attention to the Hebridean islands of Gighay and Gigha, which Peder Gammeltoft has derived from ON *guð*, though he does not commit himself to whether this means 'god' or 'God'.[102] If there were Norse gods in Scotland, we might well ask whether this was where they lived.

Conclusion

Overall, the evidence for Norse paganism in Scotland, let alone the cult of individual gods, is not well attested. To some extent this is simply a function of the fragmentary and inconclusive evidence from so long ago – even if paganism had been rife in Viking and Norse Scotland, it would be difficult to demonstrate this conclusively. If we avoid the dubious evidence of the sagas, we are left with archaeology, onomastics, poetry and folklore, all of which present grave problems of interpretation, as outlined above.

However, there may still be some mileage in further interdisciplinary studies. We are a long way from having a full overview of either place- or personal names in Scandinavian Scotland, and archaeological work continues in many areas. Both of these promise a substantial and well-distributed body of evidence, which can be studied for larger overall patterns, even when individual examples may be doubtful and difficult to interpret. There is sufficient evidence presented above to suggest that Odin and Thor were widely known, and probably venerated, in Scandinavian Scotland, even though none of the evidence is decisive on its own. It is also of interest to observe patterns of absence as well as presence. A recent study by Stefan Brink concludes that 'only a few gods and even fewer goddesses were the objects of an actual cult in Scandinavia',[103] and the range of deities appears to be even more restricted in Scandinavian Scotland, where only Odin, Thor, and just faintly possibly Frey/Freya, can be traced in the evidence. There is also little convincing evidence of cult sites in general. It is probably significant that Odin and Thor had an existence outside their cults, in poetry, narrative and iconography. They seem to have survived their translation from the theophoric landscapes of the homeland whereas other deities and mythological figures, who were perhaps too closely linked to particular landscapes and sites, did not. However, these other deities were known in Iceland and the question still remains whether the diasporic experience of paganism in Scandinavian Scotland differed from that in Iceland and elsewhere and, if so, in what ways.

The construction of an overall framework for Norse paganism, based in the first instance on onomastics and archaeology and keyed to similar frameworks from other diasporic communities in Faroe, Iceland, and Greenland, will one day provide a useful background to further study of the more problematic (because difficult to date) literary and folkloric evidence. In all cases, the evidence also has to be interpreted, or re-interpreted, in the light of the newer and developing discourses of the specialist disciplines. It is important to recognise that archaeologists are no longer so confident about the identification of 'pagan' graves, that folklorists no longer believe in unchanging beliefs and stories over a millennium, and that onomasts are constantly modifying their interpretations as the bigger picture emerges. This recognition will certainly sharpen source-criticism, which is still needed, especially at the more popular end of studies of Scandinavian Scotland. At the same time, communication between these different discourses will allow the emergence of any faint patterns which may be there but which are not obvious to those engaged in only one of them. And there are positive developments, too. Folklorists may distrust verbal lore, but increasingly acknowledge the messages of the unchanging landscape, while philologists now distinguish more carefully between the poetic sources of the sagas, which may have links of some kind with the pagan period, and the sagas themselves, which are rather to be seen as medieval constructions of that period. Even such later constructions can play their part in the bigger picture, as long as their nature is recognised – after all, the saga-writers struggled with the same problems of sources and evidence as modern scholars do and simply dismissing their evidence is too reductive.

In short, there is still plenty of room to test and develop the historical and cultural patterns of paganism in Scandinavian Scotland that were provisionally outlined by Barbara Crawford a quarter of a century ago.

Notes

[1] Barbara E. Crawford, *Scandinavian Scotland* (Leicester, 1987), 159-69.
[2] *Ibid.*, 159-61.
[3] *Ibid.*, 171-8.
[4] *Ibid.*, 172.
[5] *Ibid.*, 177-8. More recently, Crawford has speculated on possible connections between Scottish hogbacks and the ascendant pagan, or semi-pagan, Hiberno-Norse dynasties of the late tenth century, in *The Govan Hogbacks and the Multi-Cultural Society of Tenth-Century Scotland* (Glasgow, 2005).
[6] Crawford, *Scandinavian Scotland*, 195-8.
[7] *Ibid.*, 195.
[8] Alex Woolf, *From Pictland to Alba, 789-1070* (Edinburgh, 2007), 311.
[9] 'Conversion and the Church in the Hebrides in the Viking Age: "A very difficult thing indeed" ..', in Beverley Ballin Smith *et al.* (eds), *West Over Sea: Studies in Scandinavian Sea-Borne Expansion and Settlement Before 1300* (Leiden, 2007), 169-94.
[10] Woolf, *Pictland to Alba*, 311.
[11] 'Conversion and the Church', 172.
[12] Unlike Crawford, I leave the Isle of Man out of this discussion, although I am well aware that this is to impose anachronistic modern territorial boundaries on the subject. However, space is limited, and Man does have some distinctive features which should be given greater due than is possible here.
[13] This research has been supported by the Arts and Humanities Research Council's strategic initiative on Diasporas, Migration and Identities.
[14] Steven Vertovec as cited in Gretty M. Mirdal and Lea Ryynänen-Karjalainen, *Migration and Transcultural Identities* (Strasbourg, 2004). [www.csf.org/fileadmin/be_user/publications/Migration_and_Transcultural_Identities.pdf]
[15] James Clifford, 'Diasporas', *Cultural Anthropology* 9/3 (1994), 302-38, at 306.
[16] Michael Chesnutt, 'An unsolved problem in Old Norse-Icelandic literary history', *Mediaeval Scandinavia* 1 (1968), 122-37, at 126.
[17] James Graham-Campbell and Colleen Batey, *Vikings in Scotland* (Edinburgh, 1998), 113-54; Angela Z. Redmond, *Viking Burial in the North of England* (Oxford, 2007), 74-86, xix-xxv.
[18] Graham-Campbell and Batey, *Vikings in Scotland*, 151.

[19] 'The Scar boat burial – and the missing decades of the Early Viking Age in Orkney and Shetland', in Jonathan Adams and Katherine Holman (eds), *Scandinavia and Europe, 800-1350. Contact, Conflict and Co-Existence* (Turnhout, 2004), 3-33, at 20.

[20] *Ibid*. See also Graham-Campbell and Batey, *Vikings in Scotland*, 126, 136, 144.

[21] Christopher Morris, 'From Birsay to Brattahlíð: Recent perspectives on Norse Christianity in Orkney, Shetland, and the North Atlantic region', in Adams and Holman (eds), *Scandinavia and Europe*, 177-95, at 195.

[22] Berit Sandnes thinks the name *Evin helga* could be older than the monastic site, but whether the name could therefore have pagan significance is not clear, *Fra Starafjall til Starling Hill. Dannelse og utvikling av norrøne stedsnavn på Orknøyene* (Trondheim, 2003), 140-1. Iona is also called by this name in sagas, see Peder Gammeltoft, 'Scandinavian naming-systems in the Hebrides', in Ballin Smith *et al.* (eds), *West Over Sea*, 479-95, at 484.

[23] Hugh Marwick, *Orkney Farm-Names* (Kirkwall, 1952), 2, 26, 47, 59, 171.

[24] F. T. Wainwright, 'The Scandinavian settlement', in F. T. Wainwright (ed.), *The Northern Isles* (Edinburgh, 1964), 117-62, at 154; Sandnes, *Starafjall til Starling Hill*, 156. Marwick was more cautious in *Orkney Farm-Names* than in earlier publications, such as 'The place-names of North Ronaldsay', *Proceedings of the Orkney Antiquarian Society* 1 (1923), 53-64, at 53-4.

[25] Some of it is surveyed in Judith Jesch, 'Literature in medieval Orkney', in Olwyn Owen (ed.), *The World of Orkneyinga Saga* (Kirkwall, 2005), 11-24.

[26] Despite its inclusion in Thomas O. Clancy (ed.), *The Triumph Tree* (Edinburgh, 1998), *Eiríksmál*'s connections to Scotland are in my view too tenuous for it to be considered here.

[27] Diana Whaley, *The Poetry of Arnórr jarlaskáld. An Edition and Study* (Turnhout, 1998), 74.

[28] Bjarne Fidjestøl, 'Pagan beliefs and Christian impact: the contribution of scaldic studies', in Anthony Faulkes and Richard Perkins (eds), *Viking Revaluations* (London, 1993), 100-20.

[29] Finnbogi Guðmundsson (ed.), *Orkneyinga saga* (Reykjavík, 1965), 11-16.

[30] Ernest W. Marwick, *The Folklore of Orkney and Shetland* (London, 1975); Ernest Walker Marwick, *An Orkney Anthology*, ed. John D. M. Robertson (Edinburgh, 1991), 257-78.

[31] James Porter, 'The folklore of northern Scotland: five discourses on cultural representation', *Folklore* 109 (1998), 1-14, at 1.

[32] *Ibid.*, 4, 6-7.

[39] Stefan Brink, 'How uniform was the Old Norse religion?', in Judy Quinn *et al.* (eds), *Learning and Understanding in the Old Norse World. Essays in Honour of Margaret Clunies Ross* (Turnhout, 2007), 105-36, at 111-3, 129-31.

[34] I am grateful to Doreen Waugh for discussing some of these names with me.

[35] Frans-Arne Stylegar, '"Central places" in Viking Age Orkney', *Northern Studies* 38 (2004), 5-30, at 12.

[36] E. Marwick, *Orkney Anthology*, 318.

[37] Peter Foote, 'An Orkney myth?' in Hans Frede Nielsen (ed.), *Papers on Scandinavian and Germanic Language and Culture Published in Honour of Michael Barnes* (Odense, 2005), 73-5, at 73.

[38] For some examples, see Jakob Jakobsen, *The Place-Names of Shetland* (London, 1936, reprinted Kirkwall, 1993), 24-5; H. Marwick, *Orkney Farm-Names*, 36, 113, 173; Sandnes, *Starafjall til Starling Hill*, 152; Peder Gammeltoft, 'Scandinavian influence on Hebridean island names', in Peder Gammeltoft and Bent Jørgensen (eds), *Names through the Looking-Glass. Festschrift in Honour of Gillian Fellows-Jensen* (Copenhagen, 2006), 53-84, at 73.

[39] E Marwick, *Orkney Anthology*, 309-20; Foote, 'Orkney myth'. There is a 'Stone of Odin' on the beach in Shapinsay (H. Marwick, *Orkney Farm-Names*, 59-60) though I have been unable to discover the earliest record of this.

[40] E. Marwick, *Orkney Anthology*, 318, 370.

[41] E. Marwick, *Folklore*, 140.

[42] As most recently published in Walter Traill Dennison, *Orkney Folklore and Sea Legends* (Kirkwall, 1995), 22-5; see p. 12 for information on Dennison's collecting. The tale was first published in 1893 from 'Mr. W. Traill Dennison's MS' and frequently reprinted in Sir George Douglas (ed.), *Scottish Fairy and Folk Tales* (the edition cited here is London, 1901, 58-72). Dennison's question 'Is Odin here meant?' (*ibid.*, 301) has been rather too solidified into a statement by Marwick.

[43] Whaley, *Poetry of Arnórr*, 120.

[44] 'However mighty, goddess of Draupnir's band [lady], I learn the lord is—he rules his realm—ruler of the constellation's path will welcome me', Anthony Faulkes (ed.), *Snorri Sturluson: Edda. Skáldskaparmál* (London, 1998), 34; Anthony Faulkes (trans.), *Snorri Sturluson: Edda* (London, 1987), 89.

[45] Hermann Pálsson, *Söngvar frá Suðureyjum* (Akureyri, 1955), 23; Bibire's

translation in Clancy, *Triumph Tree*, 148.

[46] Bjarni Aðalbjarnarson (ed.), *Snorri Sturluson. Heimskringla I* (Reykjavík, 1979), 155-6; Lee M. Hollander (tr.), *Snorri Sturluson. Heimskringla* (Austin, 1964), 100. In fact, the stanza is likely to be from Glúmr's poem on Haraldr gráfeldr, Bjarne Fidjestøl, *Det norrøne fyrstediktet* (Øvre Ervik, 1982), 90-2.

[47] Finnbogi Guðmundsson, *Orkneyinga saga*, 15; Hermann Pálsson and Paul Edwards (tr.), *Orkneyinga saga* (London, 1981), 31.

[48] Russell G. Poole, *Viking Poems on War and Peace: A Study in Skaldic Narrative* (Toronto, 1991), 170.

[49] H. Marwick, 'Place-names of North Ronaldsay', 53; Hugh Marwick, *The Orkney Norn* (London, 1929), 227.

[50] Poole, *Viking Poems*, 119-25.

[51] *Ibid.*, 125, 155.

[52] *Ibid.*, 116.

[53] Karl Blind, 'Odinic songs in Shetland', *The Nineteenth Century* 5 (1879), 1091-1113, at 1093.

[54] *Ibid.*, 1095.

[55] Guðrún Nordal, 'Odinsdyrkelse på Island. Arkæologien og kilderne', in Ulf Drobin (ed.), *Religion och samhälle i det förkristna Norden* (Odense, 1999), 139-56.

[56] 'Odinsdyrkelse', 145-8.

[57] Per Stille, '*Peter* och *Tor* i svenska runinskrifter', in Lennart Elmevik and Svante Strandberg (eds), *Runor och namn. Hyllningsskrift til Lena Peterson* (Uppsala, 1999), 87-93, at 88-9. The name Thor is discussed further below.

[58] Michael P. Barnes and R. I. Page, *The Scandinavian Runic Inscriptions of Britain* (Uppsala, 2006), 120-3. It is also found on one or two of the runic crosses from the Isle of Man, see R. I. Page, 'The Manx rune-stones', in Christine Fell *et al.* (eds), *The Viking Age in the Isle of Man* (London, 1983), 133-46, at 140.

[59] Jakob Benediktsson (ed.), *Íslendingabók. Landnámabók* (Reykjavík, 1968), 387; Hermann Pálsson and Paul Edwards (tr.), *The Book of Settlements* (Winnipeg, 1972), 144.

[60] Finnbogi Guðmundsson (ed.), *Orkneyinga saga*, 244, 363. Gautr is of course also the name of a prolific maker of runic crosses in the Isle of Man, see Page, 'Manx rune-stones', 140.

[61] H. Marwick, *Orkney Farm-Names*, 98, 115, 142, 171; Jakobsen, *Place-Names of Shetland*, 150-1; W.F.H. Nicolaisen, *Scottish Place-Names* (London, 1976), 97.

[62] Jakobsen, *Place-Names of Shetland*, 154; Gammeltoft, 'Scandinavian influence', 80-1, 101.

[63] 'Odinsdyrkelse', 149-50.

[64] Graham-Campbell and Batey, *Vikings in Scotland*, 119, 133.

[65] H. Marwick, *Orkney Farm-Names*, 73.

[66] *Ibid.*

[67] Doreen Waugh, 'From Hermaness to Dunrossness: Some Shetland ness-names', in Andras Mortensen and Símun V. Arge (eds), *Viking and Norse in the North Atlantic* (Tórshavn, 2006), 250-6, at 253.

[68] Graham-Campbell and Batey, *Vikings in Scotland*, 128, 146-9. It is illustrated (without identification as a Thor's hammer) in John W. Hedges, *Bu, Gurness and the Brochs of Orkney. Part II: Gurness* (Oxford, 1984), 119.

[69] Crawford, *Govan Hogbacks*, 27.

[70] Per Thorson, 'Ancient Thurso, a religious and judicial centre', in Bjarni Niclasen (ed.), *The Fifth Viking Congress* (Tórshavn, 1968), 71-7, at 71-3.

[71] W. F. H. Nicolaisen, 'Scandinavians and Celts in Caithness: the place-name evidence', in John R. Baldwin (ed.), *Caithness: A Cultural Crossroads* (Edinburgh, 1982), 75-85, at 84; Doreen Waugh, 'Caithness: an onomastic frontier zone', in Colleen E. Batey *et al.* (eds), *The Viking Age in Caithness, Orkney and the North Atlantic* (Edinburgh, 1993), 120-8, at 125.

[72] *The Norn Language of Orkney and Shetland* (Lerwick, 1998), 19.

[73] H. Marwick, *Orkney Farm-Names*, 151, 262.

[74] *Ibid.*, 183, 262.

[75] '"Central Places"', 12.

[76] *Fra Staraffall til Starling Hill*, 225. See also Malcolm Bangor-Jones, 'Norse settlement in south-east Sutherland', in Barbara E. Crawford (ed.), *Scandinavian Settlement in Northern Britain* (London, 1995), 80-91, at 85; Gammeltoft, 'Scandinavian influence', 79.

[77] Simon Taylor, 'The Scandinavians in Fife and Kinross: the onomastic evidence', in Crawford (ed.), *Scandinavian Settlement*, 141-62, at 162; Doreen Waugh, 'A scatter of Norse names in Strathnaver', in John R. Baldwin (ed.), *The Province of Strathnaver* (Edinburgh, 2000), 13-23, at 16. See also Bangor-Jones, 'Norse settlement', 85; Gammeltoft, 'Scandinavian influence', 90. On the English names, see John Insley, *Scandinavian Personal Names in Norfolk* (Stockholm, 1994), 411-3.

[78] David Murison, 'Linguistic relationships in medieval Scotland', in G. W. S. Barrow (ed.) *The Scottish Tradition: Essays in Honours of R. G. Cant* (Edinburgh, 1974), 71-83, at p. 72.

[79] Gillian Fellows Jensen, *Scandinavian Personal Names in Lincolnshire and Yorkshire* (Copenhagen, 1968), 295-6; Insley, *Scandinavian Personal Names*, 390-1.

[80] '*Peter* och *Tor*', 91.

[81] '"Few know an earl in fishing-clothes"', in Barbara E. Crawford (ed.), *Essays in Shetland History* (Lerwick, 1984), 82-98.

[82] Douglas, *Scottish Fairy and Folk Tales*, 58-72; E. Marwick, *Folklore*, 139-44; Dennison, *Orkney Folklore and Sea Legends*, 22-5.

[83] *The Place-Names of Rousay* (Kirkwall, 1947), 95.

[84] '... it is correct to designate dwarves with reference to stones or screes and giants to mountains or rocks', Finnur Jónsson (ed.), *Edda Snorra Sturlusonar* (Copenhagen, 1931), 255. I have elsewhere (Jesch forthcoming) attempted to demonstrate some links between *Litla Skálda* and Orcadian poetry of the twelfth century. There are similar statements in *Snorra Edda*, see Anthony Faulkes (ed.), *Snorri Sturluson. Edda: Prologue and Gylfaginning* (Oxford, 1982) 15-16; Faulkes (tr.), *Snorri Sturluson. Edda*, 16-17.

[85] Hugh Marwick, *Orkney* (London, 1951), 18.

[86] George Barry, *The History of the Orkney Islands* (Edinburgh, 1805), 433-47, at 445-6.

[87] Katja Schulz, *Riesen* (Heidelberg, 2004), 57, 62, 138, 141-2.

[88] *Ibid.*, 208-10, 212-3, 296.

[89] Whaley, *Poetry of Arnórr*, 265.

[90] 'Boat-burials at Slusegaard and the interpretation of the boat-grave custom', in Ole Crumlin-Pedersen and Birgitte Munch Thye (eds), *The Ship as Symbol in Prehistoric and Medieval Scandinavia* (Copenhagen, 1995), 87-99, at 94, 97.

[91] *Vikings in Scotland*, 146, 150.

[92] Olwyn Owen and Magnar Dalland, *Scar: A Viking Boat Burial on Sanday, Orkney* (East Linton, 1999), 79, 144-5.

[93] 'Scar boat-burial', 14-6.

[94] 'Ancient Thurso', 75; '"Central places"', 12.

[95] The earliest surviving manuscript with this form is Copenhagen, Den Arnamagnæanske Samling, 325 I 4to, from around 1300. In one of the two instances of this name, it is erroneously written *Haufn* (an error shared with *Flateyjarbók*, and therefore probably introduced in an earlier version), see Sigurður Nordal (ed.), *Orkneyinga saga* (Copenhagen, 1913-6), 268.

[96] *Orkney Farm-Names*, 25.

[97] '"Central places"', 13.

[98] *Place-Names of Shetland*, 59. See also Brian Smith, 'Scandinavian place-names in Shetland with a study of the district of Whiteness', in Crawford (ed.), *Scandinavian Settlement*, 26-41, at 37.
[99] J.R.C. Hamilton, *Excavations at Jarlshof, Shetland* (Edinburgh, 1956), 110, 130, 137
[100] H. Marwick, *Orkney Farm-Names*, 2, 171; Sandnes, *Starafjall*, 156; Thorson, 'Ancient Thurso', 75.
[101] H. Marwick, *Orkney Farm-Names*, 36, 61, 93, 116.
[102] 'Scandinavian influence', 71.
[103] Brink, 'How uniform', 124.

Bibliography

Abrams, L., 2007, 'Conversion and the Church in the Hebrides in the Viking Age: "A very difficult thing indeed" ..', in Smith, B.B., et al. (eds), *West Over Sea: Studies in Scandinavian Sea-Borne Expansion and Settlement Before 1300*. Leiden, pp. 169-94.

Aðalbjarnarson, B., (ed.), 1979, *Snorri Sturluson. Heimskringla I.* Reykjavík.

Bangor-Jones, 1995, 'Norse settlement in south-east Sutherland', in Crawford, B.E., (ed.), *Scandinavian Settlement in Northern Britain*. London, pp. 80-91.

Barnes, M.P., 1998, *The Norn Language of Orkney and Shetland.* Lerwick.

Barnes, M.P., and Page, R.I., 2006, *The Scandinavian Runic Inscriptions of Britain.* Uppsala.

Barry, G., 1805, *The History of the Orkney Islands.* Edinburgh.

Bibire, P., 1984, '"Few know an earl in fishing-clothes"', in Crawford, B.E. (ed.), *Essays in Shetland History*. Lerwick, pp. 82-98.

Blind, K., 1879, 'Odinic songs in Shetland', *The Nineteenth Century* 5, pp. 1091-1113.

Brink, S., 2007, 'How uniform was the Old Norse religion?', in Quinn, J., et al. (eds), *Learning and Understanding in the Old Norse World. Essays in Honour of Margaret Clunies Ross*. Turnhout, pp. 105-36.

Chesnutt, M., 1968, 'An unsolved problem in Old Norse-Icelandic literary history', *Mediaeval Scandinavia* 1, pp. 122-37.

Clancy, T.O. (ed.), 1998, *The Triumph Tree.* Edinburgh.

Clifford, J., 1994, 'Diasporas', *Cultural Anthropology* 9/3, pp. 302-38.

Crawford, B.E., 1987, *Scandinavian Scotland.* Leicester.

Crawford, B.,E., 2005, *The Govan Hogbacks and the Multi-Cultural Society of Tenth-Century Scotland*. Glasgow.

Crumlin-Pedersen, O., 1995, 'Boat-burials at Slusegaard and the interpretation of the boat-grave custom', in Crumlin-Pedersen, O., and Thye, B.M. (eds), *The Ship as Symbol in Prehistoric and Medieval Scandinavia* Copenhagen, pp. 87-99.

Dennison, W.T., 1995, *Orkney Folklore and Sea Legends*. Kirkwall.

Douglas, Sir G. (ed.), 1901, *Scottish Fairy and Folk Tales*. London.

Faulkes, A. (trans.), 1987, *Snorri Sturluson: Edda*. London.

Faulkes, A. (ed.), 1998, *Snorri Sturluson: Edda. Skáldskaparmál*. London.

Fellows Jensen, G., 1968, *Scandinavian Personal Names in Lincolnshire and Yorkshire*. Copenhagen.

Fidjestøl, B., 1982, *Det norrøne fyrstediktet*. Øvre Ervik.

Fidjestøl, B., 1993, 'Pagan beliefs and Christian impact: the contribution of scaldic studies', in Faulkes, A., and Perkins, R. (eds), *Viking Revaluations*. London, pp. 100-20.

Foote, P., 2005, 'An Orkney myth?' in Nielsen, H.F. (ed.), *Papers on Scandinavian and Germanic Language and Culture Published in Honour of Michael Barnes*. Odense, pp. 73-5.

Gammeltoft, P., 2006, 'Scandinavian influence on Hebridean island names', in Gammeltoft, P., and Jørgensen, B. (eds), *Names through the Looking-Glass. Festschrift in Honour of Gillian Fellows-Jensen*. Copenhagen, pp. 53-84.

Gammeltoft, P., 2007, 'Scandinavian naming-systems in the Hebrides', in Smith, B.B., et al. (eds), *West Over Sea: Studies in Scandinavian Sea-Borne Expansion and Settlement Before 1300*. Leiden, pp. 479-95.

Graham-Campbell, J. and Batey, C., 1998, *Vikings in Scotland*. Edinburgh.

Guðmundsson, F., (ed.), 1965, *Orkneyinga saga*. Reykjavík.

Hamilton, J.R.C., 1956, *Excavations at Jarlshof, Shetland*. Edinburgh.

Hedges, J.W., 1984, *Bu, Gurness and the Brochs of Orkney. Part II: Gurness*. Oxford.

Hollander, L.M. (tr.), 1964, *Snorri Sturluson. Heimskringla*. Austin.

Insley, J., 1994, *Scandinavian Personal Names in Norfolk*. Stockholm.

Jakobsen, J., 1936/1993, *The Place-Names of Shetland*. London/Kirkwall.

Jesch, J., 2005, 'Literature in medieval Orkney', in Owen, O. (ed.), *The World of Orkneyinga Saga*. Kirkwall, pp. 11-24.

Jesch, J., forthcoming, 'The Orcadian links of Snorra Edda', in Jørgensen, J.G. (ed.) *Snorra Edda i europæisk og islandsk kultur*. Reykholt.

Jónsson, F. (ed.), 1931, *Edda Snorra Sturlusonar*. Copenhagen.

Marwick, E.W., 1975, *The Folklore of Orkney and Shetland*. London.

Marwick, E.W., 1991, *An Orkney Anthology*, Edinburgh.

Marwick, H., 1923, 'The place-names of North Ronaldsay', *Proceedings of the Orkney Antiquarian Society* 1, pp. 53-64.

Marwick, H., 1929, *The Orkney Norn*. London.

Marwick, H., 1947, *The Place-Names of Rousay*. Kirkwall.

Marwick, H., 1952, *Orkney Farm-Names*. Kirkwall.

Mirdal, G.M., and Ryynänen-Karjalainen, L., 2004, *Migration and Transcultural Identities*. Strasbourg.

Morris, C., 'From Birsay to Brattahlíð: Recent perspectives on Norse Christianity in Orkney, Shetland, and the North Atlantic region', in Adams, J., and Holman, K. (eds), *Scandinavia and Europe, 800-1350. Contact, Conflict and Co-Existence*. Turnhout, pp. 177-95.

Murison, M., 1974, 'Linguistic relationships in medieval Scotland', in Barrow, G.W.S. (ed.) *The Scottish Tradition: Essays in Honours of R. G. Cant*. Edinburgh, pp. 71-83.

Nicolaisen, W.F.H., 1976, *Scottish Place-Names*. London.

Nicolaisen, W.F.H., 1982, 'Scandinavians and Celts in Caithness: the place-name evidence', in Baldwin, J.R. (ed.), *Caithness: A Cultural Crossroads*. Edinburgh, pp. 75-85.

Nordal, G., 1999, 'Odinsdyrkelse på Island. Arkæologien og kilderne', in Drobin U. (ed.), *Religion och samhälle i det förkristna Norden*. Odense, pp. 139-56.

Nordal, S. (ed.), 1913-6, *Orkneyinga saga*. Copenhagen.

Owen, O., and Dalland, M., 1999, *Scar: A Viking Boat Burial on Sanday, Orkney*. East Linton.

Owen, O., 2004, 'The Scar boat burial – and the missing decades of the Early Viking Age in Orkney and Shetland', in Adams, J., and Holman, K. (eds), *Scandinavia and Europe, 800-1350. Contact, Conflict and Co-Existence*. Turnhout, pp. 3-33.

Pálsson, H., 1955, *Söngvar frá Suðureyjum*. Akureyri.

Pálsson, H., and Edwards, P. (tr.), 1981. *Orkneyinga saga*. London.

Poole, R.G., 1991, *Viking Poems on War and Peace: A Study in Skaldic Narrative*. Toronto.

Porter, J., 1998, 'The folklore of northern Scotland: five discourses on cultural representation', *Folklore* 109, pp. 1-14.

Redmond, A.Z., 2007, *Viking Burial in the North of England*. Oxford.

Sandnes, B., 2003, *Fra Starafjall til Starling Hill. Dannelse og utvikling av norrøne stedsnavn på Orknøyene*. Trondheim.

Schulz, K., 2004, *Riesen*. Heidelberg.

Smith, B., 1995, 'Scandinavian place-names in Shetland with a study of the district of Whiteness', in Crawford, B.E. (ed.), *Scandinavian Settlement in Northern Britain*. London, pp. 26-41.

Stille, P., 1999, '*Peter* och *Tor* i svenska runinskrifter', in Elmevik, L., and Strandberg, S. (eds), *Runor och namn. Hyllningsskrift til Lena Peterson*. Uppsala, pp. 87-93.

Stylegar, F.-A., 2004, '"Central places" in Viking Age Orkney', *Northern Studies* 38, pp. 5-30.

Taylor, Simon, 1995, 'The Scandinavians in Fife and Kinross: the onomastic evidence', in Crawford, B.E. (ed.), *Scandinavian Settlement in Northern Britain*. London, pp. 141-62.

Thorson, P., 1968, 'Ancient Thurso, a religious and judicial centre', in Niclasen, B, (ed.), *The Fifth Viking Congress*. Tórshavn, pp. 71-7.

Wainwright, F.T., 1964, 'The Scandinavian settlement', in F. T. Wainwright (ed.), *The Northern Isles*. Edinburgh, pp., 117-62.

Waugh, D., 1993, 'Caithness: an onomastic frontier zone', in Batey, C.E. et al. (eds), *The Viking Age in Caithness, Orkney and the North Atlantic*. Edinburgh, pp. 120-8.

Waugh, D., 2000, 'A scatter of Norse names in Strathnaver', in Baldwin, J.R. (ed.), *The Province of Strathnaver*. Edinburgh, pp. 13-23.

Waugh, D., 2006, 'From Hermaness to Dunrossness: Some Shetland ness-names', in Mortensen, A., and Arge, S.V. (eds), *Viking and Norse in the North Atlantic*. Tórshavn, pp. 250-6.

Whaley, D., 1998, *The Poetry of Arnórr jarlaskáld. An Edition and Study*. Turnhout.

Woolf, A., 2007, *From Pictland to Alba 789-1070*. Edinburgh.

One coast - three peoples: names and ethnicity in the Scottish west during the early Viking period

Andrew Jennings and Arne Kruse

Introduction

Among the many questions and mysteries in the place-name record of the Hebrides and the West Coast of Scotland, two have struck us as particularly interesting: firstly, why do there not appear to be any surviving pre-Norse names in the Outer Hebrides and perhaps in most of the Inner Hebrides; secondly, why are Norse settlement names based on topographical appellatives, such as names in *vík*, *fjall* and *dalr*, far more widespread than names of settlements composed of Norse habitative elements like *bólstaðr* and *staðir*? By examining these two questions, it will become apparent that they are linked and that they are related to the nature of Norse settlement, which shows considerable variation depending on whether it was in the Isles or on the Mainland.

In our discussion, we will suggest that the link between these two questions and the explanation for the place-name pattern is that in the Outer Hebrides and north of Ardnamurchan the Norse probably met Picts, who disappeared as a culture and as a people, while south of Ardnamurchan and along much of the western littoral, they met Gaels, who did not. Following this initial Norse settlement, there was a subsequent linguistic shift when Gaelic, having survived the onslaught, began to replace the Norse language, a process which began along the western littoral and later spread to the Isles.

1. Background: Archaeological, Historical and Linguistic

For a number of years the argument has been advanced that, according to the archaeological record during the pre-Viking period, the western insular area of Scotland was divided into two cultural zones. The material culture of the Inner Hebrides and the mainland littoral (at least south of Ardnamurchan, corresponding to the historic kingdom of Dál Riata) forms one zone, with links south to Ireland and beyond, the area north of Ardnamurchan, including the Outer Hebrides with Skye, forms another, with close links to the Northern Isles, and east to Pictland.

Three decades ago, Leslie Alcock (1971) coined the term 'Peripheral Picts' to describe the pre-Norse inhabitants of the Outer Hebrides, to indicate both their distinctiveness in the use of pottery and lack of imported wares as well as their links with the Pictish Mainland. The distribution of pottery production is particularly instructive. The Outer Hebrides and Skye were long-standing producers of pottery, in sharp contrast to the area further south (Lane 1983).

Links with the Pictish mainland are indicated by three Pictish Class I symbol-stones from Skye and one from Raasay, and in the Outer Hebrides by an example from Benbecula and another from Pabbay, Barra. (See further discussion in Fisher 2001:11-12.) In addition, a knife inscribed with a potential Pictish ogham was discovered on Vallay, North Uist (http://nms.scran.ac.uk/ database). No symbol stones or Pictish oghams have been discovered so far in the Dalriadic area.

The distribution pattern of the brochs is similar to that of the Pictish stones. Their distribution is clearly concentrated in the Outer Hebrides and north of Ardnamurchan, suggesting a cultural divide long prior to the appearance of the historical Picts. A number of broch sites were inhabited through the Pictish period up to c.800 AD – at the time of the arrival of the Vikings – when they appear to have been abandoned (see Armit 1996: 202; Sharples and Parker Pearson 1999: 48; Gilmour and Harding 2000)

The 'Pictishness' of the area north and west of Ardnamurchan has become increasingly apparent with new discoveries from South Uist, Barra and Eigg. On South Uist, we have the quaintly named 'Cille Pheadair Kate', who was inhumed c.700AD under a type of square cairn which is not only Pictish, of a sort generally found across eastern Scotland and the Northern Isles, but which is most closely matched by two burials at Sandwick in Unst, Shetland, suggesting she, or her people, may have come from the north or have had close cultural links with the Northern Isles (See Parker Pearson 2004:118). A couple of typical Pictish burial cairns may have been identified on Sandray, Barra (Branigan & Forster 2002:103) and a series of 15 square cairns, the largest Pictish cemetery yet found in the west, has also been identified just above the beach at Laig Bay on Eigg (http://www.rcahms.gov.uk/highlighteigg.html).

The precise linguistic situation along the western seaboard on the eve of the Viking raids is hard to ascertain but, as archaeology strongly points to a Pictish-linked material culture north and west of Ardnamurchan, it is likely that the Pictish dialect of P-Celtic was still spoken in this area, while Gaelic Q-Celtic was the norm to the south. A small corpus of place-names indicates the presence of P-Celtic speakers. Watson (1926:407) recorded 4 *pit-* 'estate, land-holding' names in the west: *Pitmaglassy* in Lochaber, *Pitalmit* and *Pitchalman* in Glenelg and *Pitnean* in Lochcarron. There are also two pre-Norse names in **abor* 'confluence, river-mouth', one of which is the famous monastery of *Applecross*, whose old name is preserved only in an English form (the modern Gaelic name being *a' Chomraich*) and the other *Òb Apoldoire*, a bay at Strollamus, in southern Skye.

A story in Adamnan's *Life of Columba* (Book I, chapter 33) certainly suggests that in the 6th century, Skye was not Gaelic speaking. According to the text, Columba baptized a good pagan called Artbranan, the *primarius Geonae cohortis* 'leader of the Geona band', after having instructed him in the word of God through an interpreter: *Qui statim, verbo Dei a Sancto per interpretem recepto, credens*, [Who immediately… believing, the word of God having been received from the Saint through an interpreter/intermediary/ translator]. Although the interpreter might have been putting Columba's religious jargon into a form understood by Artbranan, the fact that Columba himself was the religious expert suggests that the interpreter was translating Columba's speech into another language, namely Pictish.

Continuing into the 7th century, a series of entries in the Annals of Ulster supports the impression that Skye was still Pictish, and presumably P-Celtic speaking:

AU668 nauigatio filiorum Gartnaidh ad Hiberniam cum plebe Sceth
[Voyage of the sons of Gartnait to Ireland with the people of Skye]
AU670 Uenit genus Gartnaith de Hibeernia
[The sept of Gartnait came back from Ireland]
AU688 Occisio Canonn filii Gartnaidh
[The slaying of Cano son of Gartnait]

Garnait is a name with definite Pictish associations (Binchy 1963: xviii), and it occurs several times in the 'Pictish King Lists'. Indeed, this Garnait may have been a king of the Picts. The Pictish king Bruide son of Maelchon, who died in 586, was succeeded by Gartnait son of Domelach who Bannerman (1974: 92-94) suggested was the son of Aedán mac Gabráin, king of Dál Ríata, Domelach being his Pictish mother. However, there are chronological difficulties. The historical content of these annals is obscure. Were the sons of Garnait driven from Skye, and if so, by whom? Why did they return? Who slew Cano, the eponymous hero of the 9th century Irish tale *Scéla Cano Meic Gartnáin* (Binchy 1963)? This saga describes conflict between Aedán mac Gabráin and Cano, which, although chronologically impossible, might reflect conflict between Dál Ríata and Skye in the second half of the 7th century. The alternative interpretation that the *genus Gartnaith* was a Gaelic kindred the *cenél Gartnait*, through descent from Aedán, who had settled in Skye, can best be refuted by their non-appearance in the *Senchus fer nAlban*, which according to Anderson (1973:160) was probably drawn up in the years around 700AD.

An obscure entry in AU672, *Deleti sunt Ibdig*. [The Ibdaig were destroyed] probably refers to the Outer Hebrides and may provide a political link between these islands and the Pictish kingdom. *Ibdaig* is the Old Irish form of *Hebudes* and probably refers to the Outer Hebrides, islands outside of Dál Ríata, because the name does not occur in the *Senchus fer nAlban*. It bears an obvious resemblance to the AU entry of 682 *Orcades delete sunt la Bruide* [Orkney destroyed by Bruide], which refers to the Pictish king enforcing his authority in the archipelago. It is possible that the 672 entry is a reference to an attack on the Outer Hebrides from the Pictish mainland, either enforcing submission or absorbing them into the Pictish Kingdom.

The Gaelic language was centred on the kingdom of Dál Riata, which according to the *Senchus fer nAlban*, by c. 700AD stretched from the Mull of Kintyre to Ardnamurchan. It would also have been spoken in monastic settlements further north, such as in the hermitage on Rum where, perhaps, Beccán mac Luigdech, who died in 677, composed poetry in praise of Saint Columba (Clancy & Márkus 1995). However, other than as a religious language, if Gaelic had not succeeded in spreading furth of Dál Riata in the 7th century, it is unlikely that it would have made much headway in the Outer Hebrides and Skye during the 8th. This was not a period conducive to the spread of the language. According to Woolf (in Lynch 2001:604) the 'smiting of Dál Riata' by Ungus map Uurguist in AU741 probably destroyed the independence of the kingdom, effectively making it a Pictish satellite. However, on the other hand, the name Argyll, 'coastline of the Gael' which is likely to be a 9th century term, may indicate that Gaelic had begun to spread north of Ardnamurchan along the littoral during the 8th.

Although the Gaelic language was perhaps starting to make an appearance in the Outer Hebrides along with missionary and merchant advances from

Dál Riata, there is no reason to believe that Gaelic was making substantial inroads into Skye or the Outer Hebrides during the course of the 8th century. It is a reasonable suggestion that c.700AD 'Cille Pheadair Kate' was speaking P-Celtic, as presumably were those interred in an identical way on Unst, hundreds of miles to the north.

2. Pre-Norse place-names

We can be reasonably confident that there were two languages still being spoken at the end of the 8th century when the Norse arrived in the Hebrides bringing a third, P-Celtic in Skye and the Outer Hebrides and Gaelic in Dál Riata and in monasteries to the north. The respective speakers of the two Celtic languages must have had a complete onomasticon for their territories. Unfortunately, most of these names were never recorded and have now disappeared without a trace.

However, a small number of pre-Norse names do survive, and these are shown on the distribution map (*Figure 4.1*). The black names are from early Irish written sources, both in Latin and in Old Irish - their modern forms are not included on the map in order not to make it appear too crowded - for example *Ailech* where Brendan of Clonfert founded a monastery in the 6th century off the south-east coast of Mull (in modern Gaelic *Na h-Eileacha Naomha,* English the Garvellachs), and *Lismoir* where the death of abbot Echuid is recorded in AU635. The blue names do not appear in early sources but on the basis of etymology can be taken as pre-Norse, for example Morvern, (*Mor-Bhearn 'Sea gap'), which Watson (1926), the main authority for these names, suggested was the pre-Norse name for Loch Sunart. The two rivers called Sheil, would be other examples. These could be pre-Celtic names from the Indo-European root *sal 'stream, flowing river' (Nicolaisen 1976: 189) The place-name Glen Elg might be corroborating evidence for the spread of some Gaelic speakers north of Ardnamurchan in the pre-Norse period. It comes from *Eilg* 'Ireland', an early Gaelic colonial name. Gaelic colonial names certainly existed in the 8th century: we have the example of *Atholl* (AU739 'Talorgan son of Drostan king of Atholl was drowned'). In contrast, the red names are names from early written sources that have not survived.

With the clear proviso that our sample may be seriously flawed because the early sources are so focused on Dál Riata, we can draw a number of tentative conclusions from the distribution of names:

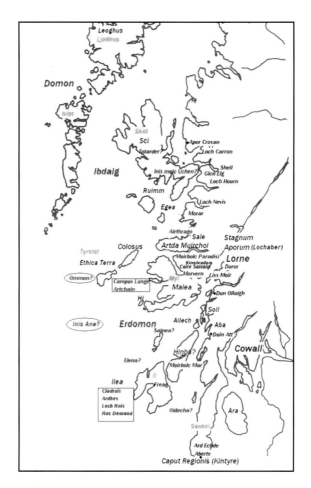

Figure 4.1 : Map of pre-Norse names in the west

- most of the surviving names are on the mainland and the names of islands themselves
- most of the pre-Norse names in the islands appear to have been lost, including those recorded in the Inner Hebrides
- the survival of the names of some of the tribal territories and some of the important tribal centres in Dál Riata suggest the survival of a polity in some form

The green names on the map are from Norse sources. Although there are no recorded pre-Norse names for the largest islands in the Outer Hebrides, Lewis and Uist, their Old Norse forms *Ljóðhús* and *Ívist* are likely to have been transformed into Norse from a pre-Norse language. Lewis may have been something like *Leoghus*, a form which occurs in the 10th century Irish saga *Caithreim Cellachain Chaisil* (Binchy 1963) while *Ívist* may be a resemanticised form of the ancient name for the archipelago itself (*Ibdaig* in Old Irish and *Hebudes* in Pliny NH IV, 103).

Ljóðhús and *Ívist* and a couple of other Hebridean island names occur in the 11th century poem *'Magnúsdrápa'* by Bjǫrn krepphendi about King Magnus Bareleg's expedition (after Finnur Jónsson 1912, B vol. I.:404-6)[1]:

Lék of Ljóðhús fíkjum
limsorg náar himni,
vítt vas ferð á flótta
fús; gaus eldr ór húsum;
ǫrr skjǫldungr fór eldi
Ívist (búendr mistu)
róggeisla vann ræsir
rauðan (lífs ok auðar).

[Over Lewis the fire played violently against the sky; all over people desired to flee; fire rose from the houses; the warlike king wasted North Uist with fire; farmers lost lives and wealth; the ruler reddened the war flash (sword).]

Hungrþverrir lét herjat
hríðar gagls á Skíði
Tǫnn rauð Tyrvist innan
teitr vargr í ben margri;
grœtti Grenlands dróttinn,
gekk hátt Skota støkkvir
(þjóð rann mýlsk til mœði)
meyjar suðr í eyjar.

[The hunger-diminisher of the goose of battle (bird of pray, warrior) harried in Skye; in Tiree the happy wolf coloured his tooth red in many a wound; the ruler over Grenland grieved young women in the south of the isles;

the banisher of the Scots was lucky; the men of Mull fled until they were exhausted.]

Vítt bar snarr á slétta
Sandey konungr randir;
rauk of Íl, þárs jóku
allvalds menn á brennur:
Santíri laut sunnar
seggja kind und eggjar;
siggœðir réð síðan
snjallr Manverja falli.

[Far and wide the keen king carries the shields on level Sanda; smoke drifted over Islay where the lord's men fueled the fires; south of Kintyre people sunk under the the sword edges; the fierce victory-increaser (warrior) later caused the fall of Manxmen.]

Ljóðhús and *Ívist* are very odd island names, meaning respectively 'house of people' and 'in-dwelling' in Old Norse. The names are unusual because they do not contain the normal Norse generic -*ey*, 'island' and are doubly atypical because they do not contain any semantic content which could relate the island to its location or its shape or to ownership in the form of a personal name. They clearly look like native originals which have been given Norse phonology and 'meanings' that may be easy to memorise, but do not refer to anything characteristic about the islands. The names are the likely products of an interaction of peoples, probably coined during the initial contact phase between natives and explorers, or early raiders from the north (Kruse 2005). It is important to note that the modern Gaelic form of the name *Leodhus* appears to come from Norse, while *Uibhist* certainly does, and not directly from earlier pre-Norse tradition.

As with the Outer Hebrides and the Northern Isles, many of the island names in the Inner Hebrides, such as *Jura, Gigha, Colonsay*, and *Staffa*, were coined by the Norse. However, there are also island names of pre-Norse origin, such as *Islay, Tiree, Coll, Mull, Arran* and *Skye*. For example, *Mull* is recorded as *Malea insula* in Adamnan (Watson 1926:38). The Norse forms of the Inner Hebridean islands have not survived. For example, *Mýl* and *Eyin Helga*, are parallel Norse forms of the Gaelic *Muile* and *Eilean I*. However, in contrast to *Lewis* and *Uist* the modern Gaelic forms of these island names appear to have developed directly from pre-Norse tradition and not via Norse.

Watson (1926:38, 503) pointed out the strange situation in Tiree where the modern Gaelic form *Tiridh* comes from the pre-Norse form, but the Gaelic for a person from Tiree, *tiristeach*, comes from the Norse form *Tyrvist*. The Norse form could have associated the Gaelic *tir* 'land' with the Norse god *Týr*, in spite of the obvious difficulty with the nominative case ending *-r*. If the modern Gaelic form of the island had come via Norse it would have been **Tirbhist*. It is important to emphasize the contrast between the Outer Hebrides where the pre-Norse forms of *Lewis* and *Uist* do not reassert themselves, and the Inner Hebrides where the modern Gaelic forms of *Islay*, *Tiree* etc appear to come directly from the pre-Norse forms.

The red names on the map show the extent to which names were lost in Dál Riata. The discontinuity is concentrated in the islands and suggests that the Norse impact on the Inner Hebrides must have been very disruptive. Johnston (1995) could not find any evidence for the survival of pre-Norse names on Coll and Tiree, while MacNiven's recent investigation of Islay (2006) suggests that the Norse disruption of the previous nomenclature was near total. He is very doubtful that any names from the *Senchus* have survived, except perhaps for *Freag*, which had twice as many *tech* 'houses' as the next biggest district and could be regarded as the 'metropolis' of early medieval Islay. There are a series of 16th, 17th and early 18th century references to a farm-district known as **Ochdamh na Freighe*, which is no longer extant.

It is possible that traces of *Odeich, Cladrois, Ardhes, Loch Rois* and *Ros Deorand* may have survived through adaptation into Old Norse, as suggested by Thomas (1881) and Lamont (1958; 1966). For example, early Gaelic *Odeich*, may be reflected in Norse *Texa*. It is just possible that the second syllable of *Odeich* has been adapted to an Old Norse word related to modern Norwegian *tikse* 'a female sheep' However, Gammeltoft sees it as 'one of the clearest examples of an outright pre-Norse to Old Norse name-change' (2006:61). Similarly, *Ros Deorand* may just conceivably lie behind the Norse *Djurey* 'Jura'.

The example of Islay raises the possibility that a stratum of pre-Norse names may lie unidentified in the Norse onomasticon. It is just possible that the Norse heard and adapted a number of names in the Hebrides. However, if they did, the names must have been given 'meaningful' semantic content, because there is no layer of peculiar names like *Ljóðhús*, nor names whose semantic content is obviously at odds with their siting or environment.

On balance, it is unlikely that much Norse adaptation of pre-Norse names took place. However, if some names do exist outside of the island names, they would still highlight a linguistic break with the past because the pre-Norse forms have not reasserted themselves.

In contrast to the red names in the insular, western portion of Dál Riata, the eastern, mainland portion shows a degree of clear continuity. The tribal names, *Cenél Loairn* and *Cenél Comgall* survived the Norse impact in present day *Lorne* and *Cowall*, while *Kinelvadon,* which was recorded in the 12th century, preserved the obscure *Cenel Baedain*, as did the tribal centres *Dunaverty*, *Dunollie* and *Dunadd.* Excavation at Dunadd has hinted that the hillfort continued in use till the 10th or later centuries (Lane & Campbell 2000:262). However, the major name *Cenél nGabrain* and *Dál Riata* itself did not survive. The sea-loch and district names north of Ardnamurchan may also owe their survival to a Dalriadan milieu, the sailors, traders and monks heading north to Applecross and beyond.

In the Outer Hebrides the Norse linguistic broom was particularly effective. The prevailing view amongst scholars since George Henderson (1910:185) is that the Norse names form the oldest stratum, there being no earlier names, indicating there was total discontinuity between the pre-Norse and the Norse periods. (See A. MacBain (1922:70), W.J. Watson (1926:38-9), I. Fraser (1974:18-19; 1984:40) and A.-B. Stahl (1999:365)). In contrast, G. Fellows-Jensen (1984:151) seems to have been in two minds although she admits none of the Gaelic place-names in the Isles can be proved to be of pre-Viking date.

In his outstanding addition to the corpus of onomastic research in the Hebrides, Cox (2002) has, in the *Place-names of Carloway* retracted his earlier advocacy for the existence of surviving pre-Norse names (Cox 1991) and now suggests that many of the Gaelic place-names are 'old', created during the Norse period, rather than before it. We have suggested elsewhere (Jennings & Kruse 2005:259-60), that these were created by Gaelic-speaking slaves imported by the Norse to the Hebrides in a similar way as to the Faroe Islands.

An interesting archaeological parallel between the Outer Hebrides and the Faroe Islands is observed by Lane (1983, 1990) and discussed further in Jennings & Kruse (2005). The 'new potters' who appear in the Outer Hebrides and Skye after *c.* AD 800 produce pottery with a completely new style and technique: 'I can see no evidence to derive the Viking-age style from the Dark-age style. The difference in form and construction methods seems overwhelming' (Lane 1983:379). The closest connections in time and style to this new Hebridean pottery are the northern Irish Souterrain Ware assemblages in Co. Antrim, and Lane suggests that the Norse themselves may have learned to make pottery in Ireland before settling in the Hebrides, or alternatively, they may have imported Irish slaves to make pots for them. He further makes the observation that pottery of a very similar type is also found in the Faroe Islands, the only other Scandinavian settlement area in the West Atlantic region with a pottery tradition (Lane 1983:348). There are Gaelic loan-words in the Faroese language and Gaelic even appears in Faroese place-names (Jakobsen 1902 and 1915). The linguistic traces of Gaelic in Faroese as well as the Irish style pottery both in the Faroe Islands and the Hebrides are most likely to be indicative of Gaelic-speaking slaves.

Cox previously (1991) seemed to assume that the pre-Norse language spoken in Lewis was Gaelic, but has lately (Cox 2007), in a response to the discussion of his findings, allowed for the possibility 'that Gaelic may have been spoken there prior to Norse settlement, but so may have Pictish'. He stresses 'that the Norse-Gaelic contact took place over several hundred years, perhaps from the earliest period of Norse settlement', and we find no problem with such a statement, as long as he now seems to accept the 'general agreement that no Gaelic names can be shown to be pre-Norse creations' (Cox 2007:142-3).

Along with the island names we have discussed previously there might be a small number of names (*pace* Henderson) that were borrowed by the Norse, because they do not readily invite Gaelic or Norse etymologies. A couple of examples are given by Oftedal (1980:188): [mu:ṇag] and [mũ:har̓], both mountains. The examples are somewhat dubious as Oftedal also gives the case [gLūmaǧ], a bay beside Stornoway, which is a Gaelic word for a 'deep pool' *glùmag* (MacLennan 1979:185). If we were to accept the mountain names as genuinely pre-Norse, the similarity in their first syllable might suggest the Norse heard a form of *monid* (OW and OI 'hill'). If these names are pre-Norse and not just names for which we cannot as yet supply a valid Norse or Gaelic etymology, then they probably indicate early contact with the natives. They are large, natural features crucial for navigational purposes, like the islands themselves, and might have been borrowed in the exploratory phase as land-marks.

Other than the possible but dubious exception of these exploratory names, we see complete discontinuity in the onomastic record, which is highly significant, as it links the nomenclature of the Outer Hebrides with that of the Northern Isles. In both places we know there were settlements when the Norse arrived but there is no evidence from the onomasticon that the inhabitants of these settlements ever existed. The Norse do not appear to have borrowed unmodified names, they are unlikely to have adapted names, apart from the strangely resemanticised island names, and, perhaps most striking, they did not even incorporate *ex-nomine* units into their own creations. The absence of names like *Abervatn (*ex-nomine* Pictish *(Aber)* + Norse *vatn)* or *Dunmórborg (*ex-nomine* Pictish *(Dunmór)* + Norse *borg*) is in complete contrast to the survival and gaelicisation of Norse names when Gaelic took over as the language of the people. There are any number of examples, but *Loch Langabhat* (Gaelic *Loch* + *ex-nomine* Norse *(langavatn)*) will suffice. Oftedal (1980:188) offers five Norse names which may have Gaelic components. They are said, a bit vaguely, to be 'from the "strong" Gaelic areas, especially the Outer Hebrides' *(ibid.*:169). However, Oftedal admits that '[t]he Gaelic-sounding components may, of course, be Gaelic popular etymologies of similar-sounding Norse components'. Cox (2007:142) provides two examples of Gaelic place-names that are used in Norse-originated names: *Camas Thairbearnais* (G *tairbeart* + ON *nes*) in Canna, and *Clach Eilistean* (G *ail* + ON *stein*, both meaning 'stone') in Lewis. The example from Canna looks like what it is meant to illustrate, and, as the name is not from the Outer Isles, it is not a total surprise. However, Cox's example from Lewis can be disputed. The first element of this name of a large stone on the shore is more likely to be Old Norse *heill*, 'luck, good omen', as in several hill-names along the coast of Norway. Alternatively, it may be the adjective *heilagr*, 'holy (also in a pagan sense)', found in many Norwegian place-names. Both elements would relate the object to belief around fishing or sea-faring. In any case, these examples – and even if there exist a handful more – illustrate how *little* influence Gaelic had on the Norse-speaking population over hundreds of years when the two languages co-existed in the Hebrides.

The lack of *ex-nomine* units in the Norse naming suggests two things: firstly, that a new population established itself in the islands, a population which had insignificant interaction with the previous inhabitants, either because they had fled, were killed or had been taken into slavery abroad (Jennings & Kruse 2005:259-60), and, secondly, when Gaelic was established alongside Norse, it must have had a very low status, probably the status characteristic of an enslaved part of the population.

To sum up, the native forms of a number of early names continue along the littoral, with one or two possible outliers in Mull and Skye, but the early names in the Outer Hebrides and most of the Inner Hebrides have been replaced. The only clearly identifiable native names which were borrowed by the Norse are the names of the islands themselves, such as *Ljóðhús* and *Ívist, Mýl* and *Íle*, which are likely to have been borrowed in an early Norse exploration phase. Within the islands themselves, there is no clear evidence of linguistic contact. If one accepts the earlier thesis that there was a linguistic division in pre-Viking western Scotland, it is clear that both the Gaelic-speaking and Pictish-speaking insular areas suffered nearly complete place-name replacement. However, within the formerly Gaelic-speaking area some of the important names on the mainland were retained and, unlike with *Ljóðhús* and *Ívist,* native forms of some of the Inner Hebrides reasserted themselves. This can be explained by, on the one hand, the survival of a Gaelic-speaking user-group of native names, perhaps in the Inner Hebrides but more certainly on the Scottish Mainland, and, on the other, the disappearance of a Pictish-speaking user-group of native names in the Outer Hebrides.

3. Norse names

The division of the western seaboard into a zone where pre-Norse names survive in a Gaelic context and a zone where they do not is mirrored by the distribution of Norse place-names ,which can also be divided roughly into two zones. The outer zone has a western and northern aspect, consisting of the Outer Hebrides, western Skye, Tiree, Coll, western Mull and Islay. Here, there are settlements bearing Norse names comprising topographical elements such as *vík, nes* and *dalr*, and settlements with habitative naming elements, such as *bólstaðr, staðir* and *setr*. The inner zone lies to the east of the outer zones and consists of eastern Mull, Arran, Kintyre and the western mainland littoral. Here, as in the outer zone, there are settlements with Norse topographical names. However, there are very few settlements bearing Norse habitative elements.

Nicolaisen was the first to identify this interesting distribution pattern, best explained in his book *Scottish Place-Names* (1976:87-96), which he used to establish a model of the chronology and intensity of Norse settlement in Scotland (*Figures 4.2 & 4.3*). According to Nicolaisen, the area with habitative Norse naming elements, i.e. the outer zone, can be described as the Norse settlement area. The distribution of the habitative element *bólstaðr* indicates, he claims, the extent of Norse settlement in the Hebrides, while the

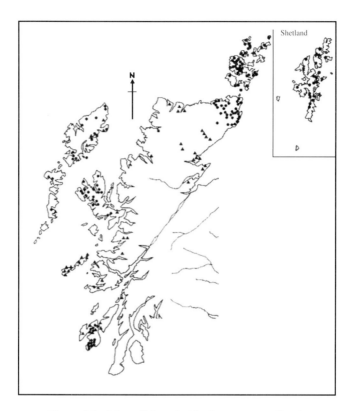

Figure 4.2 : Map of Norse habitative names ending in
bolstaðr in N. and W. Scotland (Nicolaisen,1976)

distribution of the element *dalr*, where it extends beyond the distribution of
bólstaðr, shows 'the sphere of Norse influence', not settlement. His argument
is that *bólstaðr*, as a habitative element, specifically indicates a settlement,
while *dalr*, as a topographical element, primarily indicates a topographical
feature and may never have been used to indicate a settlement. Nicolaisen
believes the existence of these Norse topographical names in the inner zone
is due to the influence of Norse seasonal visitors, making use of grassland,
timber and fish on the mainland, and bringing local Gaels with them so that
the Norse names could be passed on to the native Gaelic population.

As we have discussed in greater detail elsewhere (Jennings 2004 and
Kruse 2004), we believe the implications drawn from the division have been

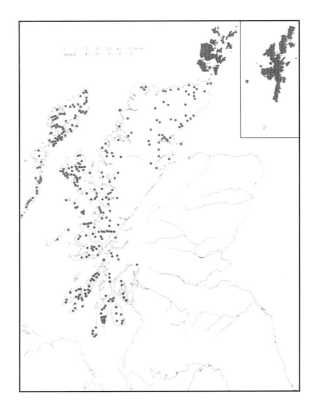

Figure 4.3 : Map of Norse topographical names ending
in *dalr* in N. and W. Scotland (Nicolaisen, 1976)

wrongly interpreted. They do indicate areas of greater and lesser Norseness, but both zones experienced Scandinavian settlement. The difference between the zones indicates a difference in the development of the settlement, primarily due to the nature of the relationship between the Scandinavians and the native population.

The underlying premise upon which Nicolaisen's hypothesis is founded is implausible, namely that Norse seasonal visitors could have left behind a large number of Norse topographical names on the Mainland without having settled there. Resident farming populations hardly ever adopt place-names from itinerant ones. Further, the idea that only habitative naming elements (such as *setr, staðir, bólstaðr*) indicate Norse settlements is rapidly losing support.

In Norway, settlements with topographical names without the definite article, such as *Vik, Haug, Nes,* as a rule of thumb, indicate the oldest, richest and most prestigious farms within a given area. There is now increasing agreement among scholars that topographical-names were also used in the Scandinavian colonies to designate settlements, indeed the very first settlements (See e.g. Crawford 1987:111 and 1995:10-13, Sandnes 2006:248.)

Marwick, as early as the 1950s, recognised the importance of settlements with topographical names, which, he said, 'have undoubtedly to be classed among the very earliest settlements' (Marwick 1952:248). With the application of archaeological, geographical and fiscal methods, scholars have been confirming this. Macgregor (1986) shows that this is the case in the Faroes and Shetland. Olson (1983), in a multidisciplinary study of the settlements in certain areas of Lewis, Skye and Islay, concluded that the settlements with Norse topographical names were amongst the oldest and first established by the Norse. In addition, Fraser (1995: fig. 21, p. 98) implicitly regards the Norse topographical names in Wester Ross as referring to settlements. Fraser lists 40 Norse names (including one single habitative name, Ullapool) from this section of the coastline and 12 Gaelic names, most of which he regards as post-medieval (ibid. 97). Most recently Sandnes (2006) has written in support of the importance and age of settlements bearing toponyms in Orkney, arguing that therefore they were amongst the most heavily taxed.

It is difficult to ascertain at this remove which of the many Norse toponyms actually represent Norse settlements, but we would suggest that those borne by present-day settlements must surely make good candidates. It is illogical to suggest that the modern *bygð* name *Strendur* in the Faroes represents an initial settlement in *strønd* 'strand', while the modern settlement called *Strond* in Harris does not. We would further suggest that a map of such settlements (*Figure: 4.4*) would show in a skeletal manner, the distribution of primary Norse settlement in the west of Scotland.

In a recent paper Graham-Campbell (2006) insists that we should proceed with caution when claiming toponyms as evidence of settlement. He is correct, as it cannot be proved that all of the individual examples originally represented *bona fide* primary Norse settlements and not simply topographical features. Only detailed archaeological study will reveal the truth. On the other hand, many of the other Norse toponyms which do not survive as the names of modern settlements may also have been primary Norse settlements. Thus, such a map can only be taken as a rough guide.

Figure 4.4 : Map of settlements with Norse names ending in *dalr* in the Hebrides and along the western seaboard (Nicolaisen, 1976)

It can immediately be seen that this map of potential Norse primary settlement provides a wider distribution of Norse settlement than that suggested by the *bólstaðr* generic. Those areas formerly regarded as having been heavily settled remain so, but there are many additional settlements on the western littoral. For example, around Kyle of Lochalsh there is a settlement in -*vik, Erbusaig,* and two in -*nes, Avernish* and *Duirinish,* while on Arran in the Clyde estuary there are two settlements with names in -*vik, Sannox* and *Brodick* and a settlement in -*dalr, Kiscadale.* This suggested distribution of Norse settlement is similar to that posited by Oftedal (1980).

The names in *vík* 'bay', we would suggest, are particularly good candidates for primary settlement sites. *Vík* was the most common topographical settlement generic in Thuesen's (1978) study of Orkney and in MacGregor's (1986) study of the Faroes. Since settlers in the west of Scotland were no less reliant on their ships nor less aware of the advantages of settling on the coast, there is no reason for supposing it was any the less popular amongst them.

The importance of *vík* in the west of Scotland has not been overlooked. Fraser (1995) examined a selected number along the west coast in an attempt to ascertain their suitability for settlement. He examined 18 examples from Enard Bay to Loch Duich, each one of which exhibits good settlement qualities. Fraser isolated the four characteristics which combine to establish a *vík* place-name:

(i)   the availability of shelter, good anchorage or beaching possibilities

(ii)   an available supply of arable land

(iii)   supplies of water for fishing, timber or game

(iv)   access to the sea-routes.

He then applied these criteria to two examples from Wester Ross, showing in the process the advantages of settling at *Scorraig,* which flourished in the last century, and *Shieldaig,* with its deep anchorage and arable land. In effect, Fraser has isolated the criteria for considering *vík* as a primary settlement name.

To recapitulate, the zones do not define areas of settlement and influence because the Norse population established itself in both the inner and the outer zone. They used prominent topographical features to name their primary settlement sites in a fashion that would also indicate important settlements in Norway. The frequency and distribution of Norse names show that this initial land-taking must have been intense and surely deeply disruptive to the local population wherever it took place in Scotland. However, the importance of the division into two zones becomes clear when habitative generics are considered.

Habitative generics generally appear to be attached to secondary settlements. The habitative element *bólstaðr* has been studied in detail by Gammeltoft (2001). With the use of linguistic and extra-linguistic criteria, he finds that the element is likely to have been productive in Shetland, Orkney and the Hebrides from the end of the 9th century. This is one hundred years after the first registered Viking raids on the West Coast of Scotland, and a couple of generations after the likely land-taking period. Therefore, *bólstaðr* was probably not used during the first settlement phase in Scotland. Gammeltoft confirms this when he analyses the topographical and economic characteristics of farms bearing this element. Rather than being used to name the first farms established by the Norse, *bólstaðr* is used to name farms that are chronologically of a secondary character, created when larger farming units were split up into several smaller units. Unfortunately, we lack similar detailed studies for the other habitative elements, but there is good reason to believe that *setr* and *staðir* are also of a similar secondary character. MacNiven (2006) argues that the complimentary distribution of *setr* and *airigh* in the west suggests it was current in the 12th century. Olson's study of Hebridean place-names (1983) supported the secondary nature of the *staðir* names. He concluded that, '*staðir* was a usual name used for 'farm' when the primary units were dismembered.'(Olson 1983:227) This is close to Fellows-Jensen's (1984:159) stated opinion on *staðir* names: 'the generic *staðir* may have had the same kind of function in the Atlantic islands as *býr* 'farm' had in the Scandinavian colonies in England. Both generics are frequently compounded with personal names and both seem to denote some kind of secondary settlement.'

It would appear, when the secondary nature of habitative generics is taken into account, that the outer zone was an area where Norse settlement, represented by the topographical generics, developed and secondary settlements were created within a Norse-speaking milieu, while the inner zone was an area where Norse settlement did not develop beyond the primary phase. Only a resident ethnic Norse community can explain today's pattern

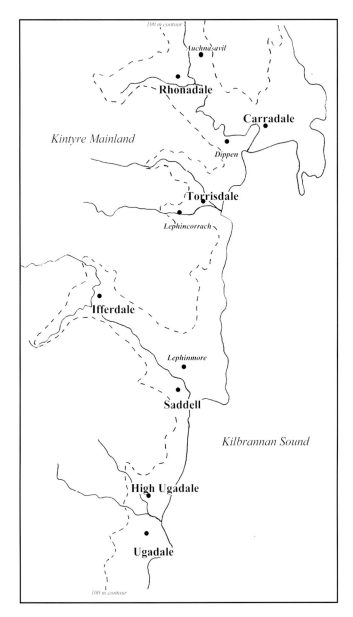

Figure 4.5 : Map of Norse names ending in *dalr*
in the Carradale area, Kintyre

and frequency of Norse place-names. This is as true of the inner as the outer zone. The Norse topographical names along the western littoral are indicative of a geographical continuum of settlements where Norse was once spoken (Kruse 2004). The invaders made use of the most prestigious naming elements that they knew from Norway in order to name farms in a rugged landscape that invited and enforced the use of topographical naming elements. There is hardly any use of the traditional habitative elements to indicate division of farms or the clearing of new land in this zone. This strongly suggests that the Norse-speaking community did not remain Norse-speaking for very long. They must have adopted the native language for the formation of secondary settlements.

The Carradale area of Kintyre provides an illustration of a scenario where the transition to Gaelic is likely to have happened at an early stage (Jennings 2004). Here, all the major settlements bear the Norse generic *dalr* (*Figure 4.5*). However, there are no Norse habitative names but there are secondary Gaelic elements, in *achadh* 'field' (*Auchnasavil*, secondary to Norse *Rhonadale*) and *peighinn* 'pennyland' (*Dippen*, secondary to Norse *Carradale*, *Lephincorrach*, secondary to Norse *Torrisdale* and likewise *Lephinmore*, secondary to Norse *Saddell*). The classifications 'primary' and 'secondary' are based on a set of favourable factors that characterise the settlements. This is usually reflected in the taxation value. For Kintyre we are lucky to have rentals from 1503. In these, *achadh* can be seen to refer to secondary farming settlements. *Auchnasavil* [Achinnasawle] is valued at 2 merks, while *Rhonadale* [Rynnadill] is valued at 4 merks. Similarly, in the case of *Dippen* and *Carradale*, the former [Dwpeyn] is valued at 3 merks while the latter [Ardcardale], is valued at 4 merks.

The Norse who settled in the inner zone appear to have settled in clusters. In any given area, there tend either to be several Norse names or none. For example, along the peninsula of Kintyre, the Norse names stretch in a continuous distribution along the east coast while they are found only in two limited clusters along the west coast. This is highly suggestive of the survival of a pre-Norse population. It is intriguing that, in the case of Kintyre, the Norse place-names appear to avoid the area with the greatest concentration of pre-Norse archaeological sites, where presumably there was the greatest density of native settlement. The duns on the western side of Kintyre were probably still inhabited during the 9th century (Alcock & Alcock 1987:131).

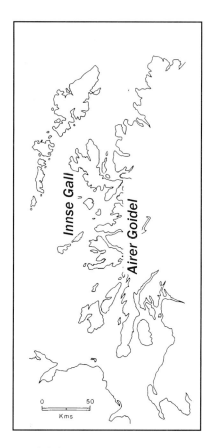

Figure 4.6 : Map defining the areas of 'Innse Gall' and 'Airer Goidel'

4. Conclusion & Gall-Gaidheil

The best explanation for the survival of pre-Norse place-names and the lack of Norse habitative generics on the mainland is the survival of the pre-Norse Gaelic-speaking society of erstwhile Dál Riata. However, it must have been much affected, because, although the tribal names *Cenél Loairn* and *Cenél Comgaill* survive in the onomasticon, that of the once most powerful, the *Cenél nGabráin,* does not; the territory where they were based now bears the Norse name *Knapdale*, from ON *nabbi*, m., 'small protruberance'. Most indicative of the Norse impact is surely the loss of the name *Dál Riata* itself.

The last contemporary record of the name is with the death of *Donncorci*, king of Dál Riata, in 798. M.O.Anderson (1976) suggested this was the time when Scottish and Irish Dál Riata were severed. Perhaps we are justified in believing that, although Gaels survived, Dál Riata did not. The topographical place-names suggest it must have been a changed society with its new resident Norse component.

The lack of pre-Norse names and the existence of many Norse habitative generics in both the Inner and Outer Hebrides suggests that the Norse impact was overwhelming and there was the establishment of a long-lasting Norse-speaking community in the formerly Dalriadic islands and in the Pictish Outer Hebrides, where we have argued there is clear evidence of a linguistic break. As in the pre-Norse period, there are clear similarities between the Outer Hebrides and the Northern Isles, only now the milieu was Norse. The Pictish Outer Hebrides, Orkney and Shetland became the most completely 'Norsified' of the Norse settlement areas in the British Isles. Norse may have continued in use in the Outer Hebrides well after the Treaty of Perth in 1266. Oftedal (1980:166) argued for the early 16th century as the date of its final demise.

A division within western Scotland between islands and mainland is corroborated by the early existence of a distinction between *Innse Gall* 'Islands of the Scandinavians' and *Airer Goidel* 'Coastline of the Gael' (*Argyll*). *Innse Gall* included the Inner as well as Outer Hebrides and *Airer Goidel* by the 13th century stretched from the Mull of Kintyre to Ullapool at least. In 1255, the parishes of Kintail to Loch Broom were described as 'the churches of Argyll belonging to the foresaid church [of Rosemarkie, base of the medieval diocese of Ross]' (Theiner, *Vetera Monumenta* No.172, here in translation after Grant 2005:88). The division has a parallel in Norse tradition where the mainland, or *Airer Goidel*, is referred to as *Skotland*, but the islands are never regarded as part of this territory. They are consistently referred to as *Suðreyjar* 'Southern Isles'. This division is confirmed in *Magnus Saga* (chapter 11), where it is stated:

Magnús konungr hélt liði sínu til Suðreyja, en er hann kom þar, tók hann þegar at herja ok brenna bygðina, en drap mannfólkit, ok ræntu alt, þar er þeir fóru; en landslýðr flýði undan víðs vegar, sumir inn í Skotlandsfjörðu, en sumir suðr í Satíri eða út til Írlands; sumir féngu grið ok veittu handgöngu.

[King Magnus and his men set course for the Suðreyjar, and when he came there he instantly began to lay waste and burn the settlements, killing the people and plundering wherever they went; and the people living in the country fled in all directions, some into the firths of Scotland, others south to Kintyre, or out to Ireland; some were granted life and safety and entered into his service.]

And in chapter 12:

Magnús konungr var um vetrinn í Suðreyjum, þá fóru menn hans um alla Skotlandsfjörðu, réru fyrir innan eyjar allar bæði bygðar ok úbygðar, ok eignuðu Noregs konungi eylönd öll.

[King Magnus stayed in the Suðreyjar during the winter, and then his men rowed around in all the firths of Scotland, they rowed inside of all islands both settled and unsettled and claimed all islands for the Norwegian king.]

A parallel is found in the name *Péttlandsfjörðr* (*Orkneyinga saga*, chapters 25-29) which refers to the Picts across the firth on the northern Mainland of Scotland.

By the 12th century there was both a *Rí Innse Gall* 'King of the Islands of the Scandinavians' and a *Rí Airer Goidel* 'King of Argyll', Somerled was the latter before his conquest of the Hebrides, when he also became the former. *Innse Gall* was in use at least by AU989 when the obit of *Gofraid mac Arailt* refers to him as *rí Innse Gall*, although it may go back to 851 with the obit of *Gofraid mac Fhergusa*, who is referred to as *toiseach Innsi Gall* in the *Annals of the Four Masters* (Sellar 1966:134). There is every reason to believe that the territorial name *Innse Gall* came into use during the 9th century when Norse settlement was taking place throughout the islands. Bruford (2005:54) is likely to have been correct when he suggested that *Airer Goidel* also came into existence during the 9th century. *Airer Goidel*, we would suggest, was the new territorial unit created by the surviving Gaelic-speaking population at some point after Dál Riata in Scotland was severed from Dál Riata in Ireland due to Norse pressure post-798. The change of name indicates the loss of the islands of the Inner Hebrides and a refocusing of the Gaelic world along the coast. Woolf (2007:64,100), in his recent interpretation of the evidence, suggests that Dál Riata was occupied from c.793 to 806 by the Norse, whom he identifies as the Hörðar from Hordaland. The kingdom then rallied briefly under its native kings, until Aed son of Boanta was killed in 839. He suggests the Frankish chronicler, Prudentius of Troyes, under 847, recorded the conquest of the island portion of Dál Riata and the effective ending of its existence: 'the Northmen also got control of the islands all around Ireland and stayed there without encountering any resistance from anyone' (Nelson 1991:65; here quoted after Woolf 2007:100).

Several things suggest the new territory of *Airer Goidel* may have allied itself with the Norse. Firstly, a Gaelic society survived, whereas the Pictish society in the Outer Hebrides did not. Secondly, after 825 there appears to have been a cessation of attacks on the monastery of Iona, until the unfortunate events of 986. Iona seems to have continued as a religious house throughout the period (Jennings 1998). There are a series of annal entries which record the obits of abbots and other important figures at the monastery, for example AU880 *Feradhach m.Cormaicc, abbas Iae, pausauit* [Feradach son of Cormac, Abbot of Iona, rested] and AU978 *Fiachra, airchinnech Ia, quieuit.* [Fiachra, superior of Iona, rested.] Thirdly, in the 850s there is the appearance of the *Gall-Gaidheil* in Ireland under the Norseman *Caitil Find.* These are surely the inhabitants of *Airer Goidel* as seen from an Irish perspective: a grouping of Norse and Gael acting together. The *Gall-Gaidheil* can only have sprung from an area where a continuing Gaelic community was in intimate contact with the Norse (Jennings & Kruse, forthcoming). The only clear option for such a situation was the mainland of the western seaboard of Scotland, where there was primary Norse settlement, shown by the topographical Norse place-names, but where the presence of a surviving Gaelic population, stopped it from developing a secondary phase.

Notes

[1] The translation is based on Finnur Jónsson's translation into Danish and on the translation of the *Morkinskinna* stanzas in Anderson and Gade: 2000:298-9.

Bibliography

Adomnán of Iona: *Life of St Columba*. Transl. by Richard Sharpe. London 1995.
Alcock, L., 1971: *Arthur's Britain: History and Archaeology*. London.

Alcock, L. & Alcock E.A., 1987: Reconnaissance excavations on Early Historic fortifications and other royal sites in Scotland, 1974-84: 2, Excavations at Dunollie Castle, Oban, Argyll, 1978. *Proc Soc Antiq Scot* 117, pp 73-101.

Anderson, M.O., 1973: *Kings and Kingship in Early Scotland.* Edinburgh.

Anderson, Th.M. and Gade, K.E.: *Morkinskinna. The Earliest Icelandic Chronicle of the Norwegian Kings (1030-1157),* Ithaca and London: Cornell University Press 2000

Armit, I., 1996: *The archaeology of Skye and the Western Isles.* Edinburgh.

Bannerman, J., 1974: *Studies in the History of Dalriada.* Edinburgh/ London.

Binchy, D.A., 1963: *Scéla Cano Meic Gartnáin.* Dublin.

Bruford, A., 2005: 'What happened to the Caledonians?' in E.J. Cowan & R.A. McDonald, eds., *Alba: Celtic Scotland in the Middle Ages.* Edinburgh pp. 43-68.

Clancy, T.O. & Márkus, G., 1995, Iona: *The Earliest Poetry of a Celtic Monastery,* Edinburgh.

Cox, R.A.V., 1987: *Place-Names of the Carloway Registry, Isle of Lewis.* . Unpublished Ph.D. thesis, University of Glasgow. Glasgow.

Cox, R.A.V., 1991: 'Norse-Gaelic Contact in the West of Lewis: The Place-Name Evidence.' In: P.S. Ureland & G. Broderick, eds., *Language Contact in the British Isles,* Eighth International Symposium on Language Contact in Europe, Douglas, Isle of Man, 1988. Tübingen, pp. 479-493.

Cox, R.A.V., 2002: *The Gaelic Place-Names of Carloway, Isle of Lewis. Their Structure and Significance.* Dublin.

Cox, R.A.V, 2007, 'Notes on the Norse Impact on Hebridean Place-names,' in *The Journal of Scottish Name Studies,* vol. 1, pp. 139-44.

Crawford, B.E., 1987: *Scandinavian Scotland.* Scotland in the Early Middle Ages 2. Leicester.

Fellows-Jensen, G., 1984: 'Viking Settlement in the Northern and Western Isles – the Place-Name Evidence as seen from Denmark and the Danelaw' in A. Fenton & H. Pálsson (eds), *The Northern and Western Isles in the Viking World: Survival, Continuity and Change.* Edinburgh pp. 148-168.

Finnur Jónsson, 1912: *Den norsk-islandske skjaldedigtning,* B, vol. I., Copenhagen and Kristiania [Oslo].

Fisher, I., 2001: *Early Medieval Sculpture in the West Highlands and Island.* Edinburgh.

Fraser, I.A., 1974: 'The Place Names of Lewis – The Norse Evidence', *Northern Studies* 4 pp. 11-21.

Fraser, I.A., 1984: 'Some Further Thoughts on Scandinavian Place-Names in Lewis', *Northern Studies* 21 pp. 34-41.

Fraser, I.A, 1995: 'Norse Settlement on the North-West Seaboard'. In: B.E. Crawford (ed.), *Scandinavian Settlement in Northern Britain*. London/ New York pp. 92-105.

Gammeltoft, P. *The place-name element* bólstaðr *in the North Atlantic area.* Copenhagen, 2001.

Grant, A., 2005: 'The Province of Ross and the Kingdom of Alba', in E.J. Cowan & R.A. McDonald, eds., *Alba: Celtic Scotland in the Middle Ages.* Edinburgh pp. 88-126.

Graham-Campbell, J., 2006: 'Some reflections on the distribution and significance of Norse place-names in northern Scotland', in P. Gammeltoft & B. Jørgensen, eds., *Names through the Looking-Glass. Festschrift in Honour of Gillian Fellows-Jensen, July 5ᵗʰ 2006.* Copenhagen. pp. 94-118.

Henderson, G., 1910: *The Norse Influence on Celtic Scotland.* Glasgow.

Jakobsen, J. 'Keltisk Indflydelse paa Færøerne', in: *Tingakrossur* 1-2, 1902. [Also in: J. Jakobsen, *Greinir og ritgerdir*, Torshavn, 1957 pp. 72- 78.]

Jakobsen, J. 'Staðanøvn í Føroyum', in: *Tingakrossur* 43, 1915. [Also in: Jakob Jakobsen, *Greinir og ritgerdir*, Torshavn, 1957 pp. 108-110.]

Jennings, A. 'Iona and the Vikings: Survival and Continuity', in: *Northern Studies* vol. 33, 1998 pp. 37-54.

Jennings, A., 2004: 'Norse Place-Names of Kintyre', in: K. Holman & J. Adams, eds., *Scandinavia and Europe 800-1350: Contact, Conflict, and Coexistence.* Turnhout pp. 109-119.

Jennings, A., & Kruse, A., 2005: 'The Ethnic Enigma', in Andras Mortensen and Símun V. Arge, eds., *Viking and Norse in the North Atlantic.* Selected papers from the Proceedings of the Fourteenth Viking Congress, Torshavn 2005.

Jennings, A., & Kruse, A., forthcoming: 'The *Gall-Gaidheil* and Dál Riata'.

Johnston, A., 1995: 'Norse Settlement Patterns in Coll and Tiree'. In: B.E. Crawford (ed.), *Scandinavian Settlement in Northern Britain.* London/ New York pp. 108-126.

Kruse, A., 2004: 'Norse Topographical Settlement Names on the Western Littoral of Scotland'. In: J. Adams & K. Holman (eds), *Scandinavia and Europe 800-1350: Contact, Conflict and Coexistence.* Turnhout pp. 97-107.

Kruse, A., 2005: 'Explorers, Raiders and Settlers. The Norse Impact upon Hebridean Place-Names', in P. Gammeltoft, C. Hough and D.Waugh, eds., *Cutural Contact in the North Atlantic*, 2005.

Lane, A., 1983: *Dark-age and Viking pottery in the Hebrides, with special reference to the Udal, North Uist.* Unpublished PhD-thesis, University College London, 1983.

Lane, A. 1990, 'Hebridean Pottery: Problems of Definition, Chronology, Presence and Absence', in Armit, I. ed., *Beyond the Brochs. Changing Perspectives on the Later Iron Age in Atlantic Scotland,* Edinburgh University Press, Edinburgh, pp. 108-30.

Lane, A. & Campbell, E. 2000: *Excavations at Dunadd: an early Dalriadic capital.* Oxbow Monographs: Oxford.

MacLennan, M., 1979: *Gaelic Dictionary*, Aberdeen.

Lynch, M., ed., 2001: *Oxford Companion to Scottish History*, Oxford.

Marwick, H., 1952: *Orkney Farm-Names*, Kirkwall.

MacBain, A., 1922: *Place-Names of the Highlands and Islands of Scotland.* Stirling.

Macgregor, L.J., 1986: 'Norse naming elements in Shetland and Faroe: A comparative study.' *Northern Studies* 23 pp. 84-101.

Macniven, A., 2006: *The Norse in Islay. A Settlement Historical Case-Study for Medieval Scandinavian Activity in Western Maritime Scotland,* Unpublished PhD dissertation, University of Edinburgh, Edinburgh.

J.L.Nelson, 1991, ed.: *The Annals of St-Bertin*, Manchester.

Oftedal, M., 1980: 'Scandinavian place-names in Celtic territory', in T. Anderson, E. Brylla & A. Rostvik, eds., *Ortnamn och språkkontakt*, NORNA-rapporter 17, Uppsala. pp. 163-191.

Olson, D., 1983: *Norse Settlement in the Hebrides, an Interdisciplinary Study*, Unpublished Cand.Philol thesis, University of Oslo, Oslo.

Pliny, NH IV, Loeb Classical Library, London, (1957).

Sandnes, B., 2006: 'Toponyms as settlement names – of no relevance in settlement history?', in P. Gammeltoft & B. Jørgensen, eds., *Names through the Looking-Glass. Festschrift in Honour of Gillian Fellows-Jensen, July 5th 2006.* Copenhagen. pp. 230-253.

Sellar, D., 1966: 'The origins and ancestry of Somerled', *SHR* xlv pp. 124-42.

Stahl, A-B., 1999: *Place-Names of Barra in the Outer Hebrides.* Unpublished Ph.D. thesis, University of Edinburgh, Edinburgh.

Thuesen, N. P., 1978: *Gardsbosetning på Orknøyene i norrøn tid. Et studium av South Ronaldsay, Rousay, Harray og Deerness.* Unpublished Cand. Philol. thesis, University of Oslo, Oslo.

Watson, W.J., 1926: *The Celtic Place-Names of Scotland.* Edinburgh.

Woolf, A., 2007: *From Pictland to Alba 789-1070*, Edinburgh.

Norse settlement in the Western Isles

Niall Sharples and Rachel Smith

When I realised that I was attending a conference to commemorate the publication of *Scandinavian Scotland* (Crawford 1987), I thought it would be good idea if I re-examined what Barbara had said about the Western Isles. On examining the index I was rather surprised to discover 66 entries on the Hebrides and 46 entries for the Western Isles. I was impressed, this was a very significant contribution and compared well with the 44 entries for Shetland and the 57 entries for Orkney; it suggested that there was a lot I had forgotten about. However, on systematically making my way through the text I was disappointed, but not surprised, to discover that the number of mentions did not represent a wealth of evidence. In the 1980s knowledge of the Norse settlement of the Western Isles was poor and this was laid out in detail in the text for *Scandinavian Scotland*:

The natural environment appeared to be conspiring against the inhabitants. The geology was forbidding: 'The hard rocks in the west make the Outer Hebrides one of the most barren landscapes in Scotland, providing hardly enough soil to cultivate' (Crawford 1987, 28). The climate was terrible: 'The patches of better land throughout the Hebrides are rarely able to realize full arable potential because of the climatic factors' (1987, 32). Even when the modern historical record suggested a relatively prosperous agricultural landscape the relevance of this record was questioned. 'Although in the seventeenth century the Hebridean farmer seems to have grown 'considerably more grain than was usual in Shetland', we cannot be certain that such a contrast would have existed at an earlier date. All it is possible to say is that neither were able to produce grain as successfully as the Orkney farmer' (1987, 34).

Any attempt to understand the region was further hampered by the poor historical record: 'There does not exist a single contemporary document from the Western Isles during the whole of the Norse period' (1987, 3). The region was totally dependent on references from other areas, in documents such as the Orkneyinga Saga and the Chronicles of the Kings of Man.

The archaeological situation was not much better '.. in the Western Isles, research lags far behind, so we cannot yet fully understand the early Medieval basis to the later settlement pattern' (1987, 151). Only three Norse settlements had been excavated Barvas on Lewis, Drimore in South Uist (Maclaren 1974) and The Udal in North Uist (Crawford and Switsur 1977). The first two sites are not mentioned in the book; Barvas was not published and though Drimore was published it was a notoriously difficult site to understand. Future progress seemed to be dependant on the publication of the Udal: 'Our understanding of Norse settlement in the Western Isles is virtually non-existent and will remain so until the site of Udal in North Uist is fully published' (1987, 5). The Udal was clearly an exceptional site that had the potential to transform the understanding of the Viking settlement not just of the Western Isles but of the North Atlantic. Provisional publications (Crawford I., 1981, 1986; Selkirk 1996) had argued that the juxtaposition of a Viking house on top of a native settlement at the Udal indicated the total obliteration of the local population by incoming Norse settlers and this was noted in *Scandinavian Scotland* though not with much enthusiasm (Crawford 1987, 140).

It is a testament to Barbara's imagination that despite the chronic lack of evidence she was able to come up with anything at all interesting to say about the Norse society in the Western Isles, but there is plenty in *Scandinavian Scotland* to consider. She suggested that despite the lack of evidence there were almost certainly administrative, taxation and legal systems comparable to those found in the Northern Isles if not equivalent to them. There is evidence that Sigurd the Stout 'laid a tax on the inhabited lands of Man' (1987, 66) which would have included the Hebrides. She also drew attention to 'the journey of Gudmund, bishop-elect of Holar in 1207, in a merchant ship from Iceland to Norway, when the ship was blown off course and landed in the Outer Hebrides'. The bailiff of the king of Man claimed land-dues 'according as the laws of the Hebrides required', which were 100 lengths of wadmell (cloth) for each man in the ship (or a monetary equivalent)' (1987, 135). The islands appear to have been taxed using a form of Ounceland system known as the *tir-unga* (1987, 88) and she suggests that this might have been introduced by Earls Sigurd or Thorfinn in the early eleventh century. Finally it was suggested that eight representatives may have been sent to the Tynwald parliament in the Isle of Man (1987, 204) which was the administrative centre for the islands.

Despite these suggestions of a sophisticated system of governance she argued that Norse society in the Hebrides was quite different from that in the Northern Isles. Distance from the political centres may have meant that

'Political control was less easily exercised over the Hebrides' (1987, 80) and the proximity to Ireland may have meant this was a more warlike society than other areas of the North Atlantic. This statement is partly justified by the presence of a group of pagan graves in the west which are markedly richer than those found in the Northern Isles (1987, 125). These suggested the presence of a group of independent warriors whose wealth, though not comparable to the political leaders on the Northern Isles, was greater than the common farmers on these islands. This wealth was based on a combination of raiding and trading in the Irish Sea province, rather than derived from the agricultural potential of the colonised landscape.

I want to demonstrate in this paper that our understanding of the Western Isles has changed for the better in the last 20 years. There is of course no increase in the historical records[1] but we now have a considerable amount of archaeological information on the Norse societies of the Hebrides, particularly for the eleventh to fourteenth centuries. The basic geology, and damp windy climate of the region, has not been transformed, but I also hope to demonstrate that the agricultural potential, of certain areas of the Western Isles at least, was underestimated.

It took a long time for work on the Norse archaeology of the Western Isles to get underway and it is possible that the importance of the Udal excavations discouraged archaeologists from researching the Norse settlement of the islands. There was little point in starting new work when it seemed that a lifetime of effort would be required to assemble a database comparable to that recovered from the Udal. However, Sharples has been involved in a long-term project (life-changing if not life-absorbing) on the island of South Uist which included the excavation of two substantial Norse settlements. Whilst most of this paper will discuss evidence from the excavations at Bornais in South Uist (Sharples 1996, 1997, 1999, 2000, 2003) frequent reference will also be made to the material from Cille Pheadair in South Uist (Brennand et al. 1998; Parker Pearson et al. 1996; Parker Pearson et al. 2004).[2] It has also been possible, through the definition of a distinctive ceramic form, the flat platter (Lane 1990), to identify a large number of Norse settlements on the machair plains of South Uist. This area was clearly densely settled in the Norse period and must have been a politically important part of the Kingdom of Man and the Isles.

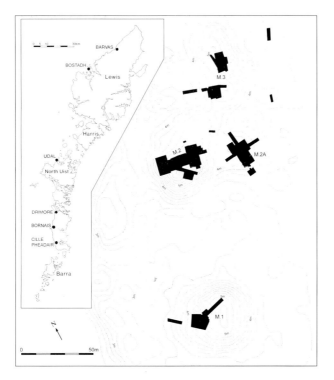

Figure 5.1 : Map of the Western Isles showing the location of the Viking and Norse settlements mentioned in the text and a plan of the areas excavated at Bornais on South Uist.

Bornais

The settlement at Bornais comprises a group of four prominent mounds currently situated in the centre of the machair plain in the middle of the island of South Uist (Figure 5.1). It lies just inland from the promontory of Ardvule which provides one of the few sheltered anchorages on the west coast of the Uists. An important fifth- to sixth-century settlement (Late Iron Age 1)[3] was exposed on Mound 1 and it is assumed that an earlier Middle Iron Age settlement lies in unexplored areas of this mound.[4] Sometime in the sixth century the settlement appears to have shifted to Mound 2 where the remains of Late Iron Age 2 settlement activity were exposed underneath a considerable depth of Norse material.

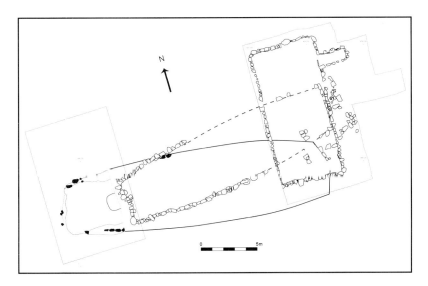

Figure 5.2 : A plan showing the sequence of three buildings on Bornais Mound 2. The stones of house 1 (tenth century) are infilled black and the outline of the house is shown by a solid line. The stones of house 2 (eleventh century) are infilled white and the outline of the house is marked by a dashed line. The stones of house 3 (fourteenth century, oriented north-south) are infilled grey.

The evidence from Mound 2 suggests that a well-connected Norse family took over the Late Iron Age (or Pictish?) settlement in the tenth century. However, the question remains over whether they took over an abandoned settlement, or evicted the occupants, and this is not a question that is easily answered by the archaeological evidence (see Sharples forthcoming). There may have been a hiatus in the ninth century caused by a violent phase of raiding, but radiocarbon dates suggest there is possibly a very ephemeral settlement of this date on mound 1 which left few diagnostic structures or material evidence. The primary settlement at the Udal (Crawford I., 1981, 1986) could belong to the phase of raiding in the ninth century AD. The material culture and buildings present on this site in the Viking periods (Selkirk 1996) are not comparable to those found at Bornais, and the pins and combs in particular suggest an early date. The location of the Udal would be an ideal base for a raiding party; it is situated at the end of a long peninsula jutting out from North Uist into the Sound of Harris and has easy access along the east and west coasts of the Hebrides.

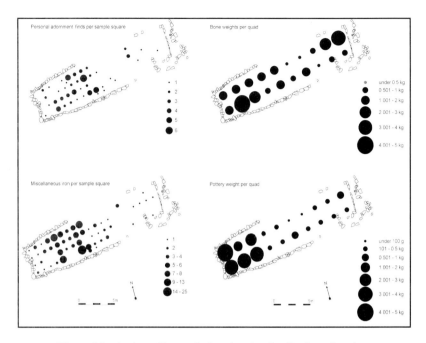

Figure 5.3 : A plan of house 2 showing the distribution of various
categories of material found in the house floor layers.

The Viking settlement at Bornais begins in the tenth century and seems to
be important from its initial establishment. On Mound 2 there is a substantial
long house, 23.1 m long, with a long central hearth area, a paved floor at
the eastern end and an entrance in the east gable (Figure 5.2). This house
was surrounded by a heavily cultivated infield which was exposed by the
excavations on Mound 2A. Large quantities of rubbish were deposited in the
cultivation soil and this provides us with good evidence for the economy of
the Viking settlement.

The later eleventh-century house on Mound 2 was much more completely
excavated and will be of considerable importance to our understanding of this
period as it has produced a substantial and spectacular collection of finds. The
house is just under 20 m long and up to 5 m wide at the centre of its interior.
A substantial internal wall was built using large stone blocks presumably
robbed from an adjacent Iron Age structure. The principal internal feature
was a central area covered in ash spreads that represent both in situ hearths,

and ash raked out of the hearths to create a compact surface that acted as a thoroughfare through the house. An analysis of the distribution of finds inside the house (Taylor 2005) indicates a threefold division of the internal space (Figure 5.3). The western half of the house is split between a cooking area at the west end and a dining and socialisation space near the centre. The eastern half of the house appears to have been given over to sleeping, or storage, and produced very few finds.

The floor of this house produced vast quantities of material which indicates the house was used for the conspicuous consumption of food, drink and material culture (see below). This is a fairly archaic way of establishing status in the eleventh century and it gives some support to the suggestion made in *Scandinavian Scotland* that the islands were relatively isolated from the political centres of the period. Isolation may have allowed the families that occupied the large farms of the island to retain an independence that enabled them to acquire and dispose of a rich and varied range of material culture that was not available to families of comparable status in the Northern Isles. They seem to have retained a "Viking" way of life longer than in the north.

This period of conspicuous consumption does not seem to continue much later than the twelfth century. It is clear that the occupants of the settlement retain a certain status as the thirteenth- to fourteenthcentury house on Mound 2 is a sizeable structure, 13 m long and 6 m wide. It was like all the late Norse houses, defined by a line of stones placed around the inside of a hollow. The wall was a consistent 0.46 m high with up to five courses of stone. It is assumed that the main structural feature of the house was a turf wall with an internal timber frame which sat on the low stone wall (See Sharples 2005 fig 107 for the reconstruction of a much smaller house on mound 3). The entrance was through a passage, 2.5 m long and 0.9 m wide, located on the east side close to the north wall. A high sill stone separated the passage from the interior of the house. The floor deposits were well preserved and included at least two separate phases of activity; there were discrete circular hearth deposits in both the southern and northern halves of the interior. Finds were less common than in the underlying, tenth- and eleventh- century house floors, and there were very few small finds (though these did include a coin of Henry III:1216-1272).

Excavations on Mounds 1, 2A and 3 have recovered evidence for lengthy sequences of occupation that had commenced at least by the eleventh century and indicate that this was a large multi-focal settlement within a hundred years of the establishment of the Viking settlement. Several thirteenth- to fourteenth-century buildings have been exposed and excavated on these mounds, but these are much less substantial than those exposed on Mound 2. In size and plan these later houses are reminiscent of the croft dwellings of the late nineteenth and early twentieth century. Their presence at this date might suggest that the agrarian system, visible when the islands emerge from prehistory in the seventeenth and eighteenth centuries, originates in the twelfth and thirteenth centuries.

Economic potential

The archaeological evidence from the recent excavations emphasises a diverse economy with access to many significant resources. The primary basis for the recent economy of South Uist is arable agriculture and Robert Dodghson (1998, tbl 1.1) has shown that Uist had a very high percentage of arable and contributed very large quantities of oat meal as rent in kind (1998, tbl 3.1). The geographical basis for this surplus was the large shell sand, or machair, plain on the west side of the Uists as this landscape is well drained and easily cultivated. However, the soils are nutrient poor and prone to erosion, which can be catastrophic.

Table 1 The density (per litre of soil) of the principal domestic crops from some of the main stratigraphic units at Bornais

Mound	Activity	Date	Phase	litres	Barley	Oats	Rye	Flax	weeds/wild seeds
1	Burnt house	5-6th cent	CB	1418.5	4.4	0.01	0	0.01	1.69
1	Midden	5-6th cent	CG	247.5	0.79	0.06	0	0	0.24
2	occupation surfaces	7-8th cent	BAB/C	219	0.8	0.01	0.01	0.1	1.47
2	House 1 floors and pits	9th-10th cent	BBA/BBC	139	3.98	3.45	1.32	0.06	5.12
2	House 2 floors	11th cent	BCC	1555	4.36	1.32	0.83	0.08	6.74
2	House 3 floors and pits	13-14th cent	BEB-D	812.5	5.29	3.74	0.51	0.26	4.52
2A	Culitivation soil	9-10th cent	GAA-C	780.5	11.49	14.07	0.44	0.17	3.28
2A	Grey sand	10th-11th	GAD	555	4.72	7.48	2.55	0.04	2.07
2A	Kiln and associated deposits	12th cent	GB-	727	4.26	72.95	1.52	0.14	2.76
2A	Structures and middens	13-14th cent	GC-/GD-	1064	4.15	4.6	0.73	0.72	2.46

The archaeological excavations confirm the importance of crop production. Detailed analysis of the carbonised plant remains from the excavations at Bornais has just been completed and provides important evidence for the crops cultivated by the inhabitants of the settlement.[5] In Table 1 the mean densities of the main cereal crops are shown for Mounds 1, 2 and 2A amalgamating a considerable amount of data into a limited number of chronological phases.

The data for barley shows an unusually high density in the burnt-down LIA1 wheelhouse. The lower densities from the LIA1 midden and the LIA2 deposits on Mound 2 are more normal. There is a very high density of barley in the Viking cultivation soil on Mound 2A which might indicate stubble burning or, more likely, the processing and disposal of waste material in the cultivated infield. The densities then remain fairly stable but at a high level through the remaining deposits. In Mound 2, in contrast, the densities of barley increase gradually through the sequence until they are slightly

Figure 5.4 : The ard marks below the cultivation soil at the base of Mound 2A when first exposed.

greater than the mound 2A densities. Oat densities are very low on all the Late Iron Age deposits but increase dramatically in the Viking deposits particularly on Mound 2A. The densities vary in different periods and phases and the very high densities, associated with the Mound 2A kiln, probably represent the accidental destruction of a crop. Rye and flax are present in the LIA but only in negligible quantities. Rye becomes a significant presence in the early Viking deposits but the densities decline gradually over time. Flax in contrast seems to take a bit longer to become established and densities increase in the later phases of the settlement. These new crops are much more tolerant of nutrient poor soils and it is possible that they indicate an expansion of arable agriculture onto the more peripheral areas of the machair in the later phases of the settlement (Church 2002).

There is also stratigraphic evidence for the increasing importance of cultivation at Bornais. The Viking deposits include an extensive cultivation soil at the base of Mound 2 that was sealed by over a metre of later deposits. The soil horizon was a rich brown sand layer that sealed a series of east-west oriented furrows (Figure 5.4) that were v-shaped in profile. This indicates cultivation was carried out by simple ards and there was no evidence for the turning of the soil that would indicate a mouldboard plough. There was some evidence for a north-south oriented series of furrows within the cultivation soil and this probably represents a change in the direction of ploughing over the years rather than contemporary cross ploughing. Work on South Uist suggests that cultivation soils are rare on the machair and where they have been located they are normally dated to the Early Bronze Age (Sharples 2009).

By the fourteenth century buildings dedicated to crop processing appear on the settlement at Bornais and a corn-drying kiln was located on Mound 3 (Sharples 2005). This was a rectangular building, 3.8 m wide by 4.6 m long, semi-subterranean, with an entrance facing west and a winnowing hole to the east. Exiting the building on the south side was a flue that leads to an external bowl where the crop would have been dried. This structure is a precursor to the diagnostic Hebridean corn-drying kilns[6] and large numbers of these corn-drying kilns are visible in the pre-Clearance settlements of South Uist (Sharples, Parker Pearson and Symonds 2004)

These kilns are quite different from the corn-drying kilns known from Orkney and appear to indicate a diverging development in the thirteenth century. The earliest known Orcadian kiln is an example partially excavated at Birsay (Morris 1996, illus 86, 87). The Orcadian kilns are larger structures and this might indicate an ability to process more grain, but the large numbers of kilns on Uist certainly confirm Dodghson's view that crop processing was an important part of the Uist economy. It seems likely that Uist was capable of producing enough oatmeal and bere barley to export a surplus to their political superiors in Man, and later the Lords of the Isles.

The excavations at Bornais and Cille Pheadair have also recovered substantial bone assemblages that provide a considerable amount of information on animal husbandry. The assemblages from the Bornais mounds have four main species present; cattle, sheep, pig and red deer, and the quantities of bone present in each of the main phases of mounds 1, 2 and 2A are shown in Table 2.[7] Cattle NISP (total number of fragments) vary between 32% and

Table 2 Bone NISP for the principal large mammals from some of the main stratigraphic units at Bornais

Mound	Activity	Date Block	Cattle		Sheep		Pig		Red deer		Total
			no	%	no	%	no	%	no	%	
1	Burnt house	5-6th cent CB	179	32.6	295	53.8	33	6	41	7.5	548
1	Midden	5-6th cent CG	521	32.1	686	42.3	81	5	332	20.5	1620
2	Occupation surfaces	7-8th cent BAB/C	110	45.8	84	35	17	7.1	29	12.1	240
2	House 1 floors and pits	9th-10th cent BBA/BBC	124	32.7	173	45.6	57	15	25	6.6	379
2	House 2 floors	11th cent BCC	422	37.6	466	45.6	159	15	75	6.6	1122
2	House 3 floors and pits	13-14th cent BEB-D	284	32.4	459	52.4	84	9.6	49	8.2	876
2A	Cultivation soil	9-10th cent GAA-C	1001	33.9	1096	37.1	617	20.9	241	8.2	2955
2A	Grey sand	10th-11th GAD	258	39.1	275	41.7	98	14.8	29	4.4	660
2A	Kiln and associated deposits	12th cent GB-	235	43	217	39.7	70	12.8	25	4.6	547
2A	Structures and middens	13-14th cent GC-/GD-/GE-	706	35.8	1050	53.3	119	6	94	4.7	1969

46% of the principal species present, whereas sheep vary between 35% and 54%. Sheep are particularly important in the later phases of the occupation, whereas the highest percentages of cattle are found in the Late Iron Age II assemblage (though it should be noted this is the smallest assemblage). Pig is a relatively small proportion of the LIA assemblage, between 5% and 7%, but in the Viking deposits they become more important, forming up to 21% of the bone assemblage from the cultivation soil on Mound 2A. Pigs are clearly important in the Viking colonisation phase and this pattern has been observed on Iceland (Vésteinsson *et al.* 2002) and on the Faroes (Church *et al.* 2005).

Red deer bones were found throughout the occupation of the settlement and make up 20% of the LIA1 midden assemblage. In the Viking and Norse periods they are fairly consistently present on both mounds with slightly higher numbers noted on Mound 2. Deer clearly made an important contribution to the diet, but they also provide an important raw material, antler, which was used to make a variety of tools and decorative objects. The ability to maintain a herd of red deer on an island as small as South Uist suggests that, though hunting had a role in this society, it was carefully controlled to maintain a viable deer population.

Another important feature of the economy of the Norse inhabitants of the Hebrides was fishing. This is an important development in the Norse period. Excavation of the Iron Age settlements at Dun Vulan (Cerón-Carrasco in Parker Pearson and Sharples 1999) and Bornais Mound 1 (Ingrem in Sharples forthcoming) clearly indicates that limited fishing for pollock and saithe was beginning to be developed in the Late Iron Age, and at Bornais there is an important assemblage of salmon bones from a limited number of LIA 1 midden layers that suggests the opportunistic exploitation of a seasonal resource. However, there is no evidence for extensive sea fishing in the LIA and the overall quantities of fish bones are low. This changes dramatically with the Viking incursions when there is a massive increase in the numbers of fish bones present and the fishing strategy becomes focussed on a limited number of species (Cerón-Carrasco 2005). In the Western Isles the catch is overwhelmingly dominated by herring (Ingrem in Sharples 2005).

This dramatic change in the nature of fishing has been the subject of detailed study in the Northern Isles and can be related to widespread changes in the nature of fish procurement and distribution in the Baltic and North Atlantic (Barrett, Nicholson and Cerón-Carrasco 1999). It is clear that the inhabitants of Orkney and Caithness are catching white fish for commercial gain and that these are being traded south to the urban centres of England and the north European plain. Some archaeologists have been reluctant to accept that the evidence for the Western Isles indicates similar evidence for commercial fishing. The principal problem is that the evidence comes from domestic settlements. The fish present are clearly there as part of the inhabitants' diet, and so far no specialist processing sites have been excavated; there is therefore no direct evidence for commercial fishing. However, it is very difficult to believe that the inhabitants would choose to commit important resources to fishing for herring if it was not for commercial benefit. Successful herring fishing involves a considerable investment of labour and resources; you need nets, boats, each manned with a skilled crew, and time to wait for the shoals to turn up. The quantities involved in a successful herring catch are also so large that no single community would be able to consume the catch; it would need to be packed and stored for redistribution. There are important markets for fish to the south; the Irish Sea towns of Dublin, Waterford and Cork would all have to import foodstuffs, and further south there is Bristol.

Other resources available to the community included wild fowl and eggs, present in fairly large quantities, and crab and sea urchins were also collected. Timber was probably the most important resource in short supply, but in the thirteenth and fourteenth centuries it seems to be available in quantities sufficient to build very large houses and one suspects it was imported from mainland Scotland. Driftwood and recycled boats would also have provided a valuable resource and there is a ready supply of deep peat on the eastern hills of South Uist that can be used for fuel.

Wealth

We hope we have demonstrated that the economic situation in the Western Isles is quite favourable to human settlement and that the Norse colonists who settled on the island were capable of generating a surplus of grain and fish, as well as probably hides and wool that enabled them to trade with the other regions of the North Atlantic. The economic significance of the islands is further demonstrated by the finds recovered from the settlements at Bornais and Cille Pheadair. We will begin with some of the more exotic finds as these include some very distinctive objects of considerable importance.

Evidence for the belief systems of the occupants of the settlements is provided by the discovery of a number of items. The settlement at Bornais has produced a small lead cross (Figures 5.5; 7). This has close parallels with crosses found in southern Scandinavia that are associated with the early spread of Christianity (Staecker 1999, 98). Two comparable objects are known from Britain: a damaged lead cross from Llanbedrgoch in Anglesey (Redknap 2004, fig 13.f) and a complete silver example which is thought to have come from the Goldsborough hoard, Yorkshire (Wilson 1957, 72-3). Coins from the Goldsborough hoard suggest it was deposited around AD920. A more enigmatic object is a rectangular piece of amber with two slightly concave sides that can be interpreted as the arm of a cross (Figure 5.5; 1). There is no definite parallel for this, as yet, but it may have been set into an elaborate Bible cover, such as the gospel of St Molaise from Devenish Island, County Fermanagh (Mitchell in Cone 1977, 57). The amber must have been imported from the Baltic or the southern North Sea coastline. The settlement at Cille Pheadair produced two carved bone crosses (Parker Pearson *et al.* 2004, fig 11), which closely resemble the jet pendants produced in workshops at York (Mainman and Rogers 2000).

Two more exotic finds that probably indicate the Christian affiliations of the inhabitants are fragments of green porphyry slabs (Figure 5.5; 2, 3). This material was quarried from Laconia in Greece to decorate the large public buildings of Rome. These buildings were stripped of this fine stone which was then distributed around the Atlantic seaboard in the later part of the first millennium AD. Large quantities of green porphyry are found in Ireland and, including these two fragments, thirteen pieces are known from Scotland. Most of these have come from sites with an ecclesiastical significance, but there is one find from a Medieval midden at Kebister (Owen and Lowe 1999, 290-

3). It seems that the Norse inhabitants of Atlantic Scotland found this stone significant and may even have considered it to have a religious importance. These finds also suggest the inhabitants of the settlement were Christians, possibly from its foundation, if the house on Mound 1 marks its foundation.

The contacts with Ireland demonstrated by the porphyry are further emphasised by the collection of nineteen copper alloy and seventeen iron stick pins from Bornais. Pins such as these are known as isolated finds on the western seaboard of Scotland (Close Brooks 1995) but the assemblage from Bornais is the largest Scottish collection outside of Whithorn, where fifty-two were discovered (Hill 1997). However, the largest assemblages are from Dublin (O'Rahilly 1998) and Waterford (Scully 1997), and suggest that these pins are produced in the Irish towns (though the author knows of no conclusive production debris), and indicate close contacts between the Hebrides and Ireland.

Imported personal ornaments include a range of small glass beads though it is difficult to say where these came from; it could be Scandinavia but York is another centre for their production (Mainman and Rogers 2000). A decorated gold strip was found at Cille Pheadair (Parker Pearson *et al.* 2004, fig 9) and a small fragment of an identical gold strip was found during the sorting of environmental residues from the floor of the eleventh-century house at Bornais. Gaming pieces were also found, and a selection of pieces, including an idiosyncratically numbered dice, is illustrated in Figure 5.5.

There is a small collection of steatite objects, mostly vessel fragments, but including a range of beads, spindle whorls and weights made from reworked vessel fragments.[8] Most of the large vessel fragments came from the floor of the tenth-century house on Mound 2, and the other large collection comes from the tenth-century ploughsoil on Mound 2A. Forster identified a minimum of eight Norwegian and a maximum of four Shetland vessels in the assemblage; this reflects the early date of the material as the Shetland steatite industry is a later development. There is no evidence for any late Norwegian forms and there are none of the distinctive steatite baking plates that appear in the later Medieval period in Shetland and Scandinavia. It is clear that vessels were being imported in the early phases of activity, but not later ones and Forster (2004) has shown that this is a pattern visible on other North Atlantic islands.

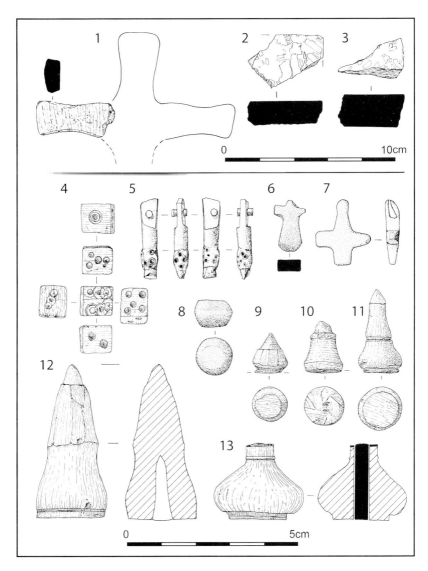

Figure 5.5 : A selection of artefacts associated with the Viking and Norse settlement at Bornais. 1 is amber; 2 and 3 are fragments of porphyry slabs; 4, 9, 10, 11, 12 and 13 are bone gaming pieces; 5 is a fragment of a copper alloy balance; 6 and 7 are lead pendants and 8 is a copper alloy weight.

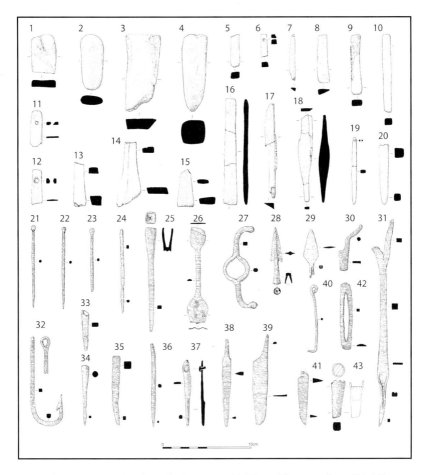

Figure 5.6 : A selection of whetstones (1-20) and iron artefacts (21-43) recovered from mounds 2 and 2A at Bornais.

An assemblage of over 40 whetstones was recovered from Bornais (Figure 5.6) and provides further evidence for the extensive contacts of the inhabitants. The assemblage is dominated by two types of stone (G Gaunt pers comm.) that are widely distributed throughout northern Europe. The most accurately located is Eidsborg schist which comes from central-southern Norway. The other important source is the Purple Phyllite and though this is not accurately located, and could come from many parts of Europe including Scotland, it probably also derives from Scandinavia. These materials are a common occurrence in Norse settlements but are unknown in British sites prior to the Viking conquest. A range of shapes and forms are being produced and these range from the very large (Figure 5.6; 4) to the small and carefully shaped (Figure 5.6; 19) and there is a relationship between form and source that suggests complete whetstones are being moved around.

A large assemblage of indigenous ceramics was recovered. Most vessels are simple tub-shaped cooking pots (Sharples 2004, fig 6) but large flat baking plates or platters are also common (Lane in Sharples 2005). A number of largely complete vessels were found on the floor at the west end of the eleventh-century house on Mound 2 and amongst the assemblage from this area was a rather unprepossessing cooking pot which was noticeably finer than the local wares. Examination by Duncan Brown and Alan Vince indicates this was produced in the Bristol area of south west England. Cille Pheadair also has a green glazed tripod pitcher from Minty in Wiltshire (Parker Pearson et al. 2004, 248). These discoveries support the documentary indications that the Scandinavian communities of the North Atlantic had close contacts with south-west England, and were probably trading through the port at Bristol.

A more direct indication of the importance of exchange are the seven coins found at Bornais and two coins from Cille Pheadair.[9] There are coins of Edgar (957-975), Æthelræd II (978-1016), Cnut (1014-1035), two coins of the Norwegian king Olaf Kyrre (1067-93), two of John (1199-1216), and two of Henry III (1248-1278). One is a counterfeit coin of Henry III produced in Westphalia, the lower Rhineland and Frisia between 1248 and 1278 (North 1995); these coins are not very common in Britain and it is rather surprising to find one in the Hebrides. This is a substantial collection of coins and it is of note that there are no Scottish coins:- they all come from either the late tenth/eleventh or the thirteenth century and there is nothing of twelfth-century date. This may indicate two periods of particularly important commercial activity on the western seaboard.

Commercial activity is also indicated by a fragment from the arm of a copper alloy balance (Figure 5.5; 5) and a small copper alloy weight (Figure 5.5; 8). The latter weighs 4.8 grams and is similar to one from Cleat in Orkney (Maleszka 2003) and to examples from London (Egan 1998 309, fig.230), though these are of iron with a covering of copper alloy. Trade weights of any form are rare in Viking Scotland but there is a particularly fine set from the grave at Kiloran Bay, Colonsay (Owen and Dalland 1999). The balance is represented by a fragment of the hinge fitting which is similar to complete examples from both Winchester (Biddle 1990: 924, no.3212 and 3211) and York (Mainman and Rogers 2000: 2560, no. 10405). Both the balance hinge and weight were from Mound 2, although the weight was unstratified.

One of the most interesting finds is a piece of antler elaborately carved in the Ringerike style (Sharples 2004, fig 8). This cylinder is quite difficult to parallel and to interpret, but it was argued that it is the mouth of a drinking flask and that it was made in Scandinavia, probably at a west Norwegian centre, in the early eleventh century. It shows evidence for considerable wear and was probably used for decades before being deposited on the floor of the eleventh-century house on Mound 2. A number of decorative antler tines were present in this floor, which are similar to examples from Jarlshof (Hamilton 1956, pl 29) and York (MacGregor, Mainman and Rogers 1999, fig 950) and though these are normally prosaically interpreted as handles this is an untenable interpretation. The shallow v-shaped socket would be a very weak point if this handle was to have any force placed upon it. We would suggest that instead these objects should be interpreted as the decorative finials from the tip of drinking horns. If this is accepted then they suggest this building was associated with feasting and drinking, in a rather clichéd Viking fashion.

This discussion of the finds from Bornais has focussed on unusual or special objects that highlight the widespread contacts of the inhabitants of the settlement, but we would like to finish this section by mentioning some of the larger assemblages of more prosaic material as these highlight the quantity and variety of material culture available to the inhabitants.[10] The principle materials used were antler and bone but there was also a considerable quantity of iron objects. The bulk of the antler and bone finds are likely to be largely locally sourced and there is evidence for extensive bone and antler working on the settlement. However, there is also a small collection of ivory waste, which probably came from Greenland (Roesdahl 2005), to be worked on at the settlement, and some of the antler and bone objects were clearly made elsewhere and imported. The iron was all imported and there is still no evidence of any significant ironworking at the settlement.

The principal antler and bone assemblages come from the production and use of composite combs and pins, and these assemblages are amongst the largest from Britain. There are about 200 pin and pin fragments, and these are associated with about 60 pieces identified as waste from the production of pins. There are 250 combs and about 500 fragments of antler waste (not including

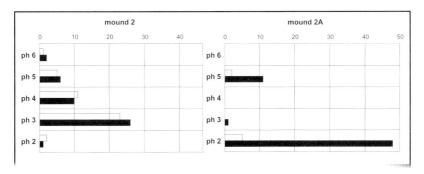

Figure 5.7 : The distribution of bone pins from Bornais Mounds 2 and 2A. Phase 2 are tenth-century deposits; Phase 3 eleventh-century deposits; Phase 4 twelfth- and thirteenth-century deposits; Phase 5 thirteenth- and fourteenth-century deposits and Phase 6 late fourteenth-century activity.

the roughly 3000 shavings recovered from environmental sampling). The antler waste is overwhelmingly concentrated in the later phases of activity on Mound 2A and indicates that comb production occurred only for a short period of time in one of the ancillary buildings in the northern part of this mound. The waste was either left on the floor or dumped in the middens lying to the east. In contrast the pin waste was concentrated in the cultivation soil at the base of the mound 2A sequence, and may indicate dumping from a nearby workshop. Debris was also found in later phases but was relatively dispersed and did not suggest any specific workshops.

Most of the pins come from Mound 2, but there is a significant assemblage from Mound 2A (Figure 5.7). On Mound 2 the largest assemblage came from the eleventh-century house and there is then a steady decline in numbers with only a small assemblage from the large fourteenth-century house. In Mound 2A the largest assemblage came from the cultivation horizon, with the only other significant assemblage from the later thirteenth- and fourteenth-century midden deposits. The character of the assemblage on each mound is also significantly different. On Mound 2 around 50% of the assemblage from all phases were complete pins, whereas on Mound 2A very few complete pins were found. The presence of so many complete pins on Mound 2 is worthy of note as it indicates a very casual approach to possessions. This was a throwaway culture where it was important to be seen to be wasteful (a culture not unlike our own perhaps).

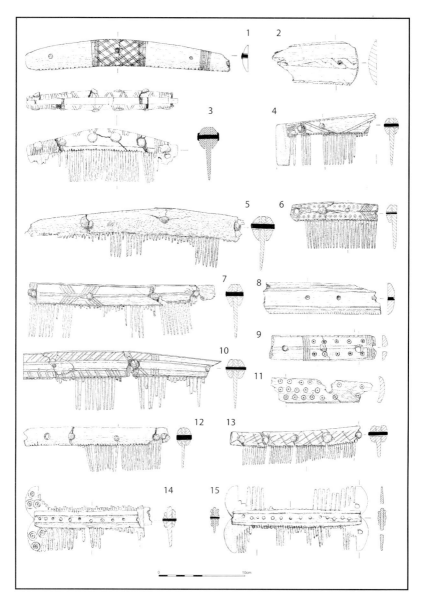

Figure 5.8 : A selection of the most complete Viking and Norse
combs from Bornais Mounds 2 and 3.

A selection of combs and comb fragments are illustrated in Figure 5.8. These range from early examples from the cultivation soil at the base of Mound 2A (Figure 5.8; 1) to the classic examples of thirteenth-century 'fish tailed' combs (Figure 5.8; 14 and 15) from the late Norse phases of the settlement. The latter were almost certainly imported from western Norway. The bulk of the complete combs came from the eleventh-century house on Mound 2 (Figure 5.8; 3, 5, 7, 10, 12 and 13), and it is noticeable that these complete combs were found concentrated in the centre of the house on the north side of the hearth. They were associated with several cutdown side plates and it seems likely that this collection of old and broken combs were in the process of being converted into decorative pendants and plaques. The only large early comb (Figure 5.8; 2) is also a fragment, trimmed probably for use as a pendant.

The iron assemblage consists of over 1500 fragments. The most common categories are structural waste materials; nails, holdfasts, fragments and strips. This is the kind of material that could be recycled and a local smith would be able to transform these broken objects into useable tools. The distribution of this material is similar to the bone pins; the largest quantities come from the floor of the eleventh-century house on Mound 2 and the quantities decline gradually in the later deposits. On Mound 2A the large assemblages come from the early cultivation soil and the later middens. This suggests that most of this material was either left where it fell, inside the abandoned houses of Mound 2, or thrown onto the middens of Mound 2A. However, most of the sheet fragments in the eleventh-century house 2 represent the cut-up remains of a large sheet iron cauldron.

Most of the iron objects can be amalgamated into four broad groups of material; weapons, pins, knives and tools, and in general these can be seen to follow the same broad general depositional trends noted above, but there are very few objects in the Mound 2A cultivation soil. A miscellaneous selection of pieces are illustrated in Figure 5.6 including three stick pins (Figure 5.6; 21-23), two arrowheads (Figure 5.6; 28, 29), one of the four fish hooks (Figure 5.6; 32), a key (Figure 5.6; 40), a possible candle stick holder (Figure 5.6; 31) and three knives (Figure 5.6; 38, 39, 41). Thirty-six knives or knife fragments were found at Bornais, and these have been classified using the blade typology developed for the Coppergate assemblage (Ottoway 1992). Surprisingly the bulk of the assemblage appears to belong to blade type B which is extremely rare at Coppergate and unknown from Whithorn (Nicholson in Hill 1997). It would appear the Hebrides had a distinctive tradition which differentiates it from other Scandinavian areas.

Conclusion

We hope we have demonstrated that the inhabitants of the Bornais settlement were well connected and relatively prosperous. The agricultural economy of the Western Isles could sustain a large settlement centred on a high status household that was capable of the most lavish entertainment and conspicuous consumption. This economy was based on the intensive cultivation of the machair plain, the extensive availability of upland grazing for sheep and cattle,[11] and access to plentiful wild resources, such as herring in the sea and red deer on the hills, though the latter required careful management. It seems more than likely that the export of cereals and fish would have enriched the island economy and enabled them to acquire resources from specialist production areas distributed across the North Atlantic.

It is probably misleading to make comparisons between the different island groups, and we have not yet attempted to make a quantified comparison with the material from other regions, but a subjective assessment suggests that there are very few sites from the Northern Isles of Scotland that have produced assemblages as rich as those from Bornais and Cille Pheadair. Furthermore, it would also seem, largely from hear-say evidence, that the material from the Udal is comparable in size and quality. This suggests that the inhabitants of the Hebrides were materially rich and fairly well connected and it supports the idea put forward in *Scandinavian Scotland* that the relatively independent farmers of the west were able to accrue wealth in a fashion that was not possible in the more controlled political centres of the north.

The strange thing about this work in the Hebrides is that it has revealed a landscape that is probably more accessible to archaeological exploration than almost any other landscape in Britain. In Orkney and Shetland the prime land with the richest farms is continually occupied from probably before the Viking colonisation, through the Norse period up to the present day or the recent past. This makes accessing the archaeological record for the Viking period very difficult. In South Uist it is clear that almost all these settlements were abandoned in the fourteenth and fifteenth centuries as people moved inland onto the "blacklands".[12] Why this movement took place is a topic for another paper but it has left us with an incredibly rich resource of settlement mounds.

Acknowledgements

This article could not have been written without the contribution of a large number of people, particularly the residents of South Uist who provided invaluable support for the excavations. The excavation, and the post excavation process, has been generously supported by Historic Scotland and the University of Cardiff. We would like to thank all the students and specialists who have worked on material from the excavations and in particular; E Besly, S Colledge, A Forster, K Forsyth, C Ingrem, F Morris, I Mulville, A Powell, K Reed, C Riley, A Rowe, H Smith and F Taylor. The illustrations were created by Ian Dennis, though he is not to be blamed for the layout which was done by NS. The text was read and helpful comments were made by Mary Davis and Alan Lane but they bear no responsibility for the opinions expressed.[13]

Notes

[1] We should note the discovery of an Ogham inscribed plaque from Bornais (Forsyth 2007).

[2] Another significant excavation of a Norse settlement has been undertaken at the site of Bostaidh in west Lewis (Neighbour forthcoming).

[3] This terminology is derived from Barrett and Foster 1991.

[4] Isolated sherds of Middle Iron Age ceramics have been found on mound 1 and are assumed to be residual material from an occupation underlying that exposed.

[5] The carbonised plant remains from Mound 1 were identified and analysed by Sue Colledge and Helen Smith and those from Mound 2 and 2A were identified by Kelly Reed

[6] The principal structural difference is that the later structures have a rectangular building that enclosed both the flue and bowl, and the adjacent rectangular working/storage space.

[7] The analysis of the animal bones was undertaken by Jacqui Mulville and Adrienne Powell.

[8] The steatite assemblage has been examined and reported on by Amanda Forster, BUFAU.

[9] The coins were all identified by Edward Besly of the National Museums of Wales.

[10] The overwhelming bulk of these finds have been catalogued and analysed by Rachel Smith, but the pins were initially catalogued and analysed by Alex

Rowe and the bone combs were catalogued and analysed by Claire Riley both for undergraduate dissertations in the School of History and Archaeology at Cardiff University
[11] The cattle may have been kept relatively close to the settlement and currently they are used to fertilise the machair and graze the Bornais machair on a two year rotation.
[12] The land to the east of the machair plain is largely rock, peat bog and heather covered moorland which has only limited agricultural potential. Most of the current settlement is located on the interface between these two landscapes where the underlying peaty soils are mixed with wind blown sand to produce a fertile and relatively stable landscape.
[13] Niall Sharples wrote this chapter but the later sections are based on work undertaken, and text written, by Rachel Smith

Bibliography

Barrett, J. and Foster, S. 1991. 'Passing the time in Iron Age Scotland'. In Hanson, E.W. and Slater E.A. (eds) *Scottish archaeology new perspectives*. Edinburgh: Aberdeen University Press, pp. 44-56.

Barrett, J., Nicholson, R. A. and Ceron-Carrasco, R. 1999. 'Archaeo-ichthyological evidence for long-term socioeconomic trends in northern Scotland: 3500 BC to AD 1500'. *Journal of Archaeological Science* 26, pp. 353-388.

Biddle, M. 1990 *Object and economy in medieval Winchester: artefacts from medieval Winchester*. Oxford: Clarendon Press.

Brennand, M., Parker Pearson M. and Smith, H. 1998. The Norse settlement and Pictish Cairn at Kilphedir, South Uist: Excavations in 1998. Unpublished manuscript, Dept of Archaeology and Prehistory, University of Sheffield.

Cerón-Carrasco, R. N. 2005. *'Of Fish and Men' ('De iasg agus dhaoine'). A Study of the Utilization of Marine Resources as Recovered from Selected Hebridean Archaeological Sites.* Oxford: British Archaeological Report (British Series 400).

Church, M. 2002. *Plants and people in the Later Prehistoric and Norse periods of the Western Isles of Scotland*. University of Edinburgh unpublished PhD thesis.

Church, M., Aarge, S., Brewington, S., McGovern, T.H., Woollett, J.M., Perdikaris, S., Lawson, I.T., Cook, G.T., Amundsen, C., Harrison, R.,

Krivogorskya, Y. and Dunbar, E. 2005. 'Puffins, pigs, cod and barley: Palaeoeconomy at Undir Junkarinsfløtti, Sandoy, Faroe Islands'. *Environmental archaeology* 10, pp. 179-197.

Close Brooks, J. 1995. 'Excavation of a cairn at Cnip, Uig, Isle of Lewis'. *Proceedings of the Society of Antiquaries of Scotland* 125, pp. 253-277.

Cone, P. 1977 *Treasures of Early Irish Art 1500 B.C. to 1500 A.D.* New York: Metropolitan Museum of Art.

Crawford, B.E. 1987. *Scandinavian Scotland*. Leicester: Leicester University Press.

Crawford, I. A. 1981. 'War or peace – Viking colonisation in the Northern or Western Isles of Scotland reviewed', in Bekker-Nielson, H., Foote. P. and Olsen, O. (eds) *Proceedings of the Eighth Viking Congress, Arrhus*, 1977. Odense, pp. 259-269.

Crawford, I. A. 1986. *The West Highlands and Islands: A view of 50 centuries: The Udal (North Uist) Evidence*. Cambridge.

Crawford, I.A. and Switsur, V.R. 1977. 'Sand-scaping and C14: the Udal, North Uist'. *Antiquity* 51, pp. 124-136.

Dodgshon, R. A. 1998. *From Chiefs to Landlords: Social and economic change in the western Highlands and Islands, c. 1493-1820*. Edinburgh: Edinburgh University Press.

Egan, G. 1998. *The medieval household: daily living c.1150-c.1450*. London: HMSO.

Forster, A. K. 2004. *Shetland and the trade of steatite goods in the North Atlantic region during the Viking and early Medieval period*. University of Bradford Unpublished PhD thesis.

Forsyth, K. 2007. 'An ogham-inscribed plaque from Bornais, South Uist'. In Smith, B.B., Taylor, S. And Williams, G. (eds) *West over sea: Studies in Scandinavian sea-borne expansion and settlement before* 1300. Leiden: Brill, pp. 461-478.

Graham-Campbell, J. and Batey, C. E. 1998. *Vikings in Scotland: An Archaeological Survey*. Edinburgh: Edinburgh University Press.

Hamilton, J. R. C. 1956. *Excavations at Jarlshof, Shetland*. Edinburgh: HMSO.

Hill, P. 1997. *Whithorn and St Ninian: The Excavation of a Monastic Town, 1984-91*. Stroud: Sutton Publishing.

Hurley, M. F. and Scully, O. M. B. 1997. *Late Viking Age and Medieval Waterford: excavations 1986-1992*. Waterford: Waterford Corporation.

Lane, A. 1990. 'Hebridean pottery: problems of definition, chronology, presence and absence'. In Armit, I (ed) *Beyond the brochs*. Edinburgh: Edinburgh University Press pp. 108-130.

MacGregor, A., Mainman, A. J., and Rogers, N. S. H. 1999. *Craft, Industry and Everyday Life: Bone, antler, ivory and horn from Anglo-Scandinavian and Medieval York*. York: Council for British Archaeology/ York Archaeological Trust.

MacLaren, A. 1974. 'A Norse house on Drimore machair, South Uist'. *Glasgow Archaeogical Journal* 3, pp. 9-18.

Mainman, A.J. and Rogers, N.S.H. 2000. *Craft, industry and everyday life: finds from Anglo-Scandinavian York*. York: Council for British Archaeology/ York Archaeological Trust.

Maleszka, M. 2003. 'A Viking age weight from Cleat, Westray, Orkney'. *Proceedings of the Society of Antiquaries of Scotland*, 133, pp. 283-91.

McGovern, T.H. and Ogilvie, A.E.J. 2000. 'Sagas and science: Climate and human impacts in the North Atlantic'. Fitzhugh, W.H. and Ward, E.I. (eds.) *Vikings. The North Atlantic Saga*. Washington: Smithsonian Institution Press.

Morris, C. D. 1996. *The Birsay Bay project volume 2: Sites in Birsay Village and on the Brough of Birsay*. Durham: University of Durham.

North, J.J. 1995. 'Some imitations and forgeries of the English and Irish Long Cross Pence of Henry III'. *British Numismatic Journal* 65, pp. 83-119.

O'Rahilly, C. 1993. 'A classification of the bronze stick pins from the Dublin excavations 1962-72'. In Manning, C (ed) *Dublin and Beyond the Pale: Studies in honour of Patrick Healy*. Bray: Worwell, 23-33.

Ottoway, P. 1992. *Anglo-Scandinavian ironwork from 16-22 Coppergate*. London: Council for British Archaeology/ York Archaeological Trust.

Owen, O. and Dalland, M. 1999. *Scar: A Viking boat burial on Sanday, Orkney*. Edinburgh: Historic Scotland.

Owen, O. and Lowe, C. 1999. *Kebister: the four-thousand-year-old story of one Shetland township*. Edinburgh: Society of Antiquaries of Scotland.

Parker Pearson, M. and Sharples, N. M. 1999. *Between Land and Sea: Excavations at Dun Vulan, South Uist*. Sheffield: Sheffield Academic Press

Parker Pearson, M. Brennand, M. and Smith, H. 1996. *Sithean Biorach (Fairy Point), Cille Pheadair, South Uist: A Viking Age and Late Norse settlement*. Unpublished Manuscript, Dept of Archaeology and Prehistory, University of Sheffield.

Parker Pearson, M., Smith, H., Mulville, J. and Brennand, M. 2004. 'Cille Pheadair: The life and times of a Norse-period farmstead c. 1000-1300'. In Hines, J, Redknap, M and Lane, A (eds) *Land, Sea and Home*. Leeds: Maney, pp. 236-254.

Redknap, M. 2004. 'Viking-Age settlement in Wales and the evidence from Llanbedrgoch'. In Hines, J, Redknap, M and Lane, A (eds) *Land, Sea and Home*. Leeds: Maney, pp. 138-175.

Roesdahl, E. 2005. 'Walrus ivory – demand, supply, workshops and Greenland'. In Mortensen, A. and Aarge, S.V. (eds.) *Viking and Norse in the North Atlantic*. Torshavn: Foroya Frodskaparfelag

Scully, O. M. B. 1997. 'Metal artefacts'. In Hurley, M. F. and Scully, O. M. B. (eds) *Late Viking Age and Medieval Waterford. Excavations 1986-1992*. Dublin: Waterford Corporation, pp. 438-489.

Selkirk, A. 1996 'The Udal' *Current Archaeology* 147, 84-94

Sharples, N. M. 1996. *The Iron Age and Norse settlement at Bornais, South Uist: An interim report on the 1996 excavations*. Cardiff Studies in Archaeology Specialist Report Number 1. http://www.cf.ac.uk/uwcc/hisar/archaeology/reports/hebrides96/

Sharples, N. M. 1997. *The Iron Age and Norse settlement at Bornais, South Uist: An interim report on the 1997 excavations*. Cardiff Studies in Archaeology Specialist Report Number 4. http://www.cf.ac.uk/uwcc/hisar/archaeology/reports/hebrides97/

Sharples, N. M. 1999. *The Iron Age and Norse settlement at Bornish, South Uist. An interim report on the 1999 excavations*. Cardiff Studies in Archaeology Specialist Report no 16. http://www.cf.ac.uk/uwcc/hisar/archaeology/reports/hebrides99/

Sharples, N. M. 2000. *The Iron Age and Norse settlement at Bornish, South Uist. An interim report on the 2000 excavations*. Cardiff Studies in Archaeology Specialist Report no 18. http://www.cf.ac.uk/uwcc/hisar/archaeology/reports/hebrides00/

Sharples, N. M. 2003. *The Iron Age and Norse settlement at Bornish, South Uist. An interim report on the 2003 excavations*. Cardiff Studies in Archaeology Specialist Report no 26.

Sharples, N. M. 2004. 'A find of Ringerike art from Bornais in the Outer Hebrides'. In Hines, J, Redknap, M and Lane, A (eds) *Land, Sea and Home*. Leeds: Maney pp. 255-272.

Sharples, N. M. 2005 *A Norse farmstead in the Hebrides: Excavations at Bornais Volume 1*. Oxford: Oxbow Books.

Sharples, N. M. 2009. 'Beaker settlement in the Western Isles'. In Allen, M., O'Connor, T. And Sharples, N. M. (eds) *Land and People*. London: Prehistoric Society.

Sharples, N. M. forthcoming. *A Late Iron Age farmstead in the Hebrides: Excavations at Bornais Volume 2*. Oxford: Oxbow Books

Sharples, N. M. and Parker Pearson, M. 1999. 'Norse settlement on the Outer Hebrides'. *Norwegian Archaeological Review* 1999, 32.1, pp. 41-62.

Sharples, N M, Parker Pearson, M and Symonds, J 2004. 'The archaeological landscape of South Uist'. In Housley, R A and Coles, G (eds) *Atlantic connections and adaptations: economics, environments and subsistence in the North Atlantic*. Oxford: Oxbow Books (Symposia for the Association for Environmental Archaeology No. 21).

Staecker, J. 1999. *Rex regum et dominus dominorum. Die wikingerzeitlichen Kreuz- und Kruzifixanhänger als Ausdruck der Mission in Altdänemark und Schweden*. Stockholm: Almqvist & Wiksell International.

Taylor, F. 2005. *An analysis of the finds from an eleventh century house at Bornais, South Uist*. Cardiff University Unpublished Dissertation.

Vesteinsson, O., McGovern, T.H. and Keller, C. 2002. 'Enduring impacts: social and environmental aspects of Viking Age settlement in Iceland and Greenland'. *Archaeologia Islandica* 2, pp. 98-136.

Wilson, D. M. 1957. 'An unpublished fragment from the Goldsborough hoard'. *Antiquaries Journal* 37, pp. 72-73.

CHAPTER 6

Sveinn Ásleifarson and the Irish Sea

Mestan Ójafnaðarmann í Vestrlöndum

Barbara Crawford's *Scandinavian Scotland* underlines interconnections from Shetland to Dublin, especially also the interplay of political and economic factors in this large area. This theme shall be expanded here, in a discussion of the coherence of the Insular Scandinavian world *after* the traditionally given end of the Scandinavian Age in the mid-eleventh century. An analysis of the activities of a twelfth-century Orcadian in the Irish Sea allows us to argue that the close links established by the Scandinavians were maintained and adjusted to fit the changing political and economic landscape of post-'Viking' times.

The Orcadian in question, Sveinn Ásleifarson, is one of *Orkneyinga Saga's* best-known characters.[1] Sveinn was a young adult by about 1135, and he was killed when he was getting on in years, presumably in 1171.

A caveat needs to be raised first, however: Sveinn hardly appears in other sources. Some scholars therefore see the account of his life as literary fiction, written with a propagandistic aim in mind. On the other hand, *Orkneyinga Saga*, once one leaves the mythical beginnings, is considered to be one of the more reliable kings' sagas. It cannot really be doubted that Sveinn, who was related to well-documented real people, was a historical person (his son Andrés married Fríða, daughter of Bishop Bjarni Kolbeinsson of Orkney[2]). Another matter is the details of Sveinn's exploits. There is a certain amount of confusion, and some care is required when the Saga is used as a historical source.[3]

Historical or fictional, Sveinn is usually discussed under the heading Orkney. Scholars focus on Sveinn there, especially on his career as an earl-maker in the 1130s and 50s, which involved earls Páll Hákonarson (1123-1136), Rögnvaldr Kalason (1136-1158), Haraldr Maddaðarson (1138-1206), and Erlendr Haraldsson (1151-1154).

However, the Saga also notes Sveinn's activities elsewhere. He raided occasionally down the Scottish east coast, but more frequently in the west, in the Irish Sea; in fact, in the whole area from Lewis in the north to the Isles of Scilly in the south. The Sveinn of the Irish Sea might be considered quite a modern businessman *cum* political mover. This, in turn, could shed a different light on to our ideas of the historical or literary Sveinn, either as an enemy of social progress, or as an enlightened practitioner of maritime commercial principles.[4] This paper shall therefore turn matters upside down, and Sveinn the Orcadian shall be considered through Irish Sea eyes. Three main episodes shall be discussed in detail.

Sveinn in the Irish Sea in the 1140s

Orkneyinga Saga's version of Sveinn's exploits during his first serious venture into the Irish Sea in the 1140s can be summed up as follows. Sveinn received a call for help from Holdboði in Tiree, who was attacked by Hölðr from Wales. Sveinn set off and eventually caught up with Holdboði in Man, where Hölðr had killed Andrés, husband of Ingiríðr. Sveinn and Holdboði then chased Hölðr around Wales to Lundy Island, where Hölðr was safe from them, and Sveinn and Holdboði returned to Man. The following year, Sveinn raided alone. After his return to Man, Holdboði attacked him, because Holdboði had by then joined Hold. Sveinn defeated Holdboði, but afterwards Sveinn left the Isle of Man and retired back north. Altogether, Sveinn spent about two years in the Irish Sea, according to Taylor sometime between 1140 and 1148.[5]

Why did Sveinn get involved in these Irish Sea affairs? Scholars seem happy to accept *Orkneyinga Saga*'s explanation that *þann mann* [Holdboði] *hafa sér orð sent, er sízt átti hann ní við at kveða ok honum hafði þá bezt gefizk, er hann þurfti mest við, er flestir fóru á hendr honum.*[6] This is a perfect saga-audience-compatible motivation, but should we believe it? If we consider the facts alone as the Saga puts them, Sveinn's reasons may not be quite as noble.[7]

When Sveinn met with Holdboði in Man the very first point they discussed was Sveinn's marriage to Ingiríðr, even before they set off to pursue Hölðr. If we are not 'un-medievally' romantic,[8] it is also quite clear why. *Ingiríðr húsfrú átti fé mikit ok bú stór. Þat ráð gerði Holdboði, at hann bæði hennar.*[9] This is the classic set-up in which a rich widow is offered as a reward for services still to be rendered: Sveinn only seems to start fighting after the finances had been sorted. Also when Sveinn and Holdboði set off from Man, *Orkneyinga Saga* first describes their plundering in quite some detail, before it adds in two short sentences *en hölðrinn hljóp í ey þá, er Lund heitir; þar var vígi gott. Sátu þeir Sveinn þar um nökkura hríð ok fengu ekki at gört.*[10] This failure to exact revenge does not seem to have depressed Sveinn too much, who then married Ingiríðr and enjoyed her wealth.[11] In short, Sveinn may have had friendly feelings for Holdboði, but contrary to *Orkneyinga Saga*'s claim it is unlikely that this was the sole reason for his involvement in Hebridean/Irish Sea affairs.

We should also not forget that Sveinn, although well-established in Orkney by that time,[12] did not have the means to organise the expedition alone. He had to borrow two ships from Earl Rögnvaldr, complete with crews. These men expected expeditions to be worth while, possibly the earl did as well, and the Saga certainly shows that Sveinn cared about his profit.[13]

It may even be argued that Sveinn envisaged more than just a single journey for plunder and for the moveable riches of a widow, that he probably also considered long-term economic gains. Sveinn *settled* on Ingiríðr's estates in Man. Studies of Irish Sea economy may explain why. Benjamin Hudson argues that 'in the eleventh and twelfth centuries the Irish Sea province can best be compared with the wild west of North America, with speculators and settlers rushing in to make their fortunes. One of the most desired commodities was land'. He stresses 'the very real fact that one could become quite wealthy as a farmer during this period'.[14] Land provided social status and ready cash, especially if one could export its produce via near-by harbours. For fertility, the Isle of Man, as the *Poem in Praise of Raghnall* and Snorri Sturluson agree, was renowned.[15] While it would go too far to redefine Sveinn as a peaceful farmer, Ingiríðr's landed wealth was certainly one attraction for him in Man.

Man's other attraction is also evident from the information in *Orkneyinga Saga*. From his base there, Sveinn conducted profitable raids in the southern Irish Sea, 'one of the great trading areas of northern Atlantic Europe'.[16] Sveinn would have been attracted by the ships sailing between the rich port towns, Dublin, Waterford and Wexford, and on the English side Chester and, increasingly, Bristol; as well as between an increasing number of smaller ports. These ships also called at bishops' seats of which many were situated on the coast, and at rich monastic houses whose contribution to the *Commercialization of English Society* were praised by Reginald of Durham and Jocelyn of Furness.[17] Looking further afield, the Irish Sea connects to the English Channel and to the European trade network. This Eldorado began at the Isles of Scilly, 'a port of call for ships leaving and entering the Channel from prehistory, whether legitimate or pirate'.[18] Not surprisingly, the Isles of Scilly were a magnet for Sveinn as well. If plundering in the Irish Sea was lucrative for him, the prospect of plundering down into the English Channel was simply dazzling. And a base on Man would offer excellent access to both. No doubt Sveinn saw these prospects, and he therefore joined Holdboði's Irish Sea adventures.

We should also consider the follow-on episode, usually regarded as a mere aftermath. After Sveinn had returned to Orkney, Sveinn *spurði, at Holdboði var kominn í Suðrey; þá bað hann Rögnvald jarl fá sér lið til at hefna sín.*[19] Although at first sight Sveinn wanted revenge for Holdboði's betrayal, Sveinn did not catch Holdboði. He gained booty though, while Holdboði fled back to Lundy Island, never to return to the Hebrides.[20] Did Sveinn therefore fail? Perhaps he did not achieve what was expected of a 'Viking' warrior, since all that happened was that Holdboði fled. But *Orkneyinga Saga* seems quite positive about this episode, and it is proposed here that this probably *was* Sveinn's main aim. He may have intended to drive Holdboði away, so that he would not have to share a profitable patch with a competitor – in the years to come. Viewed in this light, Sveinn would have been successful. He may have given up the idea of living in Man himself, but he kept his Manx contacts for the rest of his life. There was his Manx wife Ingiríðr, for whom Sveinn had divorced his first wife from Orkney, but from whom he never separated.[21] In fact, Sveinn did not only take Ingiríðr back to Orkney, but also her children, including her son by her Manx husband, Sigmundr, and possibly Sigmundr's uncle as well.[22] Sveinn also gave his own son by Ingiríðr an unusual name, Andrés, possibly after her first Manx husband.[23] As important as marriages were for alliances, the fact that Sveinn never readjusted his relations must mean that it was useful for him to keep his Manx wife than to take another Orcadian one.[24] Sveinn kept a lifelong interest in the Irish Sea.

In answer to the question hitherto ignored, why did Sveinn join Holdboði's Hebridean/Irish Sea adventures? A less 'noble' and rather more 'modern' answer can be given: Sveinn did it for sound economic reasons.

What exactly Sveinn involved himself in, has been discussed to some extent, although possibly a vital part has been overlooked here as well (Fig. 6.1.). Scholars have proposed a connection with the struggle between Owain Gwynedd and his brother Cadwaladr in 1143/44. Cadwaladr had fled Wales and recruited a fleet from Dublin. But before battle was joined, Cadwaladr and Owain came to an agreement. The Dublin fleet, which would have been left unpaid, then seized Cadwaladr and only released him after he had promised

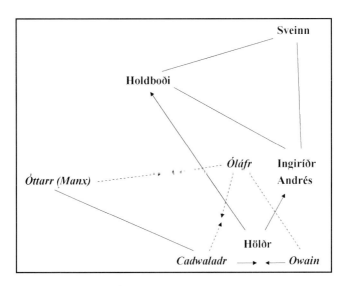

Figure 6.1 : Sveinn Ásleifarson and the Irish Sea Alliances, 1140s
Lines indicate alliances (if broken: conjectural),
arrows indicate opposition (if broken: conjectural).
Italics: not mentioned in Orkneyinga Saga.

a substantial reward. But the Dubliners miscalculated. Owain heard of this arrangement, and he attacked and defeated the fleet. Sveinn, via Holdboði, probably got involved in this political infighting in Gwynedd.[25]

What has not been asked is why Holdboði, a chieftain from rather far-away Tiree, should have backed one Gwynedd-dynast against the other. It is proposed here that the vital link was Dublin. There, Óttarr, whose family apparently came from Man, had just assumed the kingship. This allows two inferences: Óttarr was probably not universally accepted in Dublin, and he probably had enemies in Man and the Isles. The latter can be assumed because Óttarr cannot have been the uncontested maritime king. The 'official' king of Man and the Isles was Óláfr son of Guðröðr Cróbán. But Óttarr may have had a rival claim to at least Man, which he may have wished to press with backing from Dublin. By contrast Óláfr had reversed his father Guðröðr Cróbán's policy: Óláfr attempted to disengage from Dublin. What this very short overview shows is that it is highly unlikely that Óláfr supported Óttarr as king of Dublin, and that they were probably rivals for Man and the Isles as well.[26]

This explains why the Dublin fleet under Óttarr and his ally Cadwaladr *en route* to Gwynedd settled a score in Man, and why *hölðr af Bretlandi*[27] attacked Man and Tiree. Hölðr may either have co-operated with Cadwaladr and Óttarr, attacking Man and Tiree in order to weaken Óttarr's opponents there, before or while Óttarr was moving to Gwynedd. Or the opposite, Hölðr may have helped Owain, by attacking Óttarr's men in Man and Tiree, to keep Óttarr from supporting Cadwaladr.[28]

In short, Holdboði in Tiree and Andrés in Man, opponents or allies of Óttarr's in Man and the Isles, were drawn into the struggles in Gwynedd, because with Óttarr a Manx/Islesman ruled Dublin at a time when Cadwaladr required the services of the fleet of that town. And Sveinn from Orkney saw that these political upheavals offered economic opportunities for him.

Sveinn in the Irish Sea in the 1150s

After Sveinn's Irish Sea exploits in the 1140s, there is a certain lull in the early 1150s when saga-author and scholars alike are spell-bound by Sveinn's involvement in Orcadian politics.[29] Then however the Saga notes what may be called Sveinn's second Irish Sea venture, in the mid-1150s. This episode is particularly difficult to discuss because the evidence is unclear at both geographical ends. While *Orkneyinga Saga*'s account of Sveinn's later dealings with Sumarliði (Somairle/Somerled) of Argyll is clearly wrong, the *Manx Chronicle* and the Irish Annals know nothing of Sveinn, but have conflicting information on Guðröðr Óláfsson of Man and Sumarliði. A possible interpretation of this confused evidence shall be proposed here.

Orkneyinga Saga notes how in spring 1155 Sveinn sailed to Sumarliði and spent Easter with him. Afterwards Sveinn returned shortly to Orkney, travelled to Lewis, and back to Orkney.[30] The Saga then has a confused note on Sveinn's Hebridean exploits in about 1156/57, where a Gilla Oðran was mustering forces, and the erroneous information that Sveinn later killed Sumarliði in a fierce battle.[31] This is clearly wrong since Sumarliði only died in 1164.[32] Still, the description of a battle in the Saga might provide a starting-point for the discussion of Sveinn's Irish Sea activities in the 1150s.

The only battle recorded after 1155 and – since Earl Rögnvaldr was still alive when Sveinn returned from this battle – before August 1158, is that noted by the *Manx Chronicle* between Guðröðr Óláfsson and Sumarliði in January 1157.[33] Guðröðr had heard that Sumarliði, together with the Manx chieftain Þorfinnr, was preparing to attack him, and moved first, forcing Sumarliði into battle. This would agree well with the Saga account that Gilla Oðran var [...] *farinn inn í fjörðu eptir liði því, er eigi var komit.*[34] As James Barrett has also recently acknowledged, it is quite possible that Sveinn was present at this battle.[35] If one accepts this hypothesis, then once again, as in the 1140s, we would have Sveinn getting involved in others' military actions in the Irish Sea.

Once again we should ask why? The possible answer can equally be prised out of *Orkneyinga Saga.* In early June of the same year, 1155, shortly after Sveinn had visited Sumarliði at Easter, the Saga notes that Sveinn made a very successful raiding expedition via the Hebrides down to the Isles of Scilly. *Þeir fóru fyrst til Suðreyja. Þeir fóru allt vestr í Syllingar ok unnu þar sigr mikinn í Máríuhöfn Kolumbamessu ok fengu ófamikit herfang.*[36] But twelfth-century ships did not sail from Orkney to the Isles of Scilly and back non-stop; safe anchorage and fresh provisions would be required on the way. To secure these necessities, an alliance with Sumarliði in the Hebrides, and with Þorfinnr in Man, would have been very helpful indeed. Secondly, at precisely this point in the Saga, following the description of the Scilly Isles raid, we read for the first time *hvert sumar var hann* [Sveinn] *í hernaði;*[37] and again, immediately after the note on the Hebridean battle (which was, as just conjectured, presumably the one between Sumarliði and Guðröðr in January 1157): *eptir þat fór Sveinn í víking ok heim at hausti, sem hann var vanr.*[38] This may be highly significant. The Saga does not mention regular plundering expeditions of Sveinn's before, and we cannot say whether this had been Sveinn's 'custom' since the 1140s. But Sveinn's Orcadian activities in the early 1150s hardly allowed for regular longer journeys, which makes it more likely that such expeditions resumed, or even only began, in 1155.

Incidentally, in 1155 just as in the early 1140s, Sveinn would not have had any great naval strength at his disposal. His involvement in Orcadian politics shortly before had entailed a serious financial setback with, amongst other, the confiscation of his great warship. Sveinn again needed the co-operation of an Orkney earl to secure the necessary shipping, and Earls Rögnvaldr and Haraldr returned Sveinn's ship.[39]

In short, the Saga again shows Sveinn receiving a 'gift' from the Orkney earls (a point which will be taken up again below), and notes his very successful plundering activities at the same time as his contact with Sumarliði. The question of why Sveinn became involved in Irish Sea affairs can therefore be answered in the same way as for the 1140s: 'it's the economy stupid...!!'. It appears that in 1155 Sveinn arranged for a great expedition to Scilly, which duly paid off well, and that he also arranged for continued access to the Irish Sea in the future, via the Hebrides and Man. In return for these immediate and long-term economic profits, he engaged himself to support his allies in their political plots.[40]

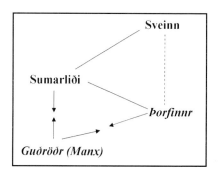

Figure 6.2 : Sveinn Ásleifarson and the Irish Sea Alliances, 1150s Lines indicate alliances (if broken: conjectural), arrows indicate opposition (if broken: conjectural). Italics: not mentioned in Orkneyinga Saga.

These plots were hatched by Þorfinnr Óttarsson and Sumarliði (Fig. 6.2.). Þorfinnr represented chiefs who were disaffected with Guðröðr Óláfsson's rule as king of Man and the Isles and, importantly, at that time as king of Dublin as well. The *Manx Chronicle* reports that Þorfinnr *postulauit ab eo* [Sumarliði] *dubgallum filium suum ut constitueret eum regem super insulas. Audiens hec sumerledus gauisus est ualde & tradidit ei dubgallum filium suum. Qui assumens eum circumduxit per omnes insulas & subiugauit ei uniuersas accipiens obsides de singulis.*[41] Þorfinnr for his part – this is however conjectural – may have coveted a place in Dublin. It is known that Guðröðr became unpopular there, and Þorfinnr has been identified as the son of the above-mentioned (Manx/Isles) Óttarr who ruled Dublin in the 1140s. Þorfinnr might therefore have hoped to follow in his father's footsteps. In the event, Guðröðr attacked Sumarliði first, but the battle in January 1157 was not the success Guðröðr required. It ended with a short-lived compromise, the split of Man and the Isles between Guðröðr and Sumarliði, and Guðröðr being driven out completely in 1158 (nothing more is heard of Þorfinnr).[42]

Since *Orkneyinga Saga* notes that Sveinn was with Sumarliði and in the Isles from 1155 on, Sveinn's stay there must have been either shortly before or parallel to Þorfinnr Óttarsson's visit. During his several travels to and through the Hebrides Sveinn must also have heard of Dubgall's royal progress. It is therefore likely that Sveinn was aware of the conspirators' plans before

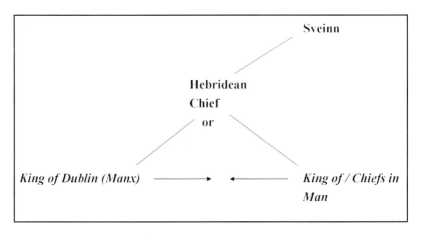

Figure 6.3 : Sveinn Ásleifarson and the Irish Sea Alliances, parallels
1140s &1150s. Lines indicate alliances, arrows indicate opposition.

matters came to a head in January 1157, which would, as proposed here, have
enabled him to consider the options and reach a deal with one of the parties.

There would appear to be obvious parallels between Sveinn's two ventures
into the Irish Sea in the 1140s and 50s (Fig. 6.3.). On both occasions Sveinn
got involved because of the prospect of serious economic benefits in areas
otherwise beyond his reach, for which he first had to organise shipping, a
'gift' from the Orkney earls: and in both cases this was connected to a specific
unstable political situation. In the 1140s, the Hebridean chief Holdboði had
asked for support when he was attacked as an ally of a Manx/Isles dynast,
Óláfr in Man or Óttarr in Dublin. In the 1150s, the Hebridean chief Sumarliði
may at least have welcomed support because he planned an attack as an
ally of a Manx/Isles dynast, Þorfinnr Óttarsson, against Guðröðr Óláfsson
in Dublin. In short, each time a Hebridean chief was in need of additional
military support because of his role in a Manx/Isles – Dublin conflict he
looked to Sveinn to supply it.

Sveinn in the Irish Sea for the last time: Dublin

After the mid-1150s, there is no more information until Sveinn's third
involvement in Irish Sea politics, which led him to Dublin and his death in
1171.

Sveinn's expedition to Dublin has received rather more attention, possibly because it was his last exploit. So much at least we can say. Otherwise we cannot be too specific because of serious problems with the evidence. In addition to *Orkneyinga Saga*, there is an 'Irish' collection of sources. Giraldus Cambrensis's *Expugnatio Hibernica*, the *Deeds of the Normans in Ireland*, and various sets of Irish Annals give independent evidence for activities of Orcadians in Ulster and Dublin. But this combined Irish evidence only partly corroborates, and sometimes seems to contradict, the Saga's account of Sveinn's activities.[43]

The sources and their problems can be summed up thus. *Orkneyinga Saga* describes how Sveinn on one of his usual spring-trips took two English merchant ships in the Irish Sea. This journey, a full success, is remembered in Orcadian history as Sveinn's famous broadcloth viking-trip. Back in Orkney Sveinn threw a banquet for Earl Haraldr, where the earl, not the only one to note how rich Sveinn has become, seemed to dislike Sveinn's grand life-style. When Haraldr told Sveinn to stop raiding, Sveinn insisted on one more autumn trip, but then agreed to the earl's request. Sveinn afterwards duly set off for this last trip which was to lead him to Dublin – and last in every sense. At first he was successful in Dublin, but overnight the Dubliners set up a trap. The next morning Sveinn and his men fell into concealed pits and most, including Sveinn, were killed. According to *Orkneyinga Saga*'s internal dating these events happened between 1165 and 1180.[44]

The Irish Annals and Giraldus note an Orcadian fleet at Inisloughlin in Ulster in 1170.[45] This might allow a more exact dating of one of Sveinn's last raiding trips. Furthermore, the Irish Annals, Giraldus and the *Deeds* note the participation and death of a 'John' in Asculf mac Torcaill's assault on Dublin, who arrived *cum Norwagiensibus et insulanis* according to Giraldus, *de Norwiche* according to the *Deeds*, and following the Irish Annals *a h-Innsibh Orc.* In the Irish Annals he is also given the byname *Lochlandach* or *Orcach.*[46] These descriptions point very strongly to a Norseman from Orkney – to Sveinn? But this person ('John') is consistently called *Johan le Devé* in the *Deeds*, and *Iohannus þe Wode* by Giraldus, who explains that his soubriquet *Latine sonat 'insano' vel 'vehementi'.*[47] The Irish Annals give his name as *Eoan.*[48] This, therefore, is the first problem with the sources: Sveinn and Iohannus/Eoan are different names.

The second problem concerns the leader's death. Following *Orkneyinga Saga*, Sveinn had been all but established in Dublin, and he then died, betrayed, in the pits. But the Iohannus/Eoan of the Irish sources fell in open battle when he assaulted the town.[49] The details of Sveinn's and Iohannus/ Eoan's death do not match

Thirdly, there is a problem of dating. *Orkneyinga Saga* is clear that Sveinn's last trip was an autumn trip, *haustvíking*. The Irish sources equally clearly date Iohannus/Eoan's death to spring, to May 1171 (in the modern Irish received opinion).[50] Since the dating is in both cases internally coherent and convincing, the contradiction between *Orkneyinga Saga*'s autumn and the Irish sources' mid-May is puzzling.

The first two problems will be discussed here only briefly. More research is needed to decide whether Norse Sveinn could become Irish Eoan (via Seán?) and then Latin Iohannus.[51] However, it seems very unlikely that there were two independent Orkney fleets operating in Ulster and Dublin, with two leaders dying there; *Orkneyinga Saga* only notes Sveinn's death and does not say a single word on the supposed other one in 1170/71, while the Irish sources only record Iohannus/Eoan's, but completely overlook Sveinn's between 1165 and 1180. The Irish characterisation of the fleet's leader as a 'mad Norseman/Orcadian' could also point to Sveinn. Alternatively it might refer to Hákon Haraldsson, Earl Haraldr's son who accompanied Sveinn. The *Deeds* in particular may speak of him in the line *neveu ert cil [al] riche reis de Norwiche*[52] A third possibility is that Sveinn's mother Ásleif had unknown connections. The latter is speculation encouraged by Sveinn's unusual preference for *Ásleifarson* over *Óláfsson*, which would have been his patronymic.[53] In the end however, whether the actions of Sveinn's and Hákon's have been partially conflated or not is not very important in the context here, since both men were part of the same expedition. The Irish sources would therefore also give evidence for Sveinn's presence.

As regards the details of Sveinn's or Iohannus/Eoan's death, the divergence might be explained by simple confusion. The Irish sources contain a large number of vile betrayals and courageous and honourable attacks in the years 1170 and 1171. Dublin alone switched sides four times in 1170/71 between Diarmait Mac Murchada king of Leinster and the Irish high king Ruaidrí Ua Conchobair. All submissions included the swearing of oaths, and discussions about hostages and tribute.[54] Especially interesting are the events in autumn 1170, when the Irish sources agree that the Dubliners took a rather long time to decide about the hostages they would give to Diarmait as part of their submission. Here, the account of the *Deeds* is very close to that of

Orkneyinga Saga. The Dubliners were led by Asculf, and *Hesculf ad dunc remandé * A Dermod, li rei preisé, * Que l'endemain hastivement * Freit tut son commandement*. This is suspiciously similar to *Orkneyinga Saga*'s *En um morgininn skyldi Sveinn koma í staðinn ok taka við fégjöldum , skipa staðinn ok taka gísla af staðarmönnum* – apart from the difference that the new incoming lord in the *Deeds* is Diarmait, in the Saga Sveinn.[55] While the negotiations (with Diarmait) were continuing, one side planned a betrayal. Diarmait's Norman allies made a surprise assault and took Dublin by force. It is possible that confused elements of these different *stories* (not necessarily facts) may have found their way into *Orkneyinga Saga*, arranged in a way that would explain Sveinn's death.[56]

This leaves the third and most vexing problem, that of the dating – or, the dating is the third hitherto *recognised* problem. There is another one which has so far not been acknowledged: a problem of the logic of Sveinn's behaviour. If this is considered first, we can then solve the dating problem.

The point of departure is Sveinn's broadcloth viking-trip in spring. *Orkneyinga Saga* notes that Sveinn did not get much plunder in the Hebrides and Man. Sveinn's luck only improved when he *nær suðr undir Dyflinn* hit upon the two English ships carrying English broadcloth.[57] After that, Sveinn returned to the Orkneys, laden with riches, which he displayed ostentatiously.[58] When Sveinn then threw a banquet for Earl Haraldr at his home at Gairsay, Haraldr eyed Sveinn's conspicuous consumption with envy and alarm, demanding unequivocally that Sveinn stop the raiding. The next few lines are crucial, and their importance has arguably been overlooked so far. Sveinn put up a token resistance to Haraldr's demand, and then simply yielded. All he asked for was to make one last trip in autumn. This is incongruous. Are we really to believe that Sveinn was so easily prepared to give up his long-standing, well-organised and exceedingly lucrative raiding and trading business, which guaranteed his social position? Sveinn's claim - that he was getting too old anyway, is equally unconvincing, whether as historical fact or as literary fiction. Sveinn had sons and daughters, some of whom would surely have liked to inherit his profitable trade. Sveinn's behaviour clashes with the image of him otherwise portrayed by the saga-writer, of the last man to take early retirement and to live on a reduced income simply because an earl wanted it.[59] This is one question concerning the logic of Sveinn's behaviour.

The other one immediately follows. Sveinn's insistence on a last autumn trip, equally glorious, is just as puzzling. Why should he have risked another adventure when the previous one had been so exceedingly successful? Plundering was a dangerous business with a large element of luck. After the broadcloth Viking trip in spring, chances were rather high that the next voyage would be a comparative let-down. In addition, if Sveinn had been serious about retiring, the broadcloth trip would have been a suitable finale to ensure his place in history. Sveinn cannot simply have hoped to be even luckier in autumn.

In short, Sveinn's easy agreement to cease raiding, and his insistence on one last expedition do not make sense. If the former was just lip-service, what lay behind the latter? To answer this, we should consider Sveinn's position. The broadcloth trip had been glorious, but it must have been obvious to Sveinn that he had by then over-fished the Hebridean waters. To quote *Orkneyinga Saga: Þá var fólk svá hrætt við hann í Suðreyjum, at menn fálu allt lausafé sitt í jörðu eða urðum*; or in more modern language: 'raiding is a strategy with diminishing returns'.[60] As the Vikings' long experience throughout Europe shows, this sometimes required moving hunting-grounds, and / or reconsidering strategies.

Sveinn's position within Orkney may also have been changing. We could ask to what extent Sveinn might actually have been a licensed privateer? Or, in earlier mode, which kind of gift-giving mechanism was at work there? As underlined above, for quite some time Sveinn received ships as 'gifts' from the earls. Earl Rögnvaldr *may* of course on the first occasion (in the 1140s) have given Sveinn ships as a counter-gift because he was still indebted to Sveinn for his support when he gained the earldom in the 1130s. For his second journey in the 1140s (the 'aftermath') Sveinn received five ships from Earl Rögnvaldr, but was saddled with four co-commanders who were not his friends, and who then duly quarrelled over the distribution of the booty. Also on the Isles of Scilly expedition in the 1150s two other leaders came along, one of whom, Þorbjörn klerkr, was the 'councillor-in-chief' of Earl Haraldr.[61] And after each independent trip Sveinn immediately sought out an earl. Did Sveinn on these occasions repay the 'gift' of the ships? And after the 1150s, when he did not seem to depend on Earl Haraldr for ships anymore, was Sveinn required to pay 'income tax'? After the broadcloth trip Sveinn invited Haraldr to a feast and the earl left *með sæmiligum gjöfum*.[62] It is likely that various earls of Orkney invested in and benefitted financially from Sveinn's adventures.

Nevertheless, Haraldr by then seemed to think that Sveinn had become too rich – and probably also again too dangerous. For Sveinn this meant that he may have wondered how long he would still be able to hold his own against Haraldr, who, since Rögnvaldr's death in 1158, had been the single well-established earl.

In sum, there seems to be a situation where Sveinn's marginal returns were decreasing, but where his wealth and secured position was so great that it displeased the earl.[63] The solution to this problem is obvious: move somewhere where business would be better and where your property, or even your life, would be safe from the earl – Dublin.

It would not be the first time that Sveinn the Orcadian considered emigration. When *Orkneyinga Saga* describes Sveinn's first Irish Sea venture in the 1140s it it is made quite plain that *Þenna vetr gerði Sveinn brúðkaup til Ingiríðar ok sat þá með sœemð mikilli.*[64] Sveinn settled in the Isle of Man. He stayed in the Irish Sea for two years, and only when his position there became untenable did he return to Orkney. Following this reversal, Sveinn later made sure of continuing access to the Irish Sea via his alliance with Sumarliði.

The hypothesis now being put forward is that Sveinn for a second time planned to set himself up further south when it seemed opportune, in 1170. Hence Sveinn could promise Earl Haraldr that the autumn raid would be his last one – it would be, at least from Orkney. Of course, Sveinn had to offer some resistance to the earl's wishes; otherwise Haraldr would have become suspicious and might have second-guessed Sveinn's intentions. Hence Sveinn promised to retire in return for the concession that he could make one last raid, which was of course all he really needed, and *skildusk þeir Sveinn með miklum kærleikum.*[65] Of course Sveinn might have been genuine about giving up raiding himself altogether to avoid the physical hardships, but only to enjoy an easier way of making profit from Dublin, not to become a harmless elderly pensioner.

This is the one scenario in which Sveinn's otherwise very odd behaviour is perfectly logical: if he planned a move where he could expect *at hon yrði eigi með minnum afburðum en várvíkingen var;*[66] a move which would be a most illustrious journey – setting himself up in Dublin.[67]

If we approach *Orkneyinga Saga* and the Irish Sources for the years 1170/71 after this interpretation of Sveinn's behaviour, after these considerations of *why* Sveinn behaved as he did, the problem of the contradictory dating simply disappears. That was that *Orkneyinga Saga* dates Sveinn's last trip to autumn, whereas the Irish sources record that Sveinn died in May. Which version is wrong?

The answer is that both the Orcadian and the Irish evidence are correct. There is no logical contradiction at all between Sveinn departing from Orkney on his last Viking trip in autumn 1170, and being killed in Dublin in May 1171. The only problem lies with scholars whose underlying assumption has always been that Sveinn came back, or rather, would have come back to Orkney from his autumn 1170 trip. If however Sveinn did not return, because he did not *intend* to return, then for the people of Orkney, and for the informant of the Icelander who composed *Orkneyinga Saga*, Sveinn departed on his last Viking trip in autumn 1170. And the following spring – at the earliest in late May – information reached Orkney that Sveinn had been killed in Dublin.

This hypothesis is open to the challenge that it relies on an appreciation of Sveinn's prior Irish Sea career and on a close reading of a conversation as recorded –or maybe invented – by the Saga author. However, *Orkneyinga Saga* also has more 'factual' information. There is the following very odd paragraph that when Sveinn and his men arrived in Dublin, they took control of the town. *Þeir gerðu þar hertekna valdsmenn þá, er þar váru í staðnum. Fóru þeira skipti svá, at þeir gáfu upp staðinn í vald Sveins ok játtaðu honum svá miklu gjaldi sem hann vildi á þá leggja. Sveinn skyldi ok skipa sínum mönnum staðinn ok hafa vald yfir. Dyflinnarmenn sverja eið at þessu. Þeir fóru til skipa um kveldit. En um morgininn skyldi Sveinn koma í staðinn ok taka við fégjöldum, skipa staðinn ok taka gísla af staðarmönnum.*[68] This looks like a long-term arrangement, indicating more than just a plundering expedition. Upon closer consideration, a successful straightforward 'Viking' hit-and-run raid of Sveinn's on Dublin would also have been unlikely. Dublin had never been a target for Sveinn's raids. Since the 1140s he had been active in the Hebrides, in Ireland in general, in the Isle of Man, in Wales, on the Cornwall and Devon coasts, but not in Dublin. It would also be surprising if Sveinn had targeted that town. Dublin had the greatest fleet in the Irish Sea, Hiberno-Norse warriors who figured regularly as professionals in Ireland, Scotland and Wales, and an impressive town wall. Even the Normans, well-versed in taking fortifications, found it a challenge.[69]

However, *Orkneyinga Saga*'s account need not be dismissed as a case of wishful thinking; there may be a kernel of truth in it. The classic way to gain

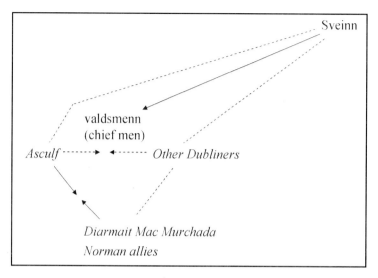

Figure 6.4 : Sveinn Ásleifarson and Dublin, 1170-1
Lines indicate alliances (if broken: conjectural), arrows indicate
opposition (if broken: conjectural).
Italics: not mentioned in Orkneyinga Saga.

access to a well-protected place is by knowing someone inside. Here matters become very complicated, and the Irish background can only be discussed summarily in this context (Fig. 6.4.). One possibility is that Sveinn had already entered into the alliance known from the Irish sources for May 1171, with Asculf, king of Dublin. Asculf's interest in Sveinn's support already in autumn 1170 is connected to the number of betrayals involving Dublin. In 1170, Asculf faced Diarmait Mac Murchada, king of Leinster with claims to be Dublin's overlord, who had just recently engaged Norman fighters, and with whom Asculf was probably not on speaking-terms.[70] In addition, Asculf seems to have faced opposition within Dublin, and the two camps were apparently quite evenly matched. It is a fair guess that Asculf's opponents were in favour of Diarmait.[71] Asculf might therefore have turned to Sveinn for help, who, according to *Orkneyinga Saga*, had seven longships in autumn 1170, a powerful enough force to tip the scales within Dublin.[72]

Troubled waters attracted Sveinn in the 1170s just as in the 1140s and 1150s. In the 1140s Sveinn's reward for his support in Irish Sea plots was marriage to Ingiríðr and settlement on Man. The kernel of truth in *Orkneyinga Saga*'s Dublin-account may therefore be an offer to Sveinn to settle respectably in

Dublin – after he had helped one party to defeat the other, *gerðu ... hertekna valdsmenn,* having 'made prisoners of the chief men'. After that, Sveinn could have quartered his men in the town, expected to collect gold and hostages, and have a say in the government of Dublin, as the Saga claims.[73]

Orkneyinga Saga's view of Sveinn's serious intentions in Dublin is therefore quite plausible and it might also not stand alone. It might in fact be corroborated by some Irish Annals, Giraldus and the *Deeds*. The *Deeds* have an interesting sentence when they describe the later May 1171 attack. *Un vassal, Johan le Devé, Ad Mac Turcul od sei mené.*[74] This may not prove anything conclusively, but it could on the other hand well represent what Diarmait and his circles, who informed the author of the *Deeds*,[75] thought of Sveinn, especially if he had been co-operating with Asculf for a longer while.

A far more instructive entry can be found in a set of Irish Annals known as *Mac Cárthaigh's Book*,[76] which notes Asculf's and Sveinn's defeat when they tried to take Dublin in May 1171. How is Sveinn referred to there? *Iohannes Orcach & Turcaill, da aramann Atha Cliath, do teacht a n-Erinn do dighailt a n-dithi & a n-innarbta a Baile Atha Cliath tri xx. long do Lochlannaibh, & cath do cur dona Lochlannachibh & dona Saxanachibh a timcill Atha Cliath, & an dis armann-sin Atha Cliath fre re do marbhadh ann go n-ar an loingis Loclannaigh.*[77] It may be ambiguous to whom exactly the possessive adjective *their* (Irish *a*) refers: only to Asculf and his Norse, or also to Sveinn? But one of the 'two officials of Dublin' was clearly Sveinn. The translation 'official' is in fact quite vague. Irish *ármann* derives from Old Norse *ármaðr*, and it also occurs in other Irish Annals.[78] Colmán Etchingham confirms that nobody has examined the use of this term as yet.[79] We therefore do not know which precise meaning *ármann* had in twelfth-century Irish. But *Mac Cárthaigh's Book* points to some recognised position which Sveinn had in Dublin prior to May 1171, and presumably also prior to Diarmait's and his Norman's take-over of the town in late September 1170. The description of Sveinn as *ármann* in *Mac Cárthaigh's Book* accords with what *Orkneyinga Saga* says of Sveinn being given power *þeir gáfu upp staðinn í vald*;[80] and it contradicts the view that Sveinn had merely embarked on a last 'Viking' raid to Dublin.

Following the interpretation advanced here, the new outline of events would therefore be as follows. Sveinn had some established position in Dublin in autumn 1170 before he suffered a reverse there. It is unlikely that Sveinn had taken Dublin on his own, without help from the inside. One candidate for this was Asculf. He (or alternatively other Dubliners) may have offered Sveinn a reward which Sveinn had already accepted at least once before, an attractive position in the place he helped to secure. Having made such an arrangement, Sveinn could easily have yielded to Earl Haraldr's demand to stop raiding, provided he would get away from Orkney with enough ships and men just one more time. Thanks to Sveinn's convincing performance at the feast for Haraldr, this was achieved. Sveinn then duly left Orkney in autumn 1170, not intending to return. He established himself in Dublin, but his plans suffered a severe set-back when shortly afterwards Diarmait and the Normans took the town.

When the Normans took Dublin Giraldus says that Asculf fled *boreales ad insulas*.[81] However, it is unlikely that these Latin northern isles correspond to Old Norse *Norðreyjar* (Orkney and Shetland). From Giraldus's perspective of a Welshman in English services, the Hebrides were sufficiently far to the north to merit this description. The Hebrides and not Orkney are also discussed as the Dubliners' refuge by Seán Duffy.[82] Considering also Sveinn's long-standing connections in the Hebrides, it is therefore proposed that he and Asculf over-wintered there. In support of this there is one other argument. Irish scholars explain that it was Diarmait's death which triggered a general uprising against the Normans, not only in Dublin. According to Giraldus, Diarmait died *circiter kalendas Maii*.[83] Giraldus says about Sveinn's and Asculf's attempt to re-gain Dublin that it occurred *eadem fere tempestate, circa Pentecostem*, which in 1171 was on 16 May.[84] Two weeks seem very short for news of Diarmait's death at Ferns to reach an Irish port, to travel up to Orkney, for Asculf and Sveinn to raise their men, make their ships seaworthy again after the winter, to provision them and to sail down to mount a major attack on Dublin. If, however, Asculf and Sveinn stayed in the (southern?) Hebrides in winter 1170/71, to await their chance to regain Dublin, such a quick move would have been more easily possible. The rest is well-known. Their assault in May 1171 was unsuccessful; Sveinn, Asculf, and most of their men died there.

If this version of events is accepted, the problem of the dating in the Irish sources and *Orkneyinga Saga* is solved. It allows a clear statement that Sveinn did indeed die in Dublin in spring 1171, having left Orkney in autumn 1170.

But this was not the only point here. Sveinn's Dublin expedition was the third example in a row of Irish Sea contacts considered here (Fig. 6.5.). It

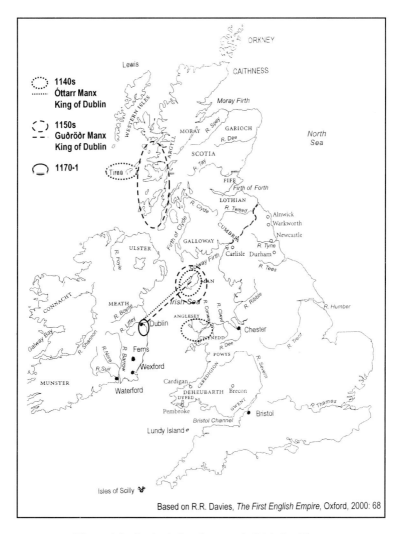

Based on R.R. Davies, *The First English Empire*, Oxford, 2000: 68

Figure 6.5 : Sveinn's involvement in Irish Sea Plots.

underlines just how serious Sveinn's continuous involvement in Irish Sea affairs was, for both sides. Sveinn's last expeditions mattered for developments in Dublin during a, if not the, most crucial period in the history of that town.[85] Before that, Sveinn may have been involved in the *causa ruine totius regnum insularum*, as the *Manx Chronicle* puts it, the break-up of the Kingdom of

Man and the Isles in the 1150s.[86] And Sveinn probably interfered in the Man-Dublin-Gwynedd conflicts of the 1140s. There was hardly any Irish Sea plot he missed.

This was because the Irish Sea mattered for Sveinn. Three times we have asked why Sveinn acted as he did, and each time economic reasons are proposed. Sveinn depended on Irish Sea riches for his life-style and status. To make sure of this source of wealth, Sveinn supported various chiefs and their plots, earning him the title *mestan ójafnaðarmann í Vestrlöndum*.[87]

This leads to a last thought. If Irish Sea raiding, secured by appropriate politicking, made Sveinn into one of the wealthiest men in Orkney, he would not have wanted to suffer from too many restrictions in Orkney, either. He would not have wanted to share his hard-earned plunder with too demanding an authority in Orkney. Apart from emigrating, the best insurance against intrusive demands would have been a weak earl; weak because he was indebted to Sveinn, or because he faced rival claims by others. To finish therefore with a provocative 'upside-down', Irish Sea-based question for Sveinn: would his economic interests there also have made him into the *ójafnaðarmann* in Orkney, would they explain his earl-making actions?

Literary or historical, *Orkneyinga Saga*'s account of Sveinn's deeds shows how much Scandinavian Scotland – and the 'Scandinavian Irish Sea' – remained a single zone of operations into the twelfth century for men of Sveinn's calibre, a rather timeless species of businessman *cum* politician.

Notes

[1] Quotes are from F. Guðmundsson (ed.), *Orkneyinga Saga*, Íslenzk Fornrit vol. 34 (Reykjavík, 1965) (OS FG). Unless otherwise indicated, the translation by A. Taylor, *The Orkneyinga Saga* (Edinburgh, 1938) (OS AT) has been preferred since it is closer to the original than that by H. Pálsson and P. Edwards, *Orkneyinga Saga* (London, 1981) (OS HP/PE). For Sveinn see especially OS chs. 73-84, 92-101, 105-108. OS's first version apparently ended with Sveinn's death, three-quarters through ch. 108. Discussion J.H. Barrett, 'Svein Asleifsson and 12th – century Orcadian Society', in O. Owen (ed.), *The World of Orkneyinga Saga* (Kirkwall, 2005), 213-223; J. Jesch, 'Literature in Medieval Orkney', in Owen *World of Orkneyinga Saga*, 11-24; R. Power, 'Scotland in the Norse Sagas', in G.G. Simpson (ed.), *Scotland and*

Scandinavia 800-1800 (Edinburgh, 1990), 15-17; P. Foote, 'Observations on Orkneyinga Saga', in B.E. Crawford (ed.), *St Magnus Cathedral and Orkney's Twelfth Century Renaissance* (Aberdeen, 1988), 192-207, at 195; M. Chesnutt, 'Haralds saga Maddarðarsonar', in U. Dronke et al. (eds.), *Speculum Norrænvm: Norse Studies in Memory of Gabriel Turville-Petre* (Odense 1981), 33-54, at 34; M. Ciklamini, 'Saint Rognvaldr and Sveinn Asleifarson, the Viking', *Scandinavian Studies* 42 (1970), 50-7; for the background W.P.L. Thomson, *History of Orkney* (Edinburgh, 1987), 60-73; J.S. Clouston, *A History of Orkney* (Kirkwall, 1932), 103-118, and esp. 119-129. Sveinn's fame is also based on less scholarly works, E. Linklater, *The Ultimate Viking* (London, 1955), more recently R.P. Gunn, *Swein Asleifson: A Northern Pirate* (Latheronwheel, Caithness, 1990), and H. Douglasson, 'Svein Asleifarsson: The Last Viking', in idem, *Saga-Men. The People Behind the Earls of Orkney* (Lulu web-publishers, http://www.lulu.com Morrisville NC & London, 2005), 136-199.

² OS ch. 108.

³ The other sources where Sveinn seems to appear are Giraldus Cambrensis, *Expugnatio Hibernica, The Conquest of Ireland*, ed A.B. Scott and F.X. Martin (Daublin, 1978) (*Expug. Hib.*), *Deeds of the Normans in Ireland, La Geste des Engleis en Yrlande*, A new edition of the chronicle formerly known as *The Song of Dermot and the Earl*, ed E. Mullally (Dublin, 2002), and the Irish Annals; overview A.O. Anderson, *Early Sources of Scottish History*, ed P. Watkins, 2 vols. (Stamford, 1990) (ES), ii. 271-3; discussed below. Both those who accept Sveinn's adventures as historical as well as those who see OS as a literary fiction seem to agree that Sveinn was, or is portrayed as, a true viking. Consequently, it has been debated whether he was the last representative of a dying age, or already only a fictive character, a memory of a way of life gone by when OS was written around 1200. See I. Beuermann, 'Orkneyinga Saga: 1195 And All That?', *Nordistica Tartuensia* 14 (2006), 113-152; shortly Barrett, 'Svein Asleifsson', 219; O. Bruhn, 'Earl Rognvald and the Rise of Saga Literature', in C. Batey et al. (eds.), *The Viking Age in Caithness, Orkney and the North Atlantic* (Edinburgh, 1995), 240-7; E.J. Cowan, 'Caithness in the Sagas, in J.R. Baldwin (ed.), *Caithness: a cultural crossroads* (Edinburgh, 1982), 25-27; idem, 'What is Orkneyinga Saga About?', *Northern Studies* 2 (1973), 19-22; OS HP/PE, 14, 15. For OS's trustworthiness and Sveinn's historicity most recently Jesch, 'Literature', 13-14; Barrett, 'Svein Asleifsson', 213-215; A. Forte et al., *Viking Empires* (Cambridge, 2005), 286; B. Fidjestøl, 'Bjarni Kolbeinsson', in P. Pulsiano et al. (eds.), *Medieval Scandinavia. An Encyclopaedia* (New York & London, 1993).

[4] Paraphrased from B.E. Crawford, *Scandinavian Scotland* (Leicester, 1987), 220.

[5] OS chs. 78, 79.

[6] 'that man [Holdboði] had sent him a message whom he ought least of all to refuse and who had stood by him best when he needed it most – when most men went against him', OS ch. 78. Taylor's translation 'all other', has been amended to 'most', to render Flateyjarbók's *flestir*. For the manuscripts shortly OS FG, 2; and OS AT, 9-13. See also OS HP/PE, 145.

[7] This might be a compromise in the discussion of whether OS is historical or fictive: the factual parts could be reasonably historical, the explanations fictive.

[8] For such a reading see Clouston, *History*, 121: Sveinn 'won the heart and hand of the fair and wealthy widow, Ingigerd Thorkel's daughter, by avenging the death of her husband Andres in true romantic, viking-errant style'. Clouston was possibly misled by these details in OS ch. 78: *þá mælti hon [Ingiríðr], at Sveinn skyldi þat til ráðahags vinna at hefna Andréss, bónda síns. Sveinn svarar, at hann mætti gera Bretum skaða nökkurn, - "en eigi má ek vita, hvers af verðr auðit um mannalát"*; 'she [Ingiríðr] said that in order to gain her hand Sweyn must avenge to the full her husband Andrew. Sweyn answers that he might do the Welshmen some harm; - "but I cannot tell what luck we shall have in man-slaying".'

[9] 'Dame Ingirid had much wealth and [many large estates]. Holdboði proposed that Sweyn should ask her to marry him', OS ch. 78.

[10] 'But the Hölðr took refuge on the island called Lundy, where there was a good natural stronghold. Sweyn and his men besieged it for some time, but to no purpose.' OS ch. 78. Also for the raiding OS ch. 78; according to Power, 'Scotland in the Norse Sagas', 16: 'an indiscriminate raiding tour of Wales'.

[11] OS ch. 79.

[12] *Eigi váru í þann tíma þeir tveir menn fyrir vestan haf, er meira háttar þætti vera en þeir Sveinn ok Þorbjörrn mágar*, OS ch. 77, 'There were not at that time two men out in the west not of higher birth who were thought more powerful than Sweyn and his brother-in-law Thorbjorn.'

[13] G. Williams, 'Land Assessment and Military Organisation in the Norse Settlements in Scotland, c. 900-1266 AD', unpublished PhD thesis (University of St Andrews, 1996), 240-245, 263, 265, underlines plunder as the reward for military service. Earl Rögnvaldr needed funds for his Kirkwall Cathedral project, OS ch. 76. See recently R. Lamb, J. Robertson, 'Kirkwall: Saga, History, Archaeology', in Owen, *World of Orkneyinga Saga*, 160-191, 165.

[14] B. Hudson, 'The Changing Economy of the Irish Sea Province', in B. Smith (ed.), *Britain and Ireland 900-1300* (Cambridge, 1999), 39-66, 55, 56.

[15] The first stanza in the *Poem in Praise of Raghnall, King of Man*, ed B. Ó Cuív, *Éigse*, vol. 8 part 4 (1957), 288, boasts about Man's fertitliy: *[B]haile suthach sith Emhna, * cruthach in chrich a ttarla, * raith chaem os cinn cech dingna * 'nab imdha craeb fhinn abhla*. ('A fruitful place is the fairy mound of Eamhain, beautiful the land in which it is found, a fair rath surpassing every dwelling in which are many bright apple-branches.'). Snorri Sturluson compares Man with Kintyre: The peninsula *er mikit land ok betra en in bezta ey í Suðreyjum nema Mön*. ('is a large land, and better than the best island in the Hebrides except Man'), *Magnúss saga Berfœtts* in Snorri Sturluson: *Heimskringla*, ed B. Aðalbjarnarsson, Íslenzk Fornrit vol. 28, (Reykjavík 1951/1979), ch.10. See P. McNeill, R. Nicholson (eds.), *An Historical Atlas of Scotland c.400-1600* (St Andrews, 1975), 105; M.A. Fullen, J. Harris, B.S. Kear, *Soils of the Isle of Man*, Centre for Manx Studies Research Report 5 (1996), 18, 19, 22.

[16] Hudson, 'Changing Economy', 40.

[17] Reginald of Durham praised the economic achievements of abbot John of Furness Abbey (which had its own harbour) in ca. 1170, in *Libellus de Admirandis Beati Cuthberti Virtutibus*, ed. J. Raine (Surtees Society, 1835), 112; Jocelyn of Furness praised Holm Cultram's first abbot Everard (1150-92) in *Vita S. Waldeni*, in *Acta Sanctorum*, August, I (Paris, 1867), 242-278. Good discussion of Irish Sea church economy K.J. Stringer, *The Reformed Church in Medieval Galloway and Cumbria: Contrasts, Connections, and Continuities*, Eleventh Whithorn Lecture 14 Sept 2002 (Whithorn, 2003), with details and further references for the stock-rearing granges of Holm Cultram and Calder, St Bees' and the salt-making industry, and Furness' and Galloway-houses' interests in Man. Cf also E. Jamroziak, 'Rievaulx Abbey as a Wool Producer in the Late Thirteenth Century: Cistercians, Sheep, and Debts', *Northern History*, 40 (2003), 197-218. For Chester's wide contacts in the late 12th century see e.g. the monk Lucian's praise poem, *Liber Luciani de Laude Cestrie*, ed M.V. Taylor, Lancashire and Chester Record Society, vol.64 (Edinburgh & London, 1912). Recent discussion of Lucian, King John's charter of liberties to Bristol in 1188, and other sources for Irish Sea Economy in Hudson, 'Changing Economy', 39-66; also idem, 'Economy and Trade', in S. Duffy (ed.), *A New History of the Isle of Man* vol.3 (Liverpool, forthcoming). For Man P. Davey, 'Medieval and Later Pottery from the Isle of Man', *IoM Natural History and Antiquarian Society* vol. 11 no.1 (2000), 91-114, examines numbers of Manx, British and Continental vessels found in Castle Rushen (95); his socio-economic evaluation (at 104ff) stresses the wide range of continental imports. For the British and Irish context R.H. Britnell, *Britain and Ireland 1050-1530. Economy and Society* (Oxford, 2004); idem,

The Commercialisation of English Society, 1000-1500 (Manchester, 1996);
C. Dyer, Making a Living in the Middle Ages (London, 2003), esp. 187-227;
for an evaluation of the various economic models J. Hatcher, M. Bailey,
Modelling the Middle Ages (Oxford, 2001), esp. 121-173.

[18] D.W. Moore, The Other British Isles. A History of Shetland, Orkney, the
Hebrides, Isle of Man, Anglesey, Scilly, Isle of Wight and the Channel Islands
(Jefferson NC, 2005), 173. Ibid. for governors appointed by successive
Plantagenet kings because of Scilly's economic and strategic importance
(167), for 12th-century tin smuggling (167, 174), and for shipwrecks as a
lucrative source of income (173), with over 600 sites of wrecks chartered
today (158).

[19] 'heard that Holdboði had come [back] to the Hebrides. Thereupon he asked
Earl Rognvald to get him a force to avenge himself [upon Holdboði]', OS
ch. 82; dated 1143 x 1148 in OS AT, 269. For Sveinn's return to Orkney OS
ch. 79.

[20] OS ch. 82.

[21] Ingiríðr Þorkelsdóttir was Sveinn's second wife. His first wife Ragnhildr is
called Ögmundardóttir / Ingimundardóttir, OS ch. 92. Sveinn and Ragnhildr's
marriage had been very short OS ch. 92.

[22] Sigmundr was a prominent member of Earl Rögnvaldr's force on the
journey to Jerusalem, fighting bravely though barely a man, and swimming in
the River Jordan with the earl; his poetry is quoted in OS chs. 87, 88. Ámundi
Hnefason, a friend of Earl Haraldr Maddaðarson and uncle of Sveinn's
stepchildren, later mediated between Sveinn and Earl Haraldr in Orkney, OS
ch. 97.

[23] This is the Andrés Sveinsson who married Fríða, daughter of Kolbeinn
Hruga and sister of Bishop Bjarni, OS ch. 108, see above.

[24] An additional reason may have been Ingiríðr's connection to Earl Haraldr:
she was frændkona jarls ('a kinswoman of the Earl') and at least on one
occasion, in winter 1154/55, seems to have protected him against Sveinn, OS
ch. 95. This would also explain why Ámundi Hnefason was able to mediate
between Sveinn and Earl Haraldr (s.a. note 22). The relations between
Sveinn, Eyvindr Melbrigðarson, Bishop William, Holdboði, Ingiríðr, and the
Atholl family of Haraldr Maddaðarson since the mid-1130s require further
research.

[25] Brut Y Tywysogion (The Chronicle of the Princes), Red Book of Hergest
Version, ed and trsl T. Jones (Cardiff, 1955), s.a.1144: Y ulwydyn racllaw, pan
welas Catwaladyr vot Ywein, y vrawt, yn y wrthlad o'e holl gyfoeth, kynullaw
llyghes o Jwerdon a oruc a dyuot y Aber Menei y'r tir. Ac yn tywyssogyon
y gyt ac ef yd oed Otter vab Otter a mab Turkyll a mab Cherwlf. ('The

following year, when Cadwaladr saw that Owain, his brother, was expelling him from all his territory, he assembled a fleet from Ireland and came to land at Abermenai. And as leaders along with him were Otir, son of Otir, and the son of Turcaill and the son of Cherwlf.'). Cf S. Duffy, 'Irishmen and Islesmen in the Kingdoms of Dublin and Man, 1052-1171', *Ériu* xliii (1992), 122, also for possible identifications of Cherwlf (n. 148); P.A. Munch (ed.), *Cronica Regum Mannie et Insularum. The Chronicle of Man and the Sudreys* (Douglas, 1874), 173-4 (CM (Munch)). Overview J.E. Lloyd, *A History of Wales from Earliest Times to the Edwardian Conquest*, (London, 1911), 489-490; and ibid, 476 for Owain and Cadwaladr's joint attack on Ceredigion in 1138, also aided by a Hiberno-Norse fleet. B.G. Charles, *Old Norse Relations With Wales* (Cardiff, 1934), 52-88, discusses Sveinn's exploits in Wales but does not consider any political background. For the 9th-11th century Irish-Welsh background C. Etchingham, 'North Wales, Ireland and the Isles: the Insular Viking Zone', *Peritia* vol. 15 (2001), 145-187, and M-T. Flanagan, *Irish Society, Anglo-Norman Settlers, Angevin Kingship. Interactions in Ireland in the Late Twelfth Century*; (Oxford, 1989), 61-67.

[26] Cf for Óttarr Duffy, 'Irishmen and Islesmen', 121-123; I. Beuermann, *Man Amongst Kings and Bishops* (Oslo, 2002), 162-164; idem, *Masters of the Narrow Sea* (Oslo, 2007), 28-29. Óttarr's father or grandfather, *Earl Óttarr*, had been killed in battle in Man in 1098, G. Broderick (ed.), *Cronica Regum Mannie et Insularum. Chronicles of the Kings of Man and the Isles* (Douglas, 1995/6), f.34r (CM (Brod)). Óttarr's position as king of Dublin would have differed from that of Guðröðr Crobán there. While Guðröðr, king of Dublin from at least 1091 to 1094, was also a Manx/Islesman (and the father of the Óláfr who probably opposed Óttarr in the 1140s), there is no evidence that he faced opposition in Man and the Isles. Like Óttarr, Guðröðr also sent a fleet to Gwynedd, in 1094, shortly before he was ousted from Dublin.

[27] OS ch. 78, cf OS AT, 264 'a "Hold" from Wales'; OS HP/PE, 145: 'a chieftain from Wales'.

[28] It has proven impossible to identify either Hölðr or Holdboði. It is unlikely that Hölðr can be identified with Cadwaladr, whose known activities in the early 1140s were in Ceredigion, Gwynedd, possibly Powys and Chester, Lincoln, and Dublin. Overview Lloyd, *History*, 476, 489-490. It is difficult to accommodate an attack on Tiree in terms of time and geography, and it is implausible that he should twice have fled to Lundy Island. Hölðr may in fact not be a personal name at all, but may simply mean 'rich farmer', as also a comparison of OS's manuscripts and the term's occurrence in other Norse contexts shows (Cf the recent discussion of *Rígspula* by F. Armory, 'The Historical Worth of *Rígspula*', *Alvíssmál* 10 (2001) 3-20, 7; and K. Helle,

Norge Blir en Stat, 1130-1319 (Oslo, 1964), 112 for *hauldar* as the highest-ranking farmers in Norway). Historians have wondered whether this *Hölðr* was Welsh, or rather a Scandinavian or an Anglo-Norman living in Wales. For the idea of an Anglo-Norman the somewhat ambiguous passage in OS is to blame: *Í þenna tíma kom til Sveins orðsending Holdboða ór Suðreyjum, at Sveinn skyldi koma til liðveizlu við hann, því at þar hafði komit hölðr af Bretlandi ok hafði eltan Holdboða ór búum sínum ok rænt fé miklu. Sá maðr hét Hróðbjartr, er sendr var, enskr at kyni.* OS ch. 78. This has been translated in OS HP/PE, 145 'Then Svein had a message from Holdbodi of the Hebrides asking for his help against a chieftain from Wales, a man called Robert, of English descent, who had arrived in the islands, driven Holdbodi off his estate and stolen a great deal of money.' The translation in OS AT, 264, avoids this mistake: 'At that time there came to Sweyn a message from Holdbodi from the Hebrides, that Sweyn should come to him with an armed force, for [to Tiree] had come a "Hold" from Wales, and had burned Holdbodi out of house and home, and had made off with much booty. The messenger was called Robert, an Englishman by birth.' Cf Charles, *Old Norse Relations*, 113; OS FG ch. 78 n. 2. The term hölðr also appears in OS ch. 80. For Holdboði OS AT, 385 n.12 offers 'probably of Celtic origin'. Jarlsness, attacked by Sveinn and Holdboði, is also unidentified. It also occurs in *Egil's saga* ch.53. Nash Point to the east of Swansea Bay has been suggested, since land there has been known as Tir-y-jarl, cf OS AT, 389 n.5. with further references. Charles, *Old Norse Relations*, 115 concurs with the general geographical placement 'somewhere on the South Wales coast in the Bristol Channel', while ES ii. 193 suggests Pembroke.

[29] OS ch. 85 focusses on Earls Rögnvaldr's and Haraldr's deeds 1148-52; Sveinn appears there but once. Chs. 86-89 recount Earl Rögnvaldr's pilgrimage to Jerusalem. The beginning of ch. 90 and chs. 92-101 describe Sveinn's activities until 1158. From this it is however clear that also in the early 1150s Sveinn kept contact with at least the Hebrides. In *ca.* 1153 Sveinn sent his brother Gunni to safety in Lewis, to his friend Ljótólfr with who Sveinn himself had been staying at some time (OS ch. 92). About a year later, when Sveinn and Earl Erlendr were hard-pressed in the war of the three earls, Sveinn spread rumours that he intended to sail to the Hebrides. Earl Rögnvaldr did not fall for Sveinn's ruse, but the fact that Sveinn tried it shows that Sveinn considered this a plausible excuse – which must be because he was known for his Hebridean and Irish Sea contacts.

[30] OS chs. 96, 97.

[31] OS ch. 101. The dating is Taylor's, OS AT: 332.

[32] A.O. and M.O. Anderson (eds.), *Chronicle of Melrose A.D.731-1275 from the Cottonian Manuscript, Faustina B.IX in the British Museum: a complete and full-size facsimile in collotype* (London, 1936), s.a.1164 (CMel); *Annals of Ulster* AU1164.4 and *Annals of Tigernach* AT1164.6, http://www.ucc.ie/celt/published/G100001A/index.html, http://www.ucc.ie/celt/published/G100002/index.html.

[33] For earl Rögnvaldr still being alive OS ch. 101, for his death in August 1158 OS chs. 103, 104. Although, following the *Manx Chronicle* (CM (Brod) f.37v., CM (Munch) 68, 69), 1156 has long been accepted as the year of the battle (A W Moore, *A History of the Isle of Man* 2 vols (London, 1900), i, 111 and later authors), it has been pointed out that, since the *Chronicle*'s dating would have been according to the Julian calendar in which the year began on 25 March, by modern reckoning the confrontation needs to be dated to January 1157, R. Oram, *The Lordship of Galloway* (Edinburgh, 2000), 76 and n.127. In 1154 the battle of Inishowen was fought by Muirchertach Mac Lochlainn against Toirrdelbach Ua Conchobair; but there is no mention of Orcadians amongst the many allies. Discussion Beuermann, *Masters*, 59-73.

[34] 'had gone into a sea-loch after a force of men that had not turned up', OS ch. 101. Cf OS HP/PE, 209: 'sailed into the lochs looking for people who had not yet turned up'. Cf OS AT, 402, note, and OS FG, 275 note 3 for the discusion whether *Myrkvafjörðr* (OS ch. 101) where Sveinn killed Gilla Oðran, is Loch Linnhe (with its alternative Gaelic name *Linne Dubh*) on the Scottish west coast, or *Loch Gleann Dubh*, the inner part of Kylestrome in Sutherland.

[35] Barrett, 'Svein Asleifsson', 218; OS ch. 101. I agree with Barrett that Sveinn may have fought in the battle between Sumarliði and Guðröðr. Contrary to Barrett, however, I think that Sveinn was on the side of Sumarliði, his friend and host according to OS ch. 97. The other possibility, that Sveinn was sent to kill Gilla-Oðran and did so, then also killing Sumarliði, which would have to be placed in 1164, does not fit OS's internal dating, cf note 33. In addition, the scenario of a battle before which Gilla-Oðran was still collecting support also agrees better with the setting of 1157 than with one of 1164.

[36] 'They sailed first to the Hebrides [and] then west to the Scilly Isles, and there won a great victory at Port St Mary on St Columba's Mass and took immense plunder.', OS ch. 100. St Columba's Mass was on 9 June, OS FG, 272 note 1.

[37] 'Every summer he spent a-harrying.', OS ch. 100.

[38] 'Sweyn went on [his] Viking cruise and [came] home in autumn as his custom was.', OS ch. 101. Later follows the famous note on Sveinn's twice-

yearly expeditions: *Þat var háttr Sveins í þann tíma, at hann sat um vetrum í Gáreksey heima ok helt þar jafnan áttatigi karla á sinn kost. Hann átti svá mikinn drykkjuskála, at engi var annarr jafnmikill í Orkneyjum. Sveinn hafði á várum starfa mikinn ok lét fœra niðr ófamikit sáð ok gekk þar mjǫk sjálfr at. En er lokit var þeim starfa, fór hann hvert vár í víking ok herjaði um Suðreyjar ok Írland ok kom heim eptir mitt sumar; þat kallaði hann várvíking. Þá var hann heima, till þess er akrar váru upp skornir ok sét var fyrir kornum. Þá fór hann í víking ok komm þá ekki fyrr heim en mánuðr var af vetri, ok kallaði hann þat haustvíking.* OS ch. 105. In the well-known translation of OS HP/PE: 215: 'This was how Svein used to live. Winter he would spend at home on Gairsay, where he entertained some eighty men at his own expense. His drinking hall was so big, there was nothing in Orkney to compare with it. In the spring he had more than enough to occupy him, with a great deal of seed to sow which he saw to carefully himself. Then when that job was done, he would go off plundering in the Hebrides and in Ireland on what he called his 'spring-trip', then back home just after mid-summer, where he stayed till the cornfields had been reaped and the grain was safely in. After that he would go off raiding again, and never came back till the first month of winter was ended. This he used to call his 'autumn-trip.'

[39] As part of his reconciliation with Earls Haraldr and Rögnvaldr, Sveinn had been required to hand over his longship, in addition to a large fine and half his lands, OS ch. 95. This did not lead to peace between Sveinn and Haraldr, and Sveinn was then 'on the run', as Hermann Pálsson and Paul Edwards entitled this chapter, using a skiff borrowed from a farmer. Later Rögnvaldr, who had not taken his share of the fine and who had ordered that Sveinn's ship be left untouched, gave the ship to Haraldr, who returned it to Sveinn, OS ch. 99.

[40] Just as discussed for the 1140s, the stress on economic reasons does not *exclude* the possibility that Sveinn may also have had feelings of gratitude towards a Hebridean who had provided a refuge when he needed it because of problems with an Orkney earl (Sveinn's problems with Earl Páll in the 1130s, his flight to Holdboði and his alliance with the latter in the 1140s, and Sveinn's problems with Earl Haraldr in the 1150s and his flight to Sumarliði and subsequent alliance with him).

[41] 'requested from [Somerled] his son Dougal, that he should make him king over the Isles. Somerled was very much pleased to hear this request and handed his son Dougal over to him, who took him and conducted him through all the Isles. He subjected them all to his sway and received hostages from each island.' CM (Brod) f.37v. and 37r.

[42] Discussion Beuermann, *Masters*, 73-80. The battle outside Dublin described at length in CM (Brod) f.37r. did in all likelihood not occur in the

1150s, but corresponds to that noted by the Irish Annals in 1162, cf discussion Beuermann ibid., 99-131. Whether the events of 1162 would have been a repetition of the possible plans of 1157, Þorfinnr Óttarsson as king of Dublin, Sumarliði/Dubgall as king of Man and the Isles, shall be discussed in my planned edition of the *Manx Chronicle*.

[43] Although Giraldus and the anonymous author of the *Deeds* were both Cambro-/Anglo-Norman and would in an Irish context be juxtaposed to native sources like the Irish Annals, here *Expug. Hib.* and the *Deeds* are classified as 'Irish', in juxtaposition to 'Norse' *Orkneyinga Saga*.

[44] OS chs. 106-108; cf Barrett, 'Svein Asleifsson', 218.

[45] AU 1170.7: *Diarmait h-Ua Ainbfheith, rí h-Ua Meith & toisech marc-sluaighi righ Ailigh, do marbadh do longais táinic a h-Innsibh Orcc isin innsi ro cumtaighedh aca féin for Loch Ruidhe, .i., for Inis Lacain.* ('Diarmait Ua Ainbfheith, king of Ui-Meith and leader of the horse-host of the king of Ailech, was killed by a fleet that came from the Islands of Orcc to the Island that was built by himself upon Loch-Ruidhe, namely, upon Inis-Lachain.') Similarly AFM 1170.25; ALC 1170.8. ES ii. 273 for the modern spelling Inisloughlin (today one of the townlands of the Parish of Magheramesk in Co. Antrim).

[46] 'with Norwegians and men from the isles' in Expug. Hib. ch. 21 (at 76, 77); 'from Norway' in *Deeds* line 2262 (at 111); 'from the Islands of Orc' in AU 1171.2, similarly AFM 1171.17; ALC 1171.2; 'the Norwegian', 'the Orcadian' AT 1171.6, MIA 'Mac Carthy's Book' 1171.2, cf AFM 1171.17 for *Lochlandach a h-Insibh h-Orc*, 'a Norwegian from the Orkney Islands' (rather than the trsl. given 'a Dane from the Insi-hOrc').

[47] 'John the Wode'; *Deeds* lines 2263, 2264 (at 111) and *passim*; 'John [...] the Wode, which means "the mad" or "the impetuous" '; Expug. Hib. ch. 21 (76, 77).

[48] *Mear*, 'the Mad' in AU 1171.2; AFM 1171.17; ALC 1171.2; AT 1171.6; *Iohannes Orcach* in MIA 'Mac Carthy's Book' 1171.2.

[49] OS chs. 107, 108; *Expug. Hib.* ch. 21 (at 76, 77); *Deeds*, lines 2369-2377 for *Johan* leaving Dublin to prevent their rearguard being routed; 2449-50 for his death, for the whole battle 2255-2458 (at 110-116); AT 1171.6, AFM 1171.17 and MIA 'Mac Carthy's Book' 1171.2 describe a battle, while AU 1171.2 and ALC 1171.2 only note Eoan's killing.

[50] OS ch. 106. The *Deeds* place Asculf's attack on Dublin *after* Ruaidrí Ua Conchobair's and his Isles' allies' unsuccessful siege of Dublin. Irish scholars had therefore earlier debated whether the attack took place later in 1171, in autumn – which would agree with OS. However, *Expug. Hib.* and the Irish Annals place the attack before the siege, and after Diarmait Mac Murchada's

death at the beginning of May, and their chronological evidence is preferred over that of the *Deeds*, cf J.F O'Doherty, 'Historical Criticism of the Song of Dermot and the Earl', *Irish Historical Studies*, 1 (1938/39), 13-19; J.F. Lydon, *The Lordship of Ireland in the Middle Ages* (Dublin, 1972/2003), 39.
[51] I am grateful to Catherine Swift for her helpful comments here.
[52] 'He was the nephew of the mighty king of Norway' *solum les Yrreis* ('according to the Irish'), *Deeds*, lines 2265-6 (at 111).
[53] Sveinn's father was Óláfr Hrólfsson, and Sveinn is called Óláfsson in OS ch. 66, during Óláfr's lifetime. Sveinn's sister is also later called Ingigerðr Óláfsdóttir, OS ch. 77. All OS says about the change is *Sveinn, er síðan var kallaðr Ásleifarson,* 'Sweyn, who was later called Asleif's son', OS ch. 66. Nothing is known about Ásleif other than that *hon var vitr ok ættstór ok in mesta fyrir sér,* 'she was a wise woman, of good family and strongest character', OS ch. 56. However, an (other) reason for Sveinn preferring his mother's name may lie in family politics. Sveinn had gone fishing, and Ásleif and her son Gunni had left, hence they all survived when Óláfr Hrólfsson was burned to death in Duncansby by opponents of Earl Páll (the eldest son, Valþjófr, had just drowned). Contrary to his father, Sveinn later opposed Earl Páll. That the opponents of Earl Páll later split into supporters of Earl Haraldr (Sveinn) and Earl Erlendr (Frakökk and her relations) however, complicates matters further.
[54] Dublin might have turned from Ruaidrí and /or Asculf to submit to Diarmait in spring 1170 (*Expug. Hib.* ch. 11 (at 52, 53); this expedition is not noted in the *Deeds*, or in the annals associated with St Mary's, Dublin (J.T. Gilbert (ed.), *Chartulary of St Mary's Abbey, Dublin,* 2 vols (Rolls Series 80, London, 1884-6) ii. 269; it may be referred to in AI 1170.4, AT 1170.6; it is accepted by A.J. Otway-Ruthven, *A History of Medieval Ireland* (London, 1980), 45, but not mentioned by Duffy, 'Irishmen and Islesmen', 131-132; cf also J.F. Lydon, 'Dublin in Transition: From Ostman Town to English Borough', in S. Duffy, (ed.), *Medieval Dublin II, Proceedings of the Second Public Friends of Medieval Dublin Symposium 2000* (Dublin, 2001), 131). Dublin turned to Ruaidrí and /or Asculf again in summer 1170 (Expug. Hib. ch. 17 (at 66, 67)); and was on the point of deciding for Diarmait again, discussing which hostages to give (AFM 1170.13, AU 1170.3, Expug. Hib. ch. 17 (at 66-69); *Deeds* lines 1598-1673 (at 94, 95) including the lightning), when the town itself was 'betrayed', by the Normans' attack in autumn 1170 while the deliberations went on (AU 1170.3, 1170.5, AFM 1170.13, Expug. Hib. ch. 17 (at 66-69), *Deeds* lines 1674-1711 (at 96, 97)). In spring 1171, before Asculf's attack, Dubliners killed some Normans in revenge for the sack of Duleek (AFM 1171.16). A first 'betrayal' in this saga would be Dublin's

turning against Diarmait in 1166, after Muirchertach Mac Lochlainn's death; Diarmait's setback which triggered all the following events. *Expug. Hib.* ch. 11 (at 52, 53) describes the submission of spring 1170: *tandem cives de pace tractantes, de fidelitate principi suo de cetero servanda et debitis exhibendis obsequiis, caucionem securam prestiterunt.* ('At last the citizens discussed peace terms and gave a firm pledge of their loyalty to their prince for the future, and promised to render him those services which were his due.')

[55] 'Asculf therefore sent back word * to Diarmait, the renowned king, * to say that he would do * all he commanded promptly the next day', *Deeds*, lines 1670-1673 (at 96) 'But in the morning Sweyn was to go to the town and take off the gold, garrison the town, and take hostages from the townsmen', OS ch. 107. The context of OS's quote is discussed in detail below, cf n. 68.

[56] In how far the version of the *Deeds* is trustworthy is not important here, since the comparison concerns the *representations* of events. The *Deeds* were probably written by a non-Latin-speaking layman of Welsh-Norman origin who was informed by Diarmait Mac Murchada's interpreter Maurice Regan, in the last decade of the 12th century (*Deeds*, 37). OS's first version was composed at the same time, cf the references in note 1.

[57] 'nearly as far south as Dublin', OS ch. 106, cf OS HP/PE's translation 'on their way south towards Dublin' (at 215).

[58] OS ch. 106. Mead and wine are also mentioned, in addition to the cloth.

[59] In how far medieval people acted like modern businessmen has been discussed. Cf Hatcher and Bailey, *Modelling*, 10: 'assumptions about the behaviour of the generality of people [...] may well be inappropriate to more distant times. For example, it is an essential underpinning of neoclassical economics that individuals and business organnizations will seek to maximise income and profit, but in the Middle Ages [...] for the great landlords the maximisation of income often took second place, because they were wariors, churchmen, politicians and dispensers of hospitality and patronage as well as owners of assets.' But Sveinn's behaviour with Earl Haraldr would also not be logic in these other medieval contexts.

[60] 'People were now so very much afraid of him in the Hebrides, that they buried all their movable property in the earth or under heaps of stones.' OS ch. 106. D. Freke, *The Peel Castle Dig* (Douglas, 1995), 17.

[61] In the 1140s Sveinn received five ships from Earl Rögnvaldr, but was put in command of only one himself. Sveinn's four co-commanders were Þorbjörn klerkr, Hafliði Þorkelsson, Dufníall Hávarðsson Gunnasonar, and Ríkarðr Þorleifarson, OS ch. 82. Earl Rögnvaldr had just recently reconciled Sveinn with Þorbjörn klerkr (a grandson of Frakökk, OS ch. 77), after their relationship had become strained since Þorbjörn moved against Sveinn's people and

supplanted him as Earl Rögnvaldr's closest ally, OS ch. 80, but Sveinn and Þorbjörn fell out again for good at the end of the expedition, with Þorbjörn divorcing Sveinn's sister, OS ch. 82. Dufníall Hávarðsson Gunnasonar was the brother of Þorsteinn, Earl Páll's man OS ch. 66. Hafliði's father Þorkel flettir had been granted the estate of Sveinn's dead brother Valþjófr by Earl Páll after Sveinn had killed Sveinn brjóstreip, OS ch. 67, and Sveinn later burned Þorkel to death, OS ch. 73. Þorbjörn klerkr, Dufníall and Hafliði are mentioned as most inimical to Sveinn when they later pursue him, OS ch. 83. Whether Ríkarðr Þorleifarson is identical with Sveinn's ally Ríkarðr of Brekkur on Stronsay (OS ch. 73) or with Sveinn's enemy Ríkarðr (OS ch. 83) is not clear. In the 1150s, Þorbjörn klerkr reappeared as co-commander and Earl Haraldr's *ráðgjafi*, OS ch. 100.

[62] 'with seemly gifts', OS ch. 106.

[63] Thomson, *History of Orkney*, 72, 73 proposed that Haraldr might have known of English moves heralding changing times, and therefore told Sveinn to stop raiding, a conjecture I find less convincing. Haraldr would not shy away from conflict with (Scottish and Norwegian) kings on later occasions. Haraldr may however have been wary of Sveinn's growing influence not only economically, but also politically/dynastically. Sveinn had close links with Hákon Haraldsson, the earl's son by his first wife, Affreca of Fife (OS ch. 107). At some stage Haraldr divorced Affreka, and in 1196/7 his son Þorfinnr with his second wife Hvarfloð, the daughter of Máel Coluim mac Alasdair was his heir (OS chs. 105, 109, 112; ES, ii. 348 n.1. A.A.M. Duncan, *Scotland. The Making of the Kingdom* (Edinburgh, 1975), 193 dates the divorce to around 1168). Haraldr may therefore, firstly, have feared Sveinn's / Hákon's opposition. He may also have feared Sveinn's very own plans: would this be an additional reason why Haraldr reacted so violently to Sveinn's brother Gunni's liaison with his mother Margaret? Any issue there would have a claim to the earldom. Margaret was later abducted by Haraldr's opponent Earl Erlendr, who married her against Haraldr's will (OS ch. 93). In 1230, Sveinn's great-grandson Snækolr Gunnason claimed part of the earldom and killed Earl Haraldr's son and successor Earl Jón (his father Gunni, son of Sveinn's stepson Andrés, had married Ragnhild, a sister of Earl Haraldr ungi, the last opponent of Earl Haraldr's, ES, ii. 350).

[64] 'that winter, Sweyn married Ingirid, and then settled down in great honour', OS ch.79.

[65] 'Sweyn and he parted the best of friends', OS ch. 106.

[66] 'it to be no less glorious than was [his] spring-cruise', OS ch. 106.

[67] Crawford, *Scandinavian Scotland*, 134, 135 points to the episode in *Egils Saga* where a visit to Dublin is called the most illustrious journey anyone can

make, in the context of Björn asking his father Brynjolfr for a warship, but getting a trading ship instead, for a journey from Norway to Dublin (where Björn in the event did not get to).

[68] 'There they made prisoners of the chief men in the town. The upshot of the affair was that they gave the town into the hands of Sweyn and promised to pay him as much money as he thought fit to demand of them; and Sweyn was to quarter his men in the town and have rule over it. The men of Dublin swore oaths to keep to these terms. They went to their ships in the evening. But in the morning Sweyn was to go to the town and take off the gold, garrison the town, and take hostages from the townsmen.' OS ch. 107. Cf already above, and n. 55, for the last sentence.

[69] Cf for Dublin's defence J. Lydon, 'The Defence of Dublin in the Middle Ages', in S. Duffy (ed.), *Medieval Dublin* IV (Dublin, 2003), 63-78; also G. Scally, 'The Earthen Banks and Walled Defences of Dublin's North-East Corner', 11-33; and A. Hayden, 'The Excavation of Pre-Norman Defences and Houses at Werburgh Street, Dublin: a Summary', 44-68, both in S. Duffy (ed.), *Medieval Dublin* III (Dublin, 2002).

[70] It was under Asculf's rule that the Dubliners turned their back on Diarmait in 1166, cf above n. 54. That there was bad blood between Diarmait and at least some Dubliners is also evident from *Expug. Hib.* ch.17 (at 66, 67), explaining that Diarmait hated the Dubliners for killing his father and burying him together with a dog. The *Deeds*, whose author was informed by Diarmait's interpreter (cf n. 56), are particularly venomous regarding Asculf, understandably more so than Giraldus who is usually critical of Diarmait.

[71] Cf discussion Duffy, 'Irishmen and Islesmen', 132.

[72] OS ch. 107.

[73] OS ch. 107.

[74] 'Mac Turcaill brought him with him a vassal called John the Wode.' *Deeds*, lines 2263, 2264 (at 111).

[75] Cf n. 56, 70.

[76] Which has to my knowledge not yet been consulted for Sveinn's Irish activities. *Mac Cárthaigh's Book*, preserved in two 15th-century manuscripts, notes mainly events from Munster, in the period 1114-c.1437. Interestingly here however, 'some [material] seems to be from the South Ulster/Oriel area'. G. MacNiocaill, *The Medieval Irish Annals* (Dublin 1975), 26-29 discusses the possible relationship between *Mac Cárthaigh's Book* and other Irish Annals (esp. AI and AT), and points out that *Mac Cárthaigh's Book* 'also draws on Giraldus Cambrensis for its account of the Anglo-Norman invasion'; quotes ibid, 26; cf overview ibid, 40 and bibliography ibid, 46, point 7. The most accessible edition is that of the CELT website, *Miscellaneous Irish Annals*

Fragment I: http://www.ucc.ie/celt/published/T100013/index.html

[77] *Mac Cárthaigh's Book* 1171.2: 'Iohannes Orcach and [Haskulf son of Raghnall son of] Thorkil, two officials of Dublin, came to Ireland with three score shiploads of Norsemen to avenge their reverse and their expulsion from Dublin. The Norse and the English fought a battle around Dublin, in which the two one-time officials of Dublin were killed, with slaughter of the Norse fleet.'

[78] E.G. Quin, *Dictionary of the Irish Language*, Royal Irish Academy (Dublin 1990), sub *ármann*, where nine other occurrences are given (including, most interestingly, Mac Gilla Muire, *ármann* of Waterford in AT 1170.8), but not the one of *Mac Cárthaigh's Book*.

[79] Etchingham, personal communication.

[80] OS ch. 107.

[81] 'to the northern isles', Expug. Hib. ch. 17 (at 68, 69).

[82] Duffy discussed whether exiled Dubliners ever returned, or remained for example in Islay. Also his reading is therefore that they fled to the Hebrides. Duffy, 'Irishmen and Islesmen', 132 note 184, based on a thirteenth-century poem about the ancestors of Angus mac Domnaill of Islay. In the *Deeds*, lines 1694, 1695 (at 96) is only the information that they defeated Dubliners fled by sea (*par marine*). *If* all this implies that they avoided Man, this may strengthen the argument above that Sveinn had been Sumarliði's ally, and was in opposition to Guðröðr of Man (who also only intervened in Dublin after Sveinn's and Asculf's death).

[83] Cf *Expug. Hib.*, 303, n. 94. 'about the kalends of May', *Expug. Hib.* (at 74, 75).

[84] 'about the same time, around Pentecost', Expug. Hib. ch.21 (at 76, 77). Ibid, 305 n. 105.

[85] I intend to return to the relations between Sveinn, Haraldr, Asculf, Diarmait, Guðröðr and Sumarliði in the future.

[86] CM (Brod) f.35v.

[87] OS ch.107, HP/PE's translation (at 217), 'the greatest troublemaker in the western lands', seems partially better than AT's (at 341), 'the most unjust man in the British Isles'. Literally, *ójafnaðr* means 'unevenness', 'inequality', something which was resented if it exceeded a certain level, cf discussion by Gunnar Karlsson, *Iceland's 1100 Years. History of a Marginal Society* (London, 2000/05), 57. The Dubliners' comment certainly suggests that Sveinn was well-known to them, supporting the argument here, that Sveinn was as much an 'Irish Sea-man' as an 'Orkney-man'.

Bibliography

Sources

Annals of Innisfallen; ed. and trsl. by S. Mac Airt, Dublin, 1988

Annals of Loch Cé, ed. and trsl. by W. Hennessy, Rolls Series, London, 1871

Annals of the Four Masters; Corpus of Electronic Texts (CELT) http://www. ucc.ie/celt/published/G100005A/index.html (Irish), http://www.ucc.ie/celt/published/T100005A/index.html (English trsl.)

Annals of Tigernach, Corpus of Electronic Texts (CELT) http://www.ucc.ie/celt/published/G100002/index.html (Irish)

Annals of Ulster, Corpus of Electronic Texts (CELT) http://www.ucc.ie/celt/published/G100001A/index.html (Irish), http://www.ucc.ie/celt/published/T100001A/index.html (English trsl.)

Annals of Ulster, otherwise Annala Senait (A.D. 431-1131 : 1155-1541); II A.D. 1057-1131 : 1155-1378, ed., with translation and notes by B. Mac Carthy, Dublin, 1893

Brut Y Tywysogion (The Chronicle of the Princes), Red Book of Hergest Version, ed. and trsl. by T. Jones (Cardiff, 1955)

Chartulary of St Mary's Abbey, Dublin, 2 vols, ed. by J.T. Gilbert, Rolls Series 80, (London, 1884-6)

Chronicle of Melrose A.D.731-1275 from the Cottonian Manuscript, Faustina B.IX in the British Museum: a complete and full-size facsimile in collotype ed. by A.O. and M.O. Anderson (London, 1936)

Cronica Regum Mannie et Insularum. Chronicles of the Kings of Man and the Isles ed. and trsl. by G. Broderick (Douglas, 1995/6)

Cronica Regum Mannie et Insularum. The Chronicle of Man and the Sudreys ed. and trsl. by P.A. Munch (Douglas, 1874)

Deeds of the Normans in Ireland, La Geste des Engleis en Yrlande, A new edition of the chronicle formerly known as *The Song of Dermot and the Earl*, ed. by E. Mullally (Dublin, 2002)

Giraldus Cambrensis, *Expugnatio Hibernica, The Conquest of Ireland*, ed. by A.B. Scott and F.X. Martin (Dublin, 1978)

Libellus de Admirandis Beati Cuthberti Virtutibus, ed. J. Raine (Surtees Society, 1835)

Liber Luciani de Laude Cestrie, ed M.V. Taylor, Lancashire and Chester Record Society, vol.64 (Edinburgh & London, 1912)

Miscellaneous Irish Annals Fragment I: "Mac Cárthaigh's Book" http://www.ucc.ie/celt/published/T100013/index.html

Orkneyinga Saga, ed. by F. Guðmundsson, Íslenzk Fornrit vol. 34 (Reykjavík, 1965)

Orkneyinga Saga, trsl. by A.B. Taylor (Edinburgh, 1938)
Orkneyinga Saga, trsl. by H. Pálsson and P. Edwards (London, 1981)
Poem in Praise of Raghnall, King of Man, ed B. Ó Cuív, Éigse, vol. 8 part 4 (1957)
Snorri Sturluson, Heimskringla, ed B. Aðalbjarnarsson, Íslenzk Fornrit vol. 28. (Reykjavík 1951/1979)
Vita S. Waldeni in Acta Sanctorum, August, I (Paris, 1867)

Secondary Studies

Anderson, A.O. Early Sources of Scottish History, ed. by P. Watkins, 2 vols. (Stamford, 1990)
Armory, F. "The Historical Worth of Rígsþula", Alvíssmál 10 (2001)
Barrett, J.H. "Svein Asleifsson and 12th – century Orcadian Society", in O. Owen (ed.), The World of Orkneyinga Saga (Kirkwall, 2005)
Beuermann, I. "A Chieftain in an Old Norse Text: Sveinn Ásleifarson and the Message behind Orkneyinga Saga" in Transgressions. Interdisciplinary Communications 2007/2008, Publications of the Senter for Grunnforskning ved Det Norske Videnskaps-Akademi (Centre for Advanced Study at the Norwegian Academy of Science and Letters), Oslo forthcoming 2008
Beuermann, I. "Orkneyinga Saga: 1195 And All That?" Nordistica Tartuensia 14 (2006)
Beuermann, I. Man Amongst Kings and Bishops (Oslo, 2002)
Beuermann, I. Masters of the Narrow Sea (Oslo, 2007)
Britnell, R.H. Britain and Ireland 1050-1530. Economy and Society (Oxford, 2004)
Britnell, R.H. The Commercialisation of English Society, 1000-1500 (Manchester, 1996)
Bruhn, O. "Earl Rognvald and the Rise of Saga Literature", in C. Batey et al. (eds.), The Viking Age in Caithness, Orkney and the North Atlantic (Edinburgh, 1995)
Charles, B.G. Old Norse Relations With Wales (Cardiff, 1934)
Chesnutt, M. "Haralds saga Maddarðarsonar", in U. Dronke et al. (eds.), Speculum Norrænvm: Norse Studies in Memory of Gabriel Turville-Petre (Odense 1981)
Ciklamini, M. "Saint Rognvaldr and Sveinn Asleifarson, the Viking", Scandinavian Studies 42 (1970)
Clouston, J.S. A History of Orkney (Kirkwall, 1932)
Cowan, E.J. "Caithness in the Sagas" in J.R. Baldwin (ed.) Caithness: a cultural crossroads (Edinburgh, 1982)

Cowan, E.J. "What is Orkneyinga Saga About?" *Northern Studies* 2 (1973)

Crawford, B.E. *Scandinavian Scotland* (Leicester, 1987)

Davey, P. "Medieval and Later Pottery from the Isle of Man", *IoM Natural History and Antiquarian Society* vol. 11 no.1 (2000)

Douglasson, H. "Svein Asleifarsson: The Last Viking", in idem, *Saga-Men. The People Behind the Earls of Orkney* (Lulu web-publishers, http://www.lulu.com Morrisville NC & London, 2005)

Duffy, S. "Irishmen and Islesmen in the Kingdoms of Dublin and Man, 1052-1171", *Ériu* xliii (1992)

Duncan, A.A.M. *Scotland. The Making of the Kingdom* (Edinburgh, 1975)

Dyer, C. *Making a Living in the Middle Ages* (London, 2003)

Etchingham, C. "North Wales, Ireland and the Isles: the Insular Viking Zone", *Peritia* vol. 15 (2001)

Fidjestøl, B. "Bjarni Kolbeinsson" in P. Pulsiano et al. (eds.), *Medieval Scandinavia. An Encyclopaedia* (New York & London, 1993).

Flanagan, M-T. *Irish Society, Anglo-Norman Settlers, Angevin Kingship. Interactions in Ireland in the Late Twelfth Century*; (Oxford, 1989)

Foote, P. "Observations on Orkneyinga Saga", in B.E. Crawford (ed.), *St Magnus Cathedral and Orkney's Twelfth Century Renaissance* (Aberdeen, 1988)

Forte, A. et al. *Viking Empires* (Cambridge, 2005)

Freke, D. *The Peel Castle Dig* (Douglas, 1995)

Fullen, M.A.; Harris, J.; Kear, B.S. *Soils of the Isle of Man*, Centre for Manx Studies Research Report 5 (1996)

Gunn, R.P. *Swein Asleifson: A Northern Pirate* (Latheronwheel, Caithness, 1990)

Hatcher, J.; Bailey, M. *Modelling the Middle Ages* (Oxford, 2001)

Hayden, A. "The Excavation of Pre-Norman Defences and Houses at Werburgh Street, Dublin: a Summary" in S. Duffy (ed.), *Medieval Dublin III* (Dublin, 2002)

Helle, K. *Norge Blir en Stat, 1130-1319* (Oslo, 1964)

Hudson, B. "Economy and Trade", in S. Duffy (ed.), *A New History of the Isle of Man* vol.3 (Liverpool, forthcoming)

Hudson, B. "The Changing Economy of the Irish Sea Province", in B. Smith (ed.) *Britain and Ireland 900-1300* (Cambridge, 1999)

Jamroziak, E. "Rievaulx Abbey as a Wool Producer in the Late Thirteenth Century: Cistercians, Sheep, and Debts", *Northern History*, 40 (2003)

Jesch, J. "Literature in Medieval Orkney", in O. Owen (ed.), *The World of Orkneyinga Saga* (Kirkwall, 2005)

Karlsson, G. *Iceland's 1100 Years. History of a Marginal Society* (London, 2000/05)

Lamb, R.; Robertson, J. "Kirkwall: Saga, History, Archaeology" in O. Owen (ed.), *The World of Orkneyinga Saga* (Kirkwall, 2005)

Linklater, E. *The Ultimate Viking* (London, 1955)

Lloyd, J.E. *A History of Wales from Earliest Times to the Edwardian Conquest*, (London, 1911)

Lydon, J.F. "Dublin in Transition: From Ostman Town to English Borough", in S. Duffy, (ed.), *Medieval Dublin II, Proceedings of the Second Public Friends of Medieval Dublin Symposium 2000* (Dublin, 2001)

Lydon, J.F. "The Defence of Dublin in the Middle Ages", in S. Duffy (ed.), *Medieval Dublin* IV (Dublin, 2003)

Lydon, J.F. *The Lordship of Ireland in the Middle Ages* (Dublin, 1972/2003)

MacNiocaill, G. *The Medieval Irish Annals* (Dublin 1975)

McNeill, P.; R. Nicholson, R. (eds.) *An Historical Atlas of Scotland c.400-1600* (St Andrews, 1975)

Moore, A.W. *A History of the Isle of Man* 2 vols (London, 1900)

Moore, D.W. *The Other British Isles. A History of Shetland, Orkney, the Hebrides, Isle of Man, Anglesey, Scilly, Isle of Wight and the Channel Islands* (Jefferson NC, 2005)

O'Doherty, J.F "Historical Criticism of the Song of Dermot and the Earl", *Irish Historical Studies*, 1 (1938/39)

Oram, R. *The Lordship of Galloway* (Edinburgh, 2000)

Otway-Ruthven, A.J. *A History of Medieval Ireland* (London, 1980)

Power, R. "Scotland in the Norse Sagas", in G.G. Simpson (ed.), *Scotland and Scandinavia 800-1800* (Edinburgh, 1990)

Quin, E.G. *Dictionary of the Irish Language*, Royal Irish Academy (Dublin 1990)

Scally, G. "The Earthen Banks and Walled Defences of Dublin's North-East Corner" in S. Duffy (ed.), *Medieval Dublin* III (Dublin, 2002)

Stringer, K.J. *The Reformed Church in Medieval Galloway and Cumbria: Contrasts, Connections, and Continuities*, Eleventh Whithorn Lecture 14 Sept 2002 (Whithorn, 2003)

Thomson, W.P.L. *History of Orkney* (Edinburgh, 1987)

Williams, G. *Land Assessment and Military Organisation in the Norse Settlements in Scotland, c. 900-1266 AD*, unpublished PhD thesis (University of St Andrews, 1996)